Subject Lite Culturally Diverse Secondary Schools

ALSO AVAILABLE FROM BLOOMSBURY

Computer Science Education, edited by Sue Sentance, Erik Barendsen and Carsten Schulte
Reflective Teaching in Schools, Andrew Pollard
Teaching and Learning the English Language, Richard Badger
Teaching English to Young Learners, edited by Janice Bland

Subject Literacy in Culturally Diverse Secondary Schools

Supporting EAL Learners

Esther Daborn, Sally Zacharias and Hazel Crichton

BLOOMSBURY ACADEMIC
Bloomsbury Publishing Plc
50 Bedford Square, London, WC1B 3DP, UK
1385 Broadway, New York, NY 10018, USA

BLOOMSBURY, BLOOMSBURY ACADEMIC and the Diana logo are trademarks of
Bloomsbury Publishing Plc

First published in Great Britain 2020

Copyright © Esther Daborn, Sally Zacharias and Hazel Crichton, 2020

Esther Daborn, Sally Zacharias and Hazel Crichton have asserted their right under the
Copyright, Designs and Patents Act, 1988, to be identified as Authors of this work.

For legal purposes the Acknowledgements on p. x constitute an extension
of this copyright page.

Cover design: Adriana Brioso
Cover image © tazytaz/iStock

All rights reserved. No part of this publication may be reproduced or transmitted
in any form or by any means, electronic or mechanical, including photocopying,
recording, or any information storage or retrieval system, without prior
permission in writing from the publishers.

Bloomsbury Publishing Plc does not have any control over, or responsibility for, any
third-party websites referred to or in this book. All internet addresses given in this
book were correct at the time of going to press. The author and publisher regret any
inconvenience caused if addresses have changed or sites have ceased to exist,
but can accept no responsibility for any such changes.

A catalogue record for this book is available from the British Library.

ISBN: HB: 978-1-3500-7393-7
PB: 978-1-3500-7362-3
ePDF: 978-1-3500-7392-0
eBook: 978-1-3500-7394-4

Typeset by Deanta Global Publishing Services, Chennai, India
Printed and bound in Great Britain

To find out more about our authors and books visit www.bloomsbury.com and sign up
for our newsletters.

Contents

Acknowledgements x
How to Use This Book xii
Glossary of Terms xiii

Introduction: Starting Points for the Book 1

How does language knowledge support learning and subject literacy development? 1
What is it like to learn in a culturally diverse classroom? 4
How can we apply this language knowledge to our classroom practice to support EAL learners and benefit *all* learners in the process? 6

1 Where Do We Start with Supporting Subject Literacies in the Classroom? 9

Starting points: Existing understandings of language and literacies 9
What language resources and social strategies do we develop from early years? 10
How does the teacher use social meanings in school settings? 12
    Establishing a professional role in the classroom 12
    Managing relations with tutors and colleagues 14
    Managing non-standard language forms in the classroom 15
How do literacy skills develop at Primary school? 16
    Word- and sentence-level knowledge 17
    Text-level knowledge to lay a foundation for subject literacies 18
An example of language in the construction of knowledge at different stages of a lesson 22
Drawing together ideas for supporting subject literacies in the classroom 26
Teaching resources 28
    Six register continuums, with examples 28
    More detailed outline of language development in first language English 29

2 What Resources Does the EAL Learner Bring to the Classroom? 31

Starting points: Identifying cultural, educational and language resources 31
Creating a school profile for the EAL learner 32
    Getting an insight into cultural expectations 33
    Building a languages profile 37
The customary language support practices in a school 44
How do EAL specialists approach language support? 45
How do EAL learners manage their languages in class? 46
    The EAL learner's pragmatic skills: Basic Interpersonal Communication Skills (BICS) 47
    The EAL learner's subject literacy skills: Cognitive Academic Language Proficiency (CALP) 49
Drawing together key areas of support for inclusive practice in the classroom 54
    Background knowledge 54
    Languages apart from English 55
    English language 55
    How EAL learners manage languages in class 55
Teaching resources 56
    Three key strategies for EAL learner engagement 56
    Planning lessons: A *language aware* teaching and learning cycle 58
    Policy documents and books for more detail on working with EAL learners 59

3 How Is Language Used to Present and Discuss Knowledge in My Subject? 61

Starting points: Your subject-oriented lens 61
What you already know about communication purpose and text organization 64
Establishing types of communication purpose of texts 65
Identifying language patterns in sample text types: Lower Secondary Geography, Maths and History 67
    Geography: The formation of volcanoes 68
    Maths: Squares and cubes 76
    History: The Norman Conquest 81
Drawing together metalanguage for language patterns to support EAL learners 88

How challenging are these Geography, Maths and History texts for
   the EAL learner?   90
Teaching resources   93
   Macro level – Questions and answers for planning the
      explanation   93
   Macro-level – How is it organized? Note-taking and writing
      templates for three types of explanation   93
   Micro-level – Language patterns for particular purposes   94

4 How Can I Support EAL Learners to Engage with New Knowledge in Challenging Texts?   97

Starting points: Identifying challenges   97
How did your receptive skills develop?   100
How do fluent language users approach a topic using prediction?   101
   Approaching a topic through visuals   101
   Approaching a topic in Listening   103
   Approaching a topic in Reading   104
Supporting the EAL learner with hearing new words   105
Supporting the EAL learner with reading new words   108
How many words do EAL learners need to know?   109
   Learning general academic words: Notice and apply to other
      subject areas   110
   Learning subject-specific words: Use reformulations to make
      synonymous phrases   111
   Learning everyday words for specialist purposes: Note them down
      and compare with other subject areas   112
Dealing with the challenges of complex language   113
   Deconstruction, paraphrasing and glossing a meaning   115
Apply these strategies systematically to engaging with
   challenging texts   118
   Subject English: A poem   119
   Subject Geography: A discussion report   125
Teaching resources   132
   High challenge/high support framework for EAL learners'
      engagement with new knowledge   132
   Answer to the title puzzle   134
   Word stress rules in English   134
   Communication purpose and sample linking words in text   134
   Questions to ask yourself FREQUENTLY about words   135

5 What Are the Key Principles for Adapting Pedagogical Tasks and Tests to Suit the EAL Learner? 137

Starting points: Opportunities for participation 137
Setting up a Science topic for small group discussion 139
    Planning: Identifying the communication goal 139
    Setting up: Preparing for the small group discussion 141
    Support for comprehension of the topic 142
    Setting up the group discussion task 144
    Opportunities and challenges in the group discussion 146
Planning, setting up and supporting a group task in subject English 151
Planning, setting up and supporting an individual test in Climate Science 157
    Supporting the synthesis of ideas for cause and effect 159
    Planned opportunities for oral rehearsal of ideas 160
    Support understanding of the purpose of a test 162
    Apply a check list for a planning, setting up and supporting a test to other subject areas 164
Drawing together principles for *language aware* task design 164
    Work on the communication purpose 165
    Model the structure and language features of a task or test 165
    Plan for engagement in a *language aware* way 166
    Be aware of the challenges and opportunities for participation in a task 167
Teaching resources 168

6 What Constitutes 'Useful Feedback' to Support EAL Learner Subject Literacy Development? 171

Starting points: The supportive role of feedback 171
What does emerging subject literacy look like? 175
How do learners manage the complexities of language to support the vocabulary of subject literacies in a test? 177
    Input for the End of Unit test 178
    Learning outcomes and success criteria: What does the teacher expect in the answer? 179
    What feedback on this test can we offer that is relevant to other subject areas? 182

How do learners use subject-specific and general academic words to explain abstract concepts in an essay?   187
   Input for History essay   187
   The essay 'The five steps leading to World War 2'   188
   What feedback on the essay can we offer that is relevant to other subject areas?   190
Drawing together features of *useful feedback* to support EAL learners   195
Teaching resources   197
   The *language aware* feedback portfolio   197
   Feedback codes for writing guidance (Make a parallel one for calculations?)   198
   The English tenses timeline chart   199

7 How Can I Monitor Emerging Subject Literacy and Plan Progression?   201

Starting points: Situating the EAL learner in the trajectory towards Upper Secondary-level study   202
Monitoring a newcomer to your class (PiE levels A–E)   203
Monitoring learners working at low level (PiE B): Wu, Sophia and Jamila   205
What are the areas to work on to reach level C?   206
Monitoring learners working at mid-level (PiE C) Alena and Yusra   208
What are the areas to work on to reach level D?   209
Monitoring learners working at upper level (PiE D) Yurek   210
What are the areas to work on to reach level E?   211
Monitoring and supporting learners working at high level (PiE E) Sabih   213
   Supporting areas of challenge for the high-level learner: Comparison and interpretation   214
Four steps in planning progression   218
Teaching resources for further study of language   222

References   225
Index   231

Acknowledgements

'I am a part of all that I have met' (Tennyson, 1833).

We acknowledge with appreciation the sources of our knowledge and experience that enabled the writing of this book.

Our team consists of teachers with English as a first language and as a second or third language. We have been educated in the UK, the Romanian and the US system. We have worked as teachers in the education systems of the UK, Malawi, Zambia, India, Latvia, Romania, France and Germany. We have taught in mainstream and private systems, for general and specialized purposes, at primary, secondary and tertiary levels.

Our learners have been those with English as a first language and as a second or third language; they have often been simultaneously learning English and learning IN English.

As reflective teachers we have learned from our learners and our peers as we have adapted our practices to the requirements of the different teaching contexts. We have gained policy insights from working with colleagues in professional bodies: BAAL, LKALE SiG, BALEAP, CLiE, SQA (ESOL), IELTS.

As researchers we can draw on evidence that knowing about language supports the knowledge building process for both mono- and multilingual users

As practising teachers we apply this knowledge to our practice.

We wish to thank the following individuals for their thoughts and works.

At the University of Glasgow: Lavinia Hirsu, Julie McAdam, Lee Dunn, Delia Wilson, Heather Macdonald, Aileen Sherry, Leon Robinson, colleagues and students at the University of Glasgow School of Education for many conversations and teaching experiences; Carole MacDiarmid, Anneli Williams, Bill Guariento, the staff and students of the University of Glasgow Language Centre 2000–13 and cross-college academic colleagues working with international students on academic programmes for insights into subject literacies across the disciplines.

In the UK: Urszula Clark, Sue Ellis, Claire Acevedo, Constant Leung, Yvonne Foley.

Thanks are due to William Zacharias for the illustrations, Peiyue Xu for tips on Chinese tones and an anonymous Chinese informant for Mandarin grammar.

Copyright permissions: the quote from Schleppegrell (2010) and data from NALDIC transcript 300509 (2009) are cited with permission of NALDIC Publications Committee; the Frogs and Frog Prince Table adapted from the University of Melbourne (2001) is used with permission of Professor Kristina Love; the poem 'Was Worm' May Swenson, from *May Swenson: Collected Poems* (Library of America, 2013), is used with permission of the Literary Estate of May Swenson. All rights reserved; the front cover image of *Wolf Brother* (2004) is used with permission of Hachette Children's books; material from Crown Copyright documents is fully referenced and used under Open Government Licence Version 3; other student and subject tutor data is used with permission of Zacharias (2018) and the University of Glasgow, College of Social Sciences Ethics Committee. All names are anonymized.

How to Use This Book

This book contains a number of features to support both students and professionals, from initial teacher training, right through their development into expert teachers.

To make the most of what this book offers, we suggest you read the **Introduction: Starting Points for the Book** on page 1 and then work your way through the chapters. Or, use the **Table of Contents** and **Index** to find what you need if you are looking to explore a particular topic or issue.

Each chapter begins with **starting points**, giving outline questions to guide you through the content.

Each chapter ends with **teaching resources**, setting out templates and key strategies.

Throughout each chapter, we have indicated where we suggest you note down your thoughts.

You will find a range of features within each chapter:

Key ideas are highlighted

Further reading and **policy documents** recommendations are provided

Reflective questions encourage you to pause and think about what you have experienced, read and learnt

Call outs give you questions to think about, models to use and examples of language features to show you how to identify the patterns to focus on

Text boxes annotate language features in subject texts

We have also provided a **glossary** to decipher key terms and acronyms on page xiii that you may find useful to refer to as you use the book.

Glossary of Terms

EAL learner	Bilingual or multilingual learner for whom English is an Additional Language. Learner who uses a language other than English as the home language
Home learner	Learner generally born and brought up in an English language context, whose main language is English
KS3/S1–3	Lower secondary level study: *Key Stage 3* in England and Wales, Northern Ireland; *Senior 1, 2 and 3* in Scotland
Metalanguage	Language for talking about language: labels for vocabulary words and grammar structures
PiE	Proficiency in English: level of language skills measured on EAL proficiency scales
Register	Appropriate style or word choice for communication context
Register continuum	Line between opposite styles of register, showing gradations of difference in appropriate word choice for a particular communication context
Word bank	Collection of useful subject-related words and phrases for learners' reference: activity sheets, workbooks, wall displays in multiple formats. A flexible resource that can be added to or referred to as necessary
Year 7,8,9	Learners aged 11–14 in England and Wales
Year 8,9,10	Learners aged 11–14 in Northern Ireland and Scotland

Introduction: Starting Points for the Book

Chapter Outline

How does language knowledge support learning and subject literacy development?	1
What is it like to learn in a culturally diverse classroom?	4
How can we apply this language knowledge to our classroom practice to support EAL learners and benefit *all* learners in the process?	6

This is a book about subject-related language for subject teachers working with EAL learners in culturally diverse classrooms at Lower Secondary school level. It sets out practical steps for the teacher to develop their language knowledge so that they can use activities to make clear to learners the patterns of language in their subject. This will support EAL learners and benefit *all* learners in the process.

To answer questions we know teachers have about subject literacy in these contexts, the book has three starting points.

- *How does language knowledge support learning and subject literacy development?*
- *What is it like to learn in a culturally diverse classroom?*
- *How can we apply our knowledge of language to support EAL learners and benefit* all *learners in the process?*

How does language knowledge support learning and subject literacy development?

Language is part of who we are and is intricately embedded in how we make sense of the world and learn. All teachers are told that 'language for learning is a central element in all teaching' (Ofsted 2012). What does this mean in practice?

On the positive side, all subject teachers have subject knowledge and intuitive understanding of how language works to make meaning in their subject. Subject literacy involves using the resources available to you that range from notations to visuals, to words and sounds to communicate the knowledge of a subject.

This book builds on what you already know and shows you how to talk about the language you need to support learning and subject literacy development in a clear way.

Think about how your own or your child's language skills developed. As a child, we start by using language to name and communicate things to each other, to categorize what we see, hear, feel, touch and smell – developing vocabulary. Then we start adding grammar patterns to make sense of strings of words. This tends to happen in more than one language at a time in a multilingual context.

These pieces of language become ways we use language in our everyday lives. Language becomes a set of social habits that shape our identity and our relationships with others, at home and then at school. By the time we get to school, we are ready to expand the range of our encounters to include the different kinds of language the teacher uses for classroom organization and learning.

In this way the child is learning language and also learning through language (Halliday 1993/2004). According to Halliday (1993/2004: 327), 'A distinctive feature of human learning is that it is a process of making meaning', and the fundamental tool for making meaning is language – whether visual, oral, aural or written mode.

Making meaning also involves cognition. The view of learning taken in this book is based on the general position of Piaget (1952); Bruner (1966) and Vygotsky (1978) that knowledge, both prior and new, initiates mental representation. Piaget saw the mental representations as the building blocks of knowledge. Our own personal version of how we understand the world is often referred to as *a schema*. Piaget saw *schemas* (plural) as a set of linked mental representations of the world which we use both to understand and to respond to situations.

Importantly, these representations are not fixed and static. They are dynamic cognitive structures that are altered over time as our learners encounter new experiences and accumulate knowledge. Much of what is triggered from our schematic knowledge by our daily interactions and the language we encounter is represented to us as a form of mental image.

This means that the teacher can use an image or word association to connect with an existing schema or mental representation as a starting point or a 'hook' for a 'new' topic. In the process, we develop language to talk about that new experience through the use of language and other resources with shared social and cognitive meanings. In this way the teacher enables the creation of new knowledge.

At Primary level, language and learning are well supported, with explicit focus on language forms (e.g. in England in the SPaG tests). As learners go through Primary school they learn to know the names of nouns, verbs, objects, etc. They will have had an introduction to text types and increased their style range in personal responses to match different audiences and communication purposes. The learner is offered many guided learning opportunities to expand self-expression, as well as to notice and develop general literacy skills.

However, the language knowledge taught at Primary level is rarely extended systematically across the curriculum at Secondary level to match the demands of subject literacy development. At Secondary level, where learners meet similar concepts in more detail, the subject knowledge becomes more complex and so do the language structures and text types.

Both the literature and policy documents underline the need for support. Learners need to become familiar with the language which defines each subject in its own right, such as appropriate mathematical and scientific language (Department for Education 2014: 11). Indeed, each subject area has specialized registers that develop over long trajectories and are not learned without instruction (Schleppegrell 2014). The more complex language structures learners encounter need just as much attention as subject-specific vocabulary (Bowyer 2018: 34).

Guidelines from the National Curriculum, for example, emphasize the need for language to be used 'flexibly with understanding in a suitable sentence structure – active or passive voice' (Department for Education 2014: 14). For example, there is a clear difference in meaning between the passive and active voices used in the following:

Passive: 'The power was transferred to the government.'

Here, the teacher is not foregrounding who or what transferred the power as it is not considered here to be important.

Active: 'It was the people, not the government, who transferred the power.'

Here, the teacher foregrounds *who* transfers the power, as it *is* considered important.

Understanding how the choice of language structure can influence the way we think is an important insight and resource for teachers. As a subject teacher, you are required to support the development of subject literacy across the curriculum. Some teachers report feeling insecure in their language knowledge (Cajkler and Hislam (2010), Foley, Sangster and Anderson (2013)). This challenge is increased by rising numbers of EAL learners in UK classrooms: those who are learning in English but who use a language other than English in their homes and communities.

Throughout this book we use discovery tasks and reflection points to extend your way of thinking and talking about how language is used in your subject to present and discuss knowledge. Starting with what you already know about how language works, how it is used in everyday contexts, in classroom processes and in learning, we move on to look at how EAL language knowledge develops.

The examples of how to notice and analyse the patterns of language we use in subject literacy for different communication purposes will help you consciously develop your own range of vocabulary and grammar. Each chapter looks at an aspect of subject literacy, selecting examples from particular subjects. It then shows how these activities can be adapted across subject areas and integrated into classroom practice to systematically develop learners' understanding of subject-specific language.

In this process we show how language supports learning, how we can identify the language of subject literacy and how we can apply that knowledge to our classroom practice to support learners.

What is it like to learn in a culturally diverse classroom?

All learners bring cultural diversity to the classroom based on the range of their home, educational and linguistic backgrounds. These resources will comprise the *knowledge schemas* we referred to in the previous section. They will also include the 'funds of knowledge' as first defined by Moll, Amanti and González (1992). These 'funds of knowledge' refer to the skills and knowledge that have been historically and culturally developed to enable an individual or household to function within a given culture.

You may have learners who are

- monolingual, have lived all their lives in the UK and use only English in their home;
- bilingual or multilingual, have lived all their lives in the UK, but use a language other than English at home and bring their own language and cultural practices to school or
- multilingual and have arrived in the UK from another country or other countries.

How they communicate, whether mono, bi or multilingual, will involve a diversity in the range and modality of the resources at their disposal.

This basic intercultural awareness allows you to see the learner as a whole person. Your school should have a system for *establishing a learner profile* for the teacher to recognize and respect assets brought by their learners, avoid fears, assumptions and possible misunderstandings. This will inform how you apply the same educational principles and procedures as to any teaching context, but with an awareness that your learners' cultural and language knowledge will be based on their home culture, previous educational experience and their assumptions about learning processes.

For the EAL learners, surrounded by different languages from their own and a different set of cultural habits, both in and out of class, the challenge is how to make sense of it. It's important not to equate language difficulty with learning difficulty. Our learners will use whatever resources they have at their disposal to interpret what we do in the classroom.

Try to visualize yourself as a New Arrival or Newcomer EAL learner in your class. Think outside the box from an objective viewpoint. What was it like when you first arrived in a country with a different language and culture from yours? What did you notice? Smells? Sounds? Sights? Behaviour?

If this is hard to do, have a look at *The Arrival* by Shaun Tan. This is a wordless book we often use with EAL learners to help them articulate their experiences, especially on arrival. It is about a man arriving in a new country to look for work before summoning his family. He is shown going about everyday life, but in a rather surreal landscape. It builds mental images of what a person from a different cultural environment experiences, encouraging us to look at ourselves from another person's perspective (see the video https://vimeo.com/74292820).

Another way we invoke this objectivity is to teach our student teachers their own subject in a foreign language for ten minutes and ask them: 'How did it feel?'

We use gesture and visuals with key words written on them, but the student comments are predictably about the confusion and lack of power they experienced because they did not have the language to understand fully. The gesture and visuals help to access the knowledge to some extent, and the key words helped because there was some linguistic similarity.

Inevitably EAL learners will use their everyday knowledge of the world and their own home language to make sense of what is going on in front of them until their English skills reach a certain level. Fortunately, as humans we share many common physical and social experiences, e.g. we understand that objects move forward when pushed, and we associate friendship with warmth and happiness. For the teacher, getting to know the geography and culture of your learners' countries will help you find *triggers to their schemas and funds of knowledge* to engage them in learning, e.g. food, sport, music. Smart phones and Google Translate are great tools to help find the words in their own language.

If our EAL learners are encouraged to see that the funds of knowledge that they bring to the task are not only interesting but also valued, they are far more likely to remain engaged. So a warm welcome is in order to support the adjustment process and provide opportunities for participation.

We integrate this approach to supporting EAL learners throughout the book. We emphasize the importance of familiarizing yourself with learners' educational, cultural and language backgrounds. We set out the basics of how language skills develop, how an EAL learner manages languages for learning in a new language, how to create a welcoming classroom environment, how to design suitable pedagogic tasks to support language development, how to provide appropriate feedback and how to monitor progression.

How can we apply this language knowledge to our classroom practice to support EAL learners and benefit *all* learners in the process?

The application of this knowledge to classroom practice will best take place in a collaborative classroom with *a culture of talk*. Our language skills develop through hearing and listening before seeing, reading and writing, so opportunities for talking, for oral participation in meaningful communication and receiving positive feedback are key. Our view is that learning is more than a simple transfer of knowledge. We see it as a reciprocal process between the teacher and learners as learning is created. Good 'dialogic teaching' offers opportunities for learners to share their views and shape their thinking out loud as they 'try out' the new ideas and language they are being offered (Alexander 2004).

The National Curriculum for science emphasizes

> the importance of spoken language in learner development across the whole curriculum: cognitively, socially and linguistically. (Department for Education 2014: 57)

From the scientists' point of view, the careful choice and the variety of the language that learners hear and speak are

> key factors in developing their scientific vocabulary and articulating scientific concepts clearly and precisely. They must be assisted in making their thinking clear, both to themselves and others, and teachers should ensure that pupils build secure foundations by using discussion to probe and remedy their misconception. (ibid)

We offer strategies such as 'exploratory talk', a term originally developed by Barnes (1996), which uses collaborative learning to draw on multimodal resources and talk. For example, to encourage the EAL learners to bring to mind mental images of the topic and what they already know, we use visuals and realia, along with open questions to initiate exploratory talk to build meaning.

We model how to initiate dialogue at each stage in plenary and in groups to identify ways of building knowledge, by listening, sharing and discussing ideas and coming up with an opinion. Reading and listening are essentially interactive processes that are best supported by purposeful talk in the classroom to build meaning and knowledge. We can set *focusing tasks* which ask the learner to listen for key points, or to talk to another learner about what they heard or read using guided questioning.

Working together with peers provides our learners with an opportunity to interact with others that a teacher-led discussion does not afford. For our EAL learners, oral confidence can be boosted by participating in group work, by listening, as much as contributing. Group work can offer the chance to hear a model of how the other learners talk fluently about their knowledge. It can also provide the opportunity to practise the language in a more private arena than in front of the whole class.

To reinforce ownership of new knowledge, we model how to vary ways of saying the same thing so that teachers guide their 'new' learners along the path towards becoming 'subject experts'. This is a similar practice to what has been called 'revoicing' by O'Connor and Michaels (1993). It means that the teacher *rephrases, rewords or reformulates* what the learner says to clarify and give status to the learner contribution. It also shows that the learner is being listened to and models how other learners should pay attention too.

This approach offers the opportunity to 'discuss the shades of meaning in similar words', which is recommended at this level in the National Curriculum for England (Department for Education 2014: 57). The document recommends that teachers should actively increase the general store of words by building systematically on the learners' current knowledge because 'acquisition and command of vocabulary' is 'key to their learning and progress across the whole curriculum'.

An Ofsted report on *Barriers to Literacy* (2011) noted that in the Secondary schools where teachers in all subject departments had received training in teaching literacy and where staff had included an objective for literacy in all the lessons, senior managers noted an improvement in outcomes across all subjects, for *all* learners. This point is reinforced by a colleague who has worked extensively with teachers in Secondary Schools with high populations of second generation EAL learners in Birmingham. She comments that

> teachers who spend time on supporting information processing by focussing on words, sentence deconstruction and guided talking for learning find that, although they may cover less content area, the area they have covered has been absorbed by the learners through use, rather than through one off exposure and memorisation. (Professor Urszula Clark personal communication)

And what better time to do this than at the transition from Primary to Secondary, as learners adjust to the learning environment at Lower Secondary level? This is an ideal stage to lay a foundation in Subject Literacy skills for the Exam stage in Upper Secondary School.

Since language is so closely involved in the creation of knowledge, we show teachers how to integrate a focus on language when they plan an explanation. The practical activities aim to establish a context that offers learners maximum exposure to language, sets up numerous planned opportunities for participation and talking to try out and build knowledge, followed by appropriate language aware feedback. This language aware approach offers a system for monitoring learners' emerging subject literacies and planning progression. It can be adapted for Upper Secondary learners. Teachers are encouraged to monitor their own practice and share ideas with colleagues.

1

Where Do We Start with Supporting Subject Literacies in the Classroom?

Chapter Outline

Starting points: Existing understandings of language and literacies	9
What language resources and social strategies do we develop from early years?	10
How does the teacher use social meanings in school settings?	12
How do literacy skills develop at Primary school?	16
An example of language in the construction of knowledge at different stages of a lesson	22
Drawing together ideas for supporting subject literacies in the classroom	26
Teaching resources	28

- *What language resources are available in the classroom to build on?*
- *How do we use it in everyday and classroom contexts to construct knowledge?*
- *How can we start to apply this knowledge to support EAL learners in the classroom?*

Starting points: Existing understandings of language and literacies

As we saw in the Introduction, language plays an important role in learning. All of us have an intuitive language knowledge that develops as we accumulate *social funds of knowledge*, along with *cognitive schemas* to build on. The approach we take in this book is that *learning is a creative process of knowledge building in an interactive context*. At the same time we have an *intercultural awareness of the cultural coding of our language habits* and our assumptions in how we use them.

Not all learners are equally familiar with how the English language works. So for this chapter, intuitive language knowledge is our starting point. It will be knowledge that teachers and learners who have been through the UK Primary system will have built up. We will see how existing knowledge lays a foundation for a way of talking about language and our habits of using language for a particular context and communication purpose. We look at different kinds of language knowledge to explore

- what language and literacies you can expect learners to bring from Primary school,
- how teachers use language in everyday and classroom contexts and
- how we use it to represent subject knowledge to learners.

This understanding will help the teacher make the role of language in different classroom processes visible to all learners, particularly those new to the UK education system or those more used to visual and oral communication than the written word. Looking at how we use it in everyday and classroom contexts for the construction of knowledge provides a starting point for subject literacies that we can build on as we move through the book. This general overview will set the scene for understanding the challenges facing EAL learners and a more detailed exploration of aspects of subject literacy that can be applied to classroom practice to support them.

What language resources and social strategies do we develop from early years?

We will start from the beginning. If you cast your mind back to what you know about child language development, at birth the first kind of language a child hears from the mother is often referred to as 'motherese', where tone of voice, body language, gesture and visual images play a large part. When we start naming things in our environment like 'Mummy', 'drink', we start to adopt social habits like learning to say 'Hi' and 'Bye', 'Please' and 'Thank you'.

As we construct our knowledge of the world, and talk about our knowledge and experience, we continue this socializing practice as we learn how to beg, borrow or steal each other's toys. In this natural process the words tend to come first and the grammar is gradually added to give further meaning to the individual words (more detail in the Teaching Resources for this chapter (page 28)). A child subconsciously notices and copies the patterns in the language she hears so that she can work out the rules (Halliday 1975, Wells 1985). Taking advantage of as much 'exposure' or 'input' as possible, the child is busy practising and playing around with language. She then tests her interpretation of the rules by using them in the next communication. She will get feedback, generally in the form of an encouraging response to show whether she is right or wrong. If there is a problem, most adults will repeat the language in a more correct form and even extend the conversation if possible; for example, 'Daddy go' might get the response 'Yes, Daddy is going' to draw attention to the right form of the verb. It takes nearly two years from birth to communicating in meaningful language with both words and grammar.

Gradually the number of words and patterns available to the child increases and the child becomes able to receive and respond to more complex patterns and meanings.

How we use language in our everyday lives shapes our identity and our relationships with others. We select different forms of language or register styles to communicate depending on context.

As we do this, we build mental images of how to manage conversation tasks successfully: how to greet family, friends and teachers. Do you remember working out how to persuade your parents to buy you a new pair of trainers?

EAL learners will have a similar system for managing personal relations in their language. So you are an 'interpreter' who can link together your language choices with those of the EAL learner.

Talking about these ways of using language allows us to ask the EAL learner, 'What about you?' 'How do you do these things in your culture?' Raising classroom awareness of how we use everyday language for social purposes is one step towards creating a supportive classroom culture for EAL learners trying to get their social bearings. This approach is significant to the growth of the learners' language, and general social and cognitive well-being. We can share our understandings, and any misunderstandings can be repaired.

How does the teacher use social meanings in school settings?

In this section we turn our attention to school settings to explore three aspects of how teachers use language with social meanings. The first is to establish a professional role in the classroom, the second is to manage relations with colleagues in the workplace and the third is managing standard and non-standard language forms in the classroom.

Establishing a professional role in the classroom

As teachers we make language choices about how to present ourselves in the classroom. Subject tutors often mention that one of the most complex aspects of becoming a teacher is the requirement for multiple roles. The teacher is a source of authority, but also a guide and a monitor, someone who gives praise and feedback. Microteaching, where a teacher watches a video of herself, is often used to raise awareness of how we use these roles. Timing is often key. Observing experienced others is another useful strategy for noticing these behaviours.

These are habits we have to learn. To explain how these social habits work in spoken mode, we refer to Kress (1982), who points out that the starting point for spoken language is an assumption that the speaker and the listener have shared experience. We have an existing schema to support how we use spoken language depending on what we know about each other and the context in which we are communicating. We make different language choices depending on the language habits of the context. As contexts vary, so do groups. How did you talk to your close friends as a child? Was it the same way you talked to your parents and older relatives?

What language choices will you make to establish your classroom role? What level of formality? There are sometimes issues with a learner addressing the teacher as a friend, using language that is more suitable for contexts outside class. Will your level of formality vary depending on whether you are speaking to the whole class, a group or an individual?

What different role choices can you recognize in the language of these examples?

(1) OK! Settle down, please! That's right! Everyone got a seat?
(2) Can you find your books please?
(3) Now, what I want you to do when we've finished this section is ….
(4) Noise level, please!

(5) Work with your partner on this.
(6) We'll stop in five minutes.
(7) Any questions?
(8) You've worked very well today. Good. Let's look over what we've covered.

This mixture of *commands, statements, suggestions, questions and praise* exemplifies language that will set the tone or classroom ethos, particularly a question like No 2 that is actually *an instruction*.

At the same time as establishing roles, the teacher is *modelling* desirable classroom language that is useful to the EAL learner. Think about the kinds of responses you would expect. Are there any kinds of language you would not accept?

When it comes to introducing and engaging learners in pedagogic tasks, we use strategies to make the class interesting and relevant. We learn a range of questioning techniques. Can you hear yourself in any of these examples? Do you have different ones?

(9) Has anyone ever wondered …?
(10) Who can tell me what … is?
(11) What can you tell me about …?

In this role, it is likely that you will accept responses and then reword them to model the language you want the learners to use. In the process of establishing roles and modelling classroom language, the teacher is aiming to set a classroom ethos that will build *confidence, interest, enjoyment* and *a sense of achievement*.

We can represent this concept in a visual image. The line below represents a *continuum* because it allows us to illustrate shades of meaning in the range of language choices between one register and another. In this case the examples range in context from *playground* to *classroom*.

Continuum (1) Professional role: Playground/friend versus classroom/professional

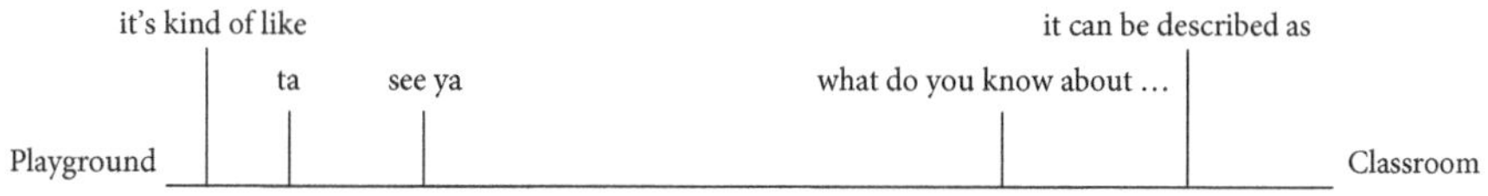

```
           it's kind of like                          it can be described as
                 ta     see ya              what do you know about …
Playground    |   |      |                         |                        | Classroom
```

The teacher and the learner take on roles using particular kinds of language in the classroom that vary from outside. An idea for how these continuums can be used in the classroom is given in Teaching Resources for this chapter (page 28).

Managing relations with tutors and colleagues

When you are in a new professional context you will have different relationships with those around you depending on their professional role and how well you know them. This is another language challenge for student teachers mentioned by subject tutors. How should students ask a tutor for something politely, without being too *familiar* or *informal*? How should they approach new colleagues to set up a good working relationship when they start school placements?

Think about *who* you are likely to be talking to, and *where*, in these examples:

(a) Sorry to bother you Mrs McVey, but could you tell me who I should ask about a staff parking permit?
(b) I wondered if I could change the time for discussion of my essay.
(c) Could you give me a hand?

Suggestions

(a) This could be you contacting the Head of Year before joining a school. This person is a stranger, a professional in a senior position. Your approach is likely to be indirect, using a number of words because you are preparing the ground, or framing the request, before asking it. You might even start with an apology for disturbance!
(b) This reflects how you might address your subject tutor: again framing the request quite politely ('I wondered if') before asking the question.
(c) This is the most direct request, with the fewest words and is likely to be you asking a colleague to help you.

These examples demonstrate how shared experience dictates the choices we make in level of formality. They depend on what we call 'social distance', i.e. *more words demonstrate indirectness and more distance*. The better you know someone, *the closer you are and the more direct* you can be. You can use fewer words. Indeed, sometimes body language or a facial expression is enough!

The continuum we use here represents a social stance that ranges between informal and formal language.

Continuum (2) Social role: Close (direct/fewer words) versus distant (indirect/more words)

Informal				Formal
hiya	thanks		thank you very much	
give us a hand	could you give me a hand	good morning	I wonder if you wouldn't mind …	

 Can you think of other examples to place on the line?

Managing non-standard language forms in the classroom

Because language is a part of who you are, it reflects your regional and social identity. Depending on where you come from, you will have associations with accent and dialect. Some people can recognize your accent from the way you say your vowels and consonants. In Scotland, they might be able to recognize which part you are from by the way you say the vowel sound 'i' in 'fish and chips'. Others can identify you by the kinds of dialect words and forms you use to express membership of a regional or social group, e.g. Geordie or London Metropolitan. Some of this language will be what we call 'non-standard' in the sense that 'standard' language forms are generally expected to be used for the public purposes that school is preparing learners for.

To raise awareness of standard and non-standard language forms, have a look at the language choices in the two text boxes below. There are four examples in the left hand column where the speakers are talking about work they 'have done' (or not) for a lecture/an essay/a class. Try to match each one with a context when you would use it from the examples in the right hand column. Think about your own choices. Which form would you use in which context?

What you said	The context
1. *I done all my reading before the lecture this time.*	a) I might say this to a mate outside school.
2. *I've did quite a lot of work for this essay.*	b) A teacher might write this to the principal.
3. *I was delighted I did my essay early.*	c) If somebody wrote this, some people might think they weren't very clever.
4. *I have done quite a lot of work for this class.*	d) I would never say this.

(Catherine Walter, personal communication 2012)

How good are you at identifying these differences? Which is it non-standard? Which is standard language?

What we can say is that '*I done*' and '*I've did*' (non-standard) are equivalent to '*I did*' and '*I have done*' (standard).

It is important to note that the non-standard forms are not 'wrong'. Indeed they are selected as everyday dialect choices in many contexts. There are strong arguments for the importance of dialect as an expression of identity and membership of a particular community. In a classroom you would probably hear a mix of accents along with both standard and non-standard language choices for different purposes at different stages of a lesson.

Many classrooms discourage the use of non-standard language, especially in written output that aims to develop subject literacies for long-term educational goals. Perhaps you allow non-standard spoken language?

This non-standard versus standard continuum allows us to demonstrate to learners where a language choice sits between the two registers.

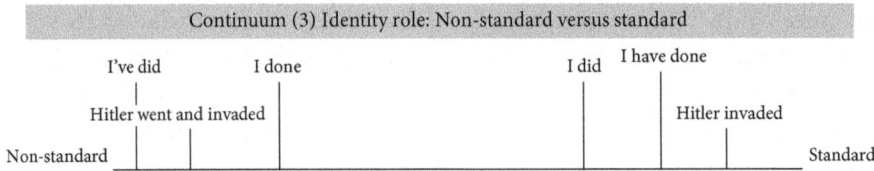

Can you think of more examples of these variations? How would you guide the EAL learner on this?

Having looked at social meanings of language choices the teacher makes in school settings, let's turn our attention to the literacy skills you can expect your learners to bring from Primary school.

How do literacy skills develop at Primary school?

When we start school the process of learning language and literacy becomes more formalized. The 'home language' a child hears before starting school is different from 'school language'. A teacher is a different kind of carer.

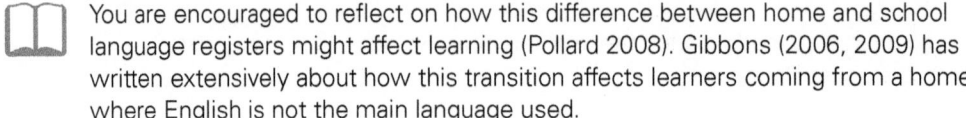

You are encouraged to reflect on how this difference between home and school language registers might affect learning (Pollard 2008). Gibbons (2006, 2009) has written extensively about how this transition affects learners coming from a home where English is not the main language used.

At Primary school the input becomes more structured because the curriculum aims to lay a foundation of language knowledge at two levels that we cover in the next two sections:

- Word- and sentence-level knowledge and
- Text-level knowledge that lays a foundation for subject literacies

Word- and sentence-level knowledge

At Primary level, where *input* is aural, written and visual, the emphasis on *output* in class is on personal response and expression, as learners speak, write and draw. This encourages a learner to articulate and expand ways of talking about new knowledge and feelings. In this way, the repertoire of words and language patterns develops and grows. A teacher will model language by repeating and extending a learner response, in a similar way to how the parent, siblings or friends did in early language communications. But the teacher's response is more structured, for example:

T: Why did the Spanish land on the coast of Mexico?
S: Gold
T: Yes, they were searching for gold.

We can see how the teacher uses *dialogic teaching* in an extended response to model the appropriate language forms. At the same time, the teacher has the opportunity to guide the child to notice and practise features of spelling and pronunciation to help with reading and writing.

Sentences are discussed in a more systematic way with labels to establish that they consist of a 'subject', 'verb' and 'object'. Learners become familiar with the idea that *simple sentences* can be expanded to form *multi-clause sentences* by using *coordination*, or *subordination*. Learners name and define parts of speech such as *noun*, *verb* and so on.

The terminology for naming 'word classes' or 'parts of speech' is helpful for explaining to a learner why some language might be appropriate and sounds right, or not, as the case may be (more details in Teaching Resources, page 29).

What is important is that learners are exposed to this terminology 'in context' so they are not only 'naming and defining' but also *understanding how the word is used in a particular type of communication*. This understanding can then be applied to how they use language themselves.

Bear in mind that EAL learners might be familiar with terminology for words and sentences if they have studied English before.

How to teach monolingual learners the patterns of English is a much debated question. Many of us in the UK joke that we only learn the grammar of our own language through learning a foreign one. But while assessment is so heavily weighted towards written text, research is leaning towards the view that

Explicit teaching of grammar and language integrated into the context of subject knowledge across the curriculum at all Key Stages can support learner outcomes in reading and writing (Myhill 2018).

You, as an adult, have already absorbed this language knowledge, even though it might not be in an explicit or analytical way. Your reading will have been key to absorbing models. But crucially you can distinguish between language that sounds 'right' and makes sense, and a *text where meaning is unclear* or *hard to work out*.

Text-level knowledge to lay a foundation for subject literacies

Moving on to text-level knowledge, we can see how the foundations of subject literacy are established at Primary school, where the learner is guided to write across the curriculum subjects and for different communication purposes. The focus is on text structure and language choices in the appropriate style or register. This is modelled by the teacher and then scaffolded in the composition process. Learners encounter the difference between *everyday and specialist terminology*, a useful preparation for the development of subject literacy at Lower Secondary stage.

This approach to writing development stemmed from the National Literacy Strategy (NLS) implemented in 1998 with subsequent updates (see Ofsted 2002). Whatever the view on these policies, the NLS guidance still offers a useful vocabulary for talking about the structure and language features of texts for different audiences and purposes.

 In 2001, the updated NLS documents offered ten fliers on teaching the different text types, six of which are archived at http://dera.ioe.ac.uk/6161/ or https://dera.ioe.ac.uk/4699/

We look at language examples from Narrative and Factual description in the next section to illustrate how we use existing schemas to recognize the language features of texts that use *everyday and specialist terms*.

Distinguishing *narrative* from *factual* description

How do you distinguish between a *narrative* and a *factual* description? Table 1.1 shows words and phrases from two texts: a story and a factual description.

 Which words and phrases belong to Text A: 'The Frog Prince'?
And which words and phrases belong to Text B: 'Frogs'?

Where Do We Start with Supporting Subject Literacies in the Classroom?

Table 1.1 Words and Phrases from 'The Frog Prince' and 'Frogs'

frogs are amphibians	Oh Master Frog!	male frogs are distinguished by	most frogs have smooth slimy skin
special characteristics	could hardly bear to touch him	she cried	on the third night
Thank Heaven!	in damp undergrowth near water	lived happily ever after	protruding eyes which allow for excellent vision
when morning came	transparent lenses	I will fetch it, said the frog, and he splashed into the water	are classified by herpetologists

Adapted from University of Melbourne (2001).

You probably found it quite easy to sort these phrases into two groups because you have *implicit* knowledge that these two texts have a different purpose. This awareness of a *different purpose* implies a different register or style, which means you can *predict* which phrases belong to the story and which ones belong to the text about Frogs.

Can you explain this *implicit* knowledge? How do you know? Can you find words to make that knowledge *explicit* to an EAL learner?

Before you look at the comments in the tables below, try to explain to yourself

'Why does "*Thank Heaven!*" belong to the story?'
'Why does "*transparent lenses*" belong to the text about frogs?'

Comments

Here are the words and phrases from Table 1.1 set out in separate groups. Table 1.2 is for Text A and Table 1.3 shows Text B, with comments on the language features in each case. Do you agree with the comments? Can you add anything else to make this understanding of different types of language clearer?

Table 1.2 Text A: Words and Phrases with Comments on Language Features

TEXT A The Frog Prince – fairy story	What are the language features?
• Oh Master Frog! • she cried • could hardly bear to touch him • on the third night • 'I will fetch it', said the frog, and he splashed into the water • when morning came • Thank Heaven! • lived happily ever after	This is a fairy story because magic is involved: the two characters, a male frog and a female princess, can speak to each other; they have feelings (*could hardly bear to touch him*), make exclamations (*Thank Heaven!*); there is a problem to solve and a happy ending. Events take place over a period of time indicated by *third night*, *morning* and the past tense.

Table 1.3 Text B: Words and Phrases with Comments on Language Features

TEXT B Frogs – a factual description	What are the language features?
• Frogs are amphibians • are classified by herpetologists • in damp undergrowth near water • most frogs have smooth slimy skin • protruding eyes which allow for excellent vision • transparent lenses • male frogs are distinguished by • special characteristics	It consists of generally true statements in the present tense about physical characteristics and habits of frogs. The term 'herpetologist' is used for the specialists who classify frogs as 'amphibians'. There is a lot of specialist vocabulary and other general terms that are unlikely to be used in everyday talk (*undergrowth, protruding, vision, lenses*).

These *story features* make use of the kind of structure and language patterns we learn to recognize and expect from schema built up through our early years at home, in school, presented in many modes (oral, written, visual).

The factual description presents slightly different challenges, but nonetheless the structure and language patterns, built up through *school years*, are predictable.

The language choices in Text B may reflect the typical classroom language the teacher uses to talk to us about the things we study. If we rewrote these parts of Text B in everyday language, it would take a lot more words.

For example,

Frogs can live on land and underwater, which means they are called 'amphibians' by scientists called herpetologists. These scientists give names to this type of animal based on what it looks like, where it lives, and what it eats. Frogs have eyes that stick out from their heads, so they are able to see very well.

Going back to using simpler words like this underlines the change in language habits that the learner has to manage in the process of learning to talk and write about Frogs in a more *specialized* way, i.e. 'amphibians', 'herpetologist', 'protruding eyes', 'excellent vision'.

This is a new set of habits, a new set of nouns to represent new mental images and a new schema. At the same time, the advantage of any specialized term is that it can carry a lot of information.

Carrying more information, or 'information density', is key to understanding the role of specialized words in subject literacies, as we will see in subsequent chapters in more detail. *Specialized words allow the user to say more in fewer words*. It also means the user can be more specific, more precise and avoid ambiguity.

This register continuum represents the range in language choices between everyday words and specialist terms.

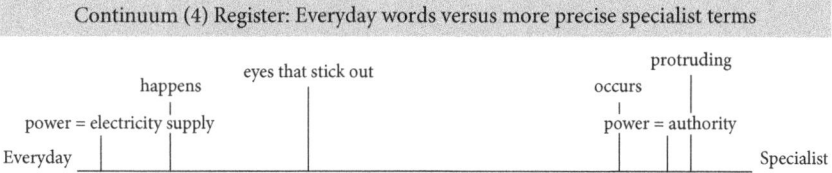

Continuum (4) Register: Everyday words versus more precise specialist terms

For learners from Primary level who are familiar with this kind of language variation to match text purpose, it is important to harness and develop that understanding at Lower Secondary level so that it continues to develop. For the EAL learners, you, as the teacher, can make these differences clear by drawing attention to how you and the other learners make the language choices.

Extending the range of vocabulary and grammar means the teacher and learner are able to move flexibly between *everyday and specialist terms* as part of normal classroom processes.

Such an awareness of style shift between registers allows the teacher to understand and manage the complexity of how knowledge is constructed and the role language plays in it.

Development of further text types

The NLS guidance shows that when learners have developed a strong sense of *narrative* structure and how to choose words for effect, the concept of text type to suit purpose is extended to include *factual descriptions*, as set out above. To this the following text types are added:

- *Instructions:* how to play a game, labelled diagram to show how to make a kite
- *Factual recounts:* of a school trip, working with magnets
- *Biography:* of Van Gogh

Reading can be a key 'input' and the teacher will deconstruct texts. Learners are then guided *to take notes, develop a flow chart, make a skeleton outline* and *think in paragraphs*. They work on *editing their writing to ensure they make the most of linking phrases and organizing devices such as headings to help the reader.*

With these underlying skills integrated into their work, the guidance recommends that at Upper Primary level there is an added focus *on clarity, conciseness, impersonal style and recording sources used.* The idea is that the broader your range of vocabulary and grammar structures, the more precise your language can be, e.g. 'amphibians' instead of 'animals that can live on land and underwater'.

Finally the learners meet

- *Persuasion:* towards a point of view
- *Discussion:* about school uniform

The text purposes of *persuasion and discussion* represent a significant developmental step towards tasks that require more *complex reasoning*. The learner has moved from merely reporting, to the process of *selecting and sequencing information, building an argument to take a stance on one point, or combine two points of view, justifying with evidence and then evaluating* in 'discussion'. We look at Secondary-level texts that exemplify these subject literacies in more detail in the following chapters.

To complete the overview of the role language plays in learning we look at different language styles at different stages of an interactive Science lesson.

An example of language in the construction of knowledge at different stages of a lesson

As set out in the Introduction, we take the view in this book that new knowledge and new language initiate a visualization or mental image of a new idea derived from some kind of stimulus and that language develops to express that new experience. Classrooms are generally active places because learning is largely socially constructed: there is a shared responsibility between teachers and learners for the co-construction of meaning and the building of knowledge. There will be scaffolding activities that involve using language in a range of modes for receiving, sharing, transmitting ideas, a lot of them oral, for the purpose of *trying out meaning* (Bruner 1978, cited in Gibbons 2015), as we shall see in this section.

Here we are working from the premise that everyday existing knowledge stored in schemas is added to and developed. There are many variables and progress is not always linear. To take account of this, the four-stage model of experiential learning developed by Kolb (1984) provides a helpful framework. It allows for a good level of repetition and recycling of words and ideas that most of us will recognize as the shape of an ideal lesson plan.

Kolb's teaching and learning cycle

Stage 1 *is drawing the students in by referring to what they already know (the old) and setting the context for the topic (the new).*

Stage 2 *involves setting up tasks to model the 'new' and deconstruct key ideas.*

Stage 3 *means drawing those ideas together to work with learners to model the construction of a product or outcome (co-construction).*

Stage 4 *sets up tasks for learners to manage their independent construction of a product or outcome.*

The following three examples of classroom language provide us with snapshots of part of this process. The data was collected in a project reported by Gibbons (2015: 7), looking at different kinds of language used in the Upper Primary class as they learn about magnets.

The language choices show

- the speaker shifting style from the shared experience perspective of talking to the more precise perspective of report writing,
- the change in level of formality (close to more distant) and
- the different language choice for **verbs (in bold)** and *nouns (in italics)*.

Example 1: We join the class at Stage 2 of the lesson (after Stage 1, where the teacher has set the context of the new topic).

Here, the learners are involved in group tasks exploring and deconstructing what magnets do with the objects. The class is supported by visuals of magnets with magnetic fields marked round the poles, along with the realia of magnets, pins and other non-ferrous objects to carry out some practical work.

One of the learners comments on what is happening,

Look, *it's* **making** *them* **move**. *Those* **don't stick**.

Language features: Speaker refers to a shared experience; uses everyday verbs in the present tense, **Look, making, move, stick**; uses informal register, talking to each other, close social distance.

> Example 2: At Stage 3 the learner relates her observations to the teacher at the end of the task, when learners start to draw ideas together.
>
> *We **found out** the pins **stuck on** the magnet.*
>
> *Language features:* Speaker uses '*we*' to refer to shared experience in the here and now (close), but uses '**found out**', a more formal (distant) register as the learners shift role to reporting to the teacher in the past tense.

> Example 3: At Stage 4 the learner has put the experience she spoke about into a written report on the experiment. The style is more scientific as the learner makes a generalization about the observation.
>
> *Our experiment **showed** that magnets **attract** some metals.*
>
> *Language features:* The learner takes a *writer perspective*. 'Our experiment' and 'magnets' refer to the topic she is writing about (more distant, formal). As Kress (1982) points out, in contrast to speaking mode, where the perspective is *shared experience*, the perspective in *written mode is the topic the writer wishes to present*. The verb '**attract**' is a specialist term that holds more specific information than '**stick**'. In writing we have to be more precise.

These examples demonstrate what Gibbons (2006) has referred to as 'language in transition through the learning process'. All the statements are carrying more or less the same information, but the language changes from a spoken commentary, to a spoken report, to a written report. As we can see, a *change in mode in the classroom implies a change of style or register*.

Continuum 5 represents the changes in style from speaking to each other to reporting to the teacher to writing a report on the experiment.

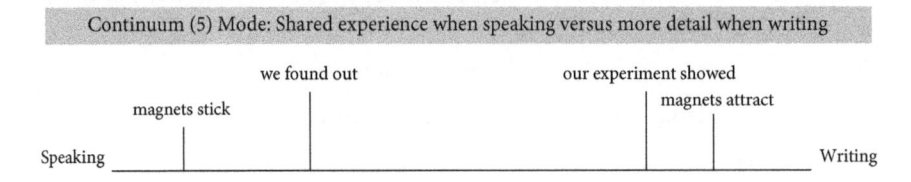

Continuum (5) Mode: Shared experience when speaking versus more detail when writing

```
                    we found out                    our experiment showed
          magnets stick                                        magnets attract
Speaking  _____|_____|_____|_____|_____ Writing
```

We do not have a further example from the lesson, but Gibbons (2015:7) offers a fourth example of language choice that is worth commenting on as it shows yet another extension to the language registers. What do you notice in this entry from a child's encyclopaedia?

Magnetic attraction **occurs** between ferrous metals.

Here we see a shift from the **verb 'attract'** to the *noun 'attraction'*. This is how the topic might be referred to in a textbook at Lower Secondary level. In a typical 'subject' text, *the writer's focus* is on the *thing* or *abstract phenomenon* that the learners have been learning about: *Magnetic attraction*. The writer therefore makes a typical *shift from using* **a** *verb for the process* (**stick, attract**) *to using a 'noun phrase' for the concept*. The process of shifting from a verb to a noun is called 'nominalization'. It is commonly used in a subject text because it has the advantage of giving more precise information in fewer words. However it does make the language of the text more complex and challenging to understand without support.

We can see from these examples how the range of language choices shifts during the different stages of the lesson, not only mixing everyday words and specialist terminology in the course of speaking and writing but also moving from talking about the concrete experience to writing more formal words, so that the event ('**stick (vb)**') is referred to as a more abstract concept ('*attraction (n)*'). These classroom processes offer the learner the building blocks for constructing knowledge, along with opportunities for articulating the experience in different forms of language.

The flow chart represents the teaching and learning process that the learners have participated in.

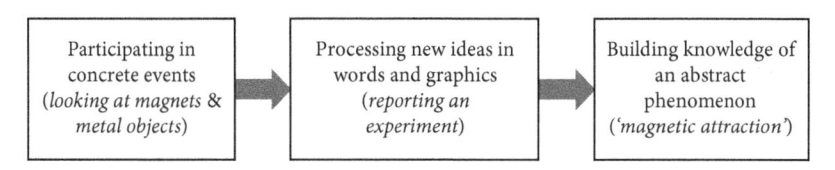

Participating in concrete events (*looking at magnets & metal objects*)	→	Processing new ideas in words and graphics (*reporting an experiment*)	→	Building knowledge of an abstract phenomenon ('*magnetic attraction*')

And so we come to the last of our continuums, which represents the change in register from talking about the concrete event to referring to an abstract concept or phenomenon.

Continuum (6) Register: Concrete versus abstract phenomenon

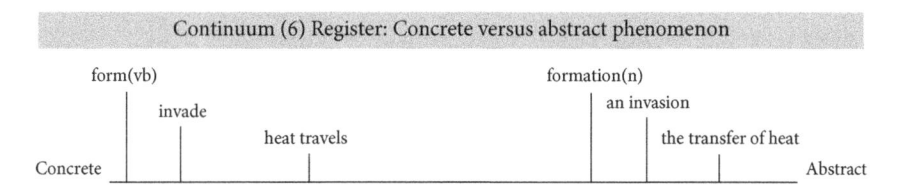

```
          form(vb)                              formation(n)
                  invade                              an invasion
                          heat travels                      the transfer of heat
Concrete  |_____|_____|        |_____|_____ Abstract
```

Does this view of the role of language in the construction of knowledge help to explain why some ideas may be hard to grasp?

Drawing together ideas for supporting subject literacies in the classroom

With these aspects of language and literacy development set out, you have a picture of the potential classroom language resources. How much has developed at Primary level is another matter. The cyclical and sometimes random nature of learning means that some of these skills are *emergent* in the sense that learner control of language and literacy might be inconsistent. Some statistics report that only one in five of the learners transitioning to Secondary school has met the Primary literacy targets (Ofsted 2011). This is one of the reasons for this book – to address subject literacy goals for all learners, as well as those for whom English is not the first language.

We have set up a reference point for the way we use language across everyday and subject-based classroom processes in the six register continuums. The first three are important for establishing language choices in a socially supportive classroom for the EAL learner. The last three, representing how classroom language ranges from everyday to specialist, from speaking to writing and from concrete to abstract, make clear the important role that language plays in learning. They show the creative flexibility in how language is used as knowledge is constructed. Learning is not just a matter of repeating a coded message to understand the knowledge held by the teacher. Importantly, knowledge building in pedagogical contexts involves much more than a simple transfer of concrete concepts of objects that we have seen or touched before, such as an apple.

Recent developments in the fields of linguistics and cognitive science have shown that we understand abstract concepts not only symbolically through our language system but also metaphorically through more concrete images and bodily experiences we have had with our physical world (Kövecses 2002). For example, our learners need to understand discipline-specific concepts such as *power, freedom, social justice, life, force*. These are very abstract concepts. In other words, they are concepts that we do not directly see or touch.

Try googling *power*. How many images do you see? Probably many *different* types of images related to representations of *strength, energy and force*.

The images the learners have in their minds would very much depend on

- what direct prior experiences her learners have had with the concept of *power*,
- what languages learners have used to refer to the idea of *power* in contexts outside the classroom and
- what the learners think their teacher wants them to understand by the word *power*.

Teachers need to make pedagogically informed language choices in the course of planning and delivering the lesson so that learners and teachers can come to some kind of shared understanding of what *power* should and could mean. This might involve discussing, negotiating and thinking through all their direct experiences and language resources to reach an understanding of this concept. Sharing and developing these meanings with the EAL learners will support reciprocal construction of language knowledge.

Some teachers use a display of relevant register continuums on the wall, to which words can be added as reference points for all learners coming to grips with representing subject knowledge at Lower Secondary level.

This range of language choices demonstrates significant aspects of how knowledge is expressed in subject literacy and makes clear the complex role that language plays in learning. We agree with Schleppegrell (2004:3) who points out that teachers need tools for helping students achieve 'greater facility with the ways language is used to create the kinds of texts that construe specialized knowledge at school'. These are the features of language use that underpin our approach to *language aware pedagogy*. As we look at these in more detail in subsequent chapters, we consider how to apply these understandings to classroom practice to support the learners in their learning task. This is part of the pedagogic rationale for an in-depth knowledge of the language involved in what you are teaching. Your recognition of the types of language involved at different stages in the learning and teaching cycle will support you as you integrate language explicitly and systematically into your lesson plans.

In Chapter 2 we get to know more about our EAL learners as we explore the cultural, language and educational resources they bring. More importantly we will see how their English language develops as a system for managing in the classroom. This background knowledge will provide further insight into how we can apply your understandings of subject-related language in the classroom to support the needs, as EAL learners learn English for learning *in* English.

Teaching resources

Six register continuums, with examples

(1) Identity role: Playground friend/classroom professional

Playground					Classroom
	it's kind of like			...can be described as	
		ta	see ya		what do you know about...

(2) Social role: Closeness (direct/fewer words) or social distance (indirect/more words)

Informal					Formal
	give us a hand	hiya	thanks	good morning	thank you very much
			could you give me a hand		I wonder if you wouldn't mind...

(3) Identity group membership role: Dialect versus standard

Dialect					Standard
	I've did	I done		I did	I have done
	Hitler went and invaded			Hitler invaded	

(4) Register: Everyday words or more precise specialist terms

Everyday					Specialist
		eyes that stickout			protruding
		happens		occurs	
	power = electricity supply			power = authority	

(5) Mode: Shared experience implicit in speaking/more detail required when writing

Speaking					Writing
		we found out		our experiment showed	
	magnets stick				magnets attract

(6) Register: Concrete or abstract phenomenon

Concrete					Abstract
	form(vb)			formation(n)	
		invade			an invasion
			heat travels		the transfer of heat

More detailed outline of language development in first language English

This section has two parts: 'birth to primary school' and 'the foundation of language knowledge in the Primary curriculum'.

Language development from birth to Primary school

This is a simplified sequence of stages of language development adapted from Brown (1973) to give a general picture.

- Receiving input in the womb and then for a year or so after birth
- Facial expression, body language, gesture
- Images linked with words
- Telegraphic – basic word forms with grammar: 'Daddy come'
- Negation – no come, not raining
- Questions – Daddy come? Why? When?
- Adding the grammar to the words, e.g.
  - '-ing' 'running';
  - plural – 'toys';
  - past tense 'wanted' and irregular past forms such as 'went' (not 'goed');
  - possessive – 'daddy's';
  - 3rd person 's' – 'he goes' (not 'he go');
  - auxiliary verb 'be' – 'is' added to make 'is coming'.
- As a child learns songs and rhymes, listening and repeating sounds and rhythms help to understand syllables, which helps spelling, and the idea of how to group words into phrases and hence manage punctuation. Word games help too.
- Before going to school the child starts speaking in groups of words that form simple sentences with a subject, verb and object: 'I like porridge'.
- The child then adds more detail: 'I like porridge for breakfast'; 'Porridge is lovely for breakfast.'

The foundation of language knowledge in the Primary curriculum at word and sentence level

Apart from providing guided practice to extend personal response and expression as learners speak, write and draw, the teacher guides the child to notice and practise:

- Regular features of spelling and pronunciation to help with reading and writing and exceptions. For example, many words in English
  - ✓ sound the same but are spelled differently (*there, their*) or
  - ✓ are spelled the same but said differently (*read, read; bow, bow*).

- Sentences are discussed in a more systematic way with labels to establish that they consist of a 'subject', 'verb' and 'object'. 'They (subject) were searching (verb) for gold (object).'
- 'Simple' sentences have a single idea. 'They were searching for gold.'
- Simple sentences can be expanded to form multi-clause sentences by
    - ✓ coordination: Joining two pieces of information (clauses) with a conjunction: 'They were searching for gold and making maps of the territory'.

    Or

    - ✓ subordination: Joining two ideas (clauses) in a more sophisticated way so that one idea becomes 'less' important (subordinate clause) because its task is to add information to the more important idea (the main clause).

    For example, 'They were making maps of the territory while they were searching for gold.' As you know, we often change the word order in a sentence like this for a more formal style to 'While they were searching for gold, they were making maps of the territory.'
- Learners name and define parts of speech such as
    - ✓ a noun to identify
        - a person (man, girl, engineer, friend)
        - a thing (horse, wall, flower, country)
        - an idea, quality or state (anger, courage, life, luck)
    - ✓ a verb to tell us about
        - an action/event (go, eat, rain, read)
        - a state (be, have)
        - a mental feeling (think, know, remember)
        - an utterance (*speak, tell*)

And so on. These *word classes* or *parts of speech* are among those currently in the Primary-level curriculum in England and Wales to be memorized for SPaG tests of Spelling, Punctuation and Grammar. For a sample glossary look at one of these sites:

https://www.gov.uk/government/uploads/system/uploads/attachment_data/file/224216/English_Glossary.pdf

https://en.oxforddictionaries.com/grammar/word-classes-or-parts-of-speech or http://www.englicious.org/glossary/multi-clause-sentence

2

What Resources Does the EAL Learner Bring to the Classroom?

Chapter Outline

Starting points: Identifying cultural, educational and language resources	31
Creating a school profile for the EAL learner	32
The customary language support practices in a school	44
How do EAL specialists approach language support?	45
How do EAL learners manage their languages in class?	46
Drawing together key areas of support for inclusive practice in the classroom	54
Teaching resources	56

- *How can we describe the EAL learner's educational and language resources?*
- *How do EAL learners' languages help them manage in class?*
- *How is language support approached in schools?*
- *What strategies can we use to engage the learner in general classroom processes and support learning?*

Starting points: Identifying cultural, educational and language resources

We are building on the objective view of the language practices for social interactions and literacies that we presented in Chapter 1 to inform our professional perspective on the cultural, education and language resources an EAL learner might bring to the classroom. The EAL learner comes with her own cultural and social background. These *funds of knowledge*, as set out in the Introduction, acknowledge the range of resources that comprise the learners' world views. As we saw in the Introduction, this objective perspective helps to visualize what it is like to be learning in a different country in a different language and in different classroom culture. At the same time, we do not see a language problem as a learning problem. A useful analogy offered by one of my colleagues for what it is like to be educated in a different culture is to suggest that the individual, who has previously been successful at cricket, now has to master a new game, e.g. football. In a different game there are different ways of measuring success. Some learners find this adjustment process interesting, while others might find it hard to interpret to begin with.

Establishing a profile of the learner will help us identify the areas of existing knowledge to build on and find the gaps where support for subject literacy from the subject teacher is needed. Then we can see how the school provision fits in, along with the assessment and monitoring that is to be done. A profile will give you an informed perspective on areas for development of language knowledge to extend your practice to maximum benefit for building and maintaining an inclusive space for subject literacy development.

We will look at

- how we create a school profile for the EAL learner,
- the descriptors used to describe EAL Proficiency in English (PiE),
- language support available in a school,
- how EAL learners manage their language in the classroom and
- how we apply this knowledge to establish an inclusive and constructive ethos in the classroom to engage the learner and support subject literacy.

Creating a school profile for the EAL learner

To develop a profile of an EAL learner entering your school, your school team will already have a whole school strategy based on the policy guidelines for inclusion.

See UK policy documents: New Arrivals Excellence Programme (2007), Count Us In (2009), Newcomer Guidelines for Schools (2010) in Teaching Resources for this chapter (page 56).

These documents, covering England and Wales, Scotland and Northern Ireland, set out the potential variables contributing to the cultural and language knowledge EAL learners bring with them. Schools have their own programmes for this welcoming process, but the aim is to develop a profile by finding out about the following:

- Where are the EAL learners from?
- What is their world view? What are their cultural and religious practices?
- What does their previous educational experience consist of? What are their likely expectations of the classroom learning and teaching processes?
- How many languages do they know? Are they literate in any of them?
- Has their education been continuous, fractured, or informal rather than in a classroom? Is this their first school in the UK?

This knowledge will be gathered in an appropriately sensitive way on entry to the school, perhaps through an induction programme with an initial interview and information exchange with the pupil, parent or interpreter.

This is a two way process. To set up an exchange of information, some schools offer a video about the school day, uniform, lessons and homework made by existing pupils. Hampshire runs a *Young Interpreters Scheme* to train learners to learn some of the newcomer language to be used in everyday situations such as tours of the school, demonstrating school routines, ensuring new arrivals are not alone at break time and generally being a good friend (see https://www.hants.gov.uk/educationandlearning/emtas/supportinglanguages/young-interpreters-guide).

As with any learner, some parents are very interested in their child's success, others are not. But it is useful to communicate a school's cultural expectations to parents for their understanding and support.

Getting an insight into cultural expectations

To get a clearer picture of cultural expectations for yourself, have a look at these four country profiles from which newcomers might arrive. These generalizations are based on knowledge we have accumulated over many years of working with individual students from different countries. They paint a picture of the diverse backgrounds that might shape the expectations an EAL leaner has. The profiles are based on two questions:

- What cultural and religious beliefs shape the world view?
- What are the expectations of the classroom learning and teaching processes likely to be?

As you read the four profiles below, ask yourself: What are the implications for my classroom practice in terms of classroom organization and inclusion?

Profile 1: Libya

World view, cultural and religious beliefs
Islamic, patriarchal world view. Female modesty important (hijab). Arabic speaking

Education and language
- Available to all at all levels. Increasing numbers of girls educated, but less rural uptake.
- Transmission model in Arabic, where teachers talk and learners listen. Large classes. Learners listen and memorize the work the teacher gives to pass the gap-fill/multiple choice exam.
- In study mode a student will memorize points rather than take notes.
- English is considered a useful asset for getting an international job. Taught from Primary.
- Speaking in English is relatively easy for students, with access to English speaking media. Communicating orally is preferred: reciting and creating poetry is popular.
- Reading classical Arabic important, writing in L1 (modern) Arabic, not so developed. Writing in English is hard: Arabic script written right to left. New script to be learned.

How similar to a typical learner profile? – very similar/on the cusp/not very similar

Profile 2: Malawi

World view, cultural and religious beliefs
'Mission Christianity' mixed with traditional spiritual practices. Patriarchal. Colonial heritage: Multilingual country with many vernaculars, all codified in Roman script. Official languages: Chichewa and English. Oral culture passes on traditional knowledge. Formal education quite 'young'.

Education and language
- Fee paying. High urban uptake. Rural areas variable: some boys may herd cattle till the age of 11, then start Primary school. Education starts in Chichewa (one of the official languages), along with the regional vernacular.
- English (the other official language) taught at Primary, used in public media and heard all around, but tends to have a formal register. English medium education from Secondary school.

- Transmission model. Large classes. Rote learning of grammar for gap-fill exams. Malawi language models for 'correct' English in the classroom and English speaking media.

How similar to a typical learner profile? – very similar/on the cusp/not very similar

Profile 3: China

World view, cultural and religious beliefs
Confucius and communism. Strong gender and family roles: grandparents may bring up children of working parents.

Education and language
- Compulsory from ages 6 to 16, free. Learning Mandarin Chinese characters (ideograms) and tones is hard, and sets the habit of memorizing word meanings and spellings when it comes to learning English and Roman script. The Mandarin sentence structure is different: there is a 'topic' and a 'comment'. The verb system for showing past, present and future is different: time is marked by words like 'before', 'now', 'in the future'.
- English is taught from Primary levels as it is seen as a requirement for a good education and a good job. Many attend fee-paying classes after school to get high exam scores. Competition is high for a place at a good university and, hopefully, a good job.
- Transmission model. Large classes. Rote learning. Many English courses have online resources for extra study, with focus on reading and writing, rather than spoken English.
- An individual student generally does not like to draw attention to themselves during class time. She is likely to ask the teacher for individual help after the class.

How similar to a typical learner profile? – very similar/on the cusp/not very similar

Profile 4: Poland

World view, cultural and religious beliefs
Predominantly Roman Catholic, linguistically homogeneous. Strong cultural heritage and work ethic.

Education and language
- Compulsory from ages 6 to 16, free. Teachers have a good level of education.
- Generally based on the Transmission model, particularly for language learning. School exams are thorough and detailed. English is relatively easy for Polish learners.

How similar to a typical learner profile? – very similar/on the cusp/not very similar

Your overall impression from the profiles is probably that newcomer learners are likely to have different expectations of classroom culture from a typical learner entering Lower Secondary school.

These educational backgrounds will influence views on the purpose of education:

> what families expect from school
> student/teacher roles within it
> different views on the value of speaking versus writing.

Cultural backgrounds with patriarchal cultures and strong gender roles will influence the views of learners about

> young people interacting with adults,
> males interacting with females.

These are generalizations. There is variation within each culture and some cultures are changing rapidly, but what are the implications for your professional work as newcomers settle into school?

- For learners from most Arabic and some African cultures, making eye contact is dependent on age, status and gender. Some female EAL learners may be less comfortable being taught by a man. Physical contact needs care.
- The view across all four profiles is that it is the responsibility of the teacher to give learners the necessary information to be memorized for success. Learners are used to being told what to do and are ready to work hard. Taking responsibility for one's own learning is a different view. Although teaching approaches are changing in Poland, the newcomers will tend to find the

dialogic approach to teaching confusing, particularly collaborating with peers in group work, unless the task is clearly structured and offers a reward they can value. How you balance plenary with group work and how you group learners will be important.

The countries profiled above all have developed education systems, though the level of teacher education might be variable. In contrast to these four profiles, a newcomer may arrive who has had no formal schooling, or whose experience has been disrupted for various reasons. Learners in this situation may well have limited or no literacy skills in any language, and may lack basic curriculum knowledge and formal learning skills. In that case the cultural gap is wider.

At the same time, there are pastoral and social aspects to a learner's background that may be straightforward, or more complex in the social and emotional sense. For example, think about:

> Why are they here? Have they lived in more than one country?
> What is their attitude to being here? What do they see as their place in this country? How do they feel about themselves?
> Are they with their family?

It is important to familiarize yourself with all aspects of the learner's background from those with responsibility for induction and pastoral care within the school. This information will allow you to be sensitive to the learner's needs in the classroom.

Building a languages profile

In this section we discuss profiling the learners' knowledge of languages apart from English and ascertaining levels of English learners are working at.

Profiling the learners' languages apart from English

Since the majority of people in the world know and use more than one language, there is a range of possibilities for your EAL learners. They might be multilingual and have many languages already, including English, or they might be monolingual and have only one to build on when they are learning English.

If they are born into a multilingual family, they have at least two language systems to master at once, but one tends to dominate the other at different stages of development. This will be what we call the 'dominant' language, which might not necessarily be the one that they learned 'first'. It is the one that is most developed, has the most resources and that the learner uses most.

The induction team will collect informal or formal evidence of language knowledge and literacy levels from previous learning by interview in the respective languages at the initial assessment if possible. If a speaker of the required language is not available, some areas can offer translations of key questions and guidance (e.g. Aberdeen City EAL service at https://acceal.org.uk/welcome-pack/).

There are known to be cognitive advantages to using more than one language. Research suggests that because multilinguals are accustomed to working out expression and meaning in more than one language pattern, they are better placed for problem-solving skills, particularly for Maths and ICT. They may also have a creative potential expressed in writing and critical understanding (see *Learning in 2(+) Languages* (2005:4) in Teaching Resources for this chapter, page 59).

It is generally acknowledged that once you have learned one language you have a good foundation to add others because you have a mental image of how language operates as a system of patterns.

As a literate individual, you also have the general idea that meaning can be carried in a system of written symbols, for example, Roman, Arabic, Urdu or ideograms such as Chinese and Japanese. Your existing literacy skills and the awareness of different language patterns are the basis for skills in the new language, especially decoding the language of new texts to work out meaning. You are likely to approach communication with a general flexibility in how you achieve your communication purpose.

Think about your own second or third language knowledge and communication skills.

- How many languages do you know? Are you a different person in each language? Are you more comfortable in one than another?
- Have you ever found yourself in a situation where the dominant language around you is not yours?
- For example, are you an English monolingual who has attended a wedding in North Wales where most of the guests were native Welsh speakers?
- For example, are you a Scottish monolingual who has gone to a shop in Lewis to buy bread and found yourself surrounded by Gaelic signs and voices? How did you feel?
- Have you ever answered a basic question in your best French in Paris, only to find yourself in a follow-up conversation where you can make out only a few words? What was your strategy? Mime? Gesture?

Do these questions help you visualize what it is like to arrive in a new country as an EAL learner?

Demonstrating familiarity with your EAL learner languages profile shows a respect for the heritage culture and knowledge resources your learner brings to your class, which in turn will contribute to developing teacher–student and student–student relationships.

Apart from establishing language and literacy skills in the learner's dominant language, it helps to think about the potential resources to draw on in the school. For example,

> Are there other bilingual learners in the school, perhaps from the same language background?
> Perhaps you are bilingual yourself?
> Perhaps you have spent some time working in another culture?
> Perhaps you appreciate aspects of the world view that your learner might bring to bear on their new situation?
> Does the school have access to EAL specialists?
> Are there tried and tested induction programmes in place?
> Have existing pupils been consulted on induction processes?

Also bear in mind the significance of life outside the classroom. There have been many ethnographic studies carried out looking at the backgrounds your EAL learners might bring as they settle into your community. They show that it helps to find out

- what after school classes they attend to support their own language;
- what languages are used at home;
- what interests do they have – music, sport, art, cooking?
- what English speaking friends they have;
- what level of support for school work is available from parents;
- how familiar school topics are to them.

If you are interested to know more, have a look at some of the studies reported by MOSAIC, the research centre for Multilingualism in Birmingham https://www.birmingham.ac.uk/schools/education/research/mosaic/index.aspx

Whatever the case, this shared knowledge is important for the teacher and the student to develop mutual intercultural awareness. It provides a starting point for assumptions about previous knowledge the learner has. It helps to identify new territory, and to manage expectations of both learners and their parents.

⭐ Visual clues in the form of signs, written words and translations in the classroom will help. Back up this welcome through gesture, mime and facial expression. If there is a shared system of signs in your school to communicate basic ideas, encourage all learners to use it.

Identifying levels of English language knowledge in your classroom

Assessment of English proficiency empowers teachers to understand and meet the learning needs of their EAL learners appropriately. In the 2016–17 School Census, schools were asked to rate their EAL learners' PiE on a five-point measure, as shown in the text box below:

> A. New to English – beginning skill
> B. Early acquisition, becoming familiar with English – emerging skill
> C. Becoming a confident user of English – expanding skill
> D. Being a competent user of English in most social and learning contexts – successful engagement in learning activities
> E. Being a fluent learner of English: equivalent competence to classmates

The statutory requirement for this assessment was withdrawn in the summer of 2018, but the five-level code generally remains the point of reference professionals use for the initial assessment to place the learner on an appropriate language and curriculum programme in schools.

The initial English language assessment may be based on a small written sample of personal and, possibly, subject-based writing, plus an oral interview. In language learning, EAL specialists tend to refer to levels of 'competence' (ability) or 'proficiency' (skill level) and have therefore developed more detailed assessment frameworks based on the five scales mentioned above, for example, Solihull levels of competence (http://socialsolihull.org.uk/schools/sab/wp-content/uploads/2016/06/HR-EAL-levels-of-Competence-Secondary-docx-amended.pdf). The Bell Foundation (2017) has published a detailed EAL Assessment Framework for Secondary-level learners that offers assessment descriptors in the four different areas of language skill: listening, speaking, reading and writing. The framework uses 'can do' statements and has tickboxes for monitoring progress of each learner in each school term, see https://www.bell-foundation.org.uk/eal-assessment-framework-version-1-1/

However, for the purposes of this book, we have adapted Table 2.1 for subject teachers to use. It has two dimensions: the five scales of PiE published by the Department for Education (2016) listed in the left hand column:

A. New to English – beginning skill
B. Early acquisition, becoming familiar with English – emerging skill
C. Becoming a confident user of English – expanding skill
D. Being a competent user of English in most social and learning contexts – successful engagement in learning activities
E. Being a Fluent learner of English: equivalent competence to classmates

The dimension across the top of Table 2.1 gives headings to describe the kind of language behaviour a subject teacher might observe in the subject classroom, along with possible background profiles for each level to help you visualize an EAL learner:

- understanding of what's going on for class participation,
- production of oral language (everyday vs. subject specific),
- dealing with reading and producing writing of different kinds,
- complexity of language evidenced and ability to deal with abstract concepts and
- possible background profiles.

Check out the descriptors in the intersecting boxes describing level and behaviour and link them to the profiles in the last column. Do you recognize any EAL learner behaviour you have come across? You may find the language of the descriptors offers ways of describing how language is used that are new to you.

The descriptors are set up so that the teacher can link language knowledge with classroom behaviour with phrases like 'student starts to follow instructions', 'participating with increasing independence', 'successful engagement in learning activities'. Similarly, the descriptors focus on words like 'managing', 'coping' and contrasting 'significant inaccuracies' with 'occasional errors'. Here, 'significant' means the inaccuracies that affect understanding of clear meaning. We will meet some EAL learners at PiE levels B, D and C later in the book when we look at learners in the classroom and ways you can evaluate progress in subject literacy in more detail.

You will notice that what the learner can do in terms of (a) *ability to participate* and (b) *level of language knowledge* is frequently linked to the *amount of time spent in the UK system*.

The emerging profile of the learner as an individual will be discussed by the school team as the basis for setting up an appropriate curriculum development and language support programme. The learner can then be welcomed into class. Progress will be monitored and reviewed from time to time with reference to such benchmarks. In the section following the table we will ask, What support is generally available in school?

Table 2.1 EAL Learners' Proficiency in English (PiE) Scales

	Understanding the culture and the language of class participation.	Oral production of everyday language and subject-specific vocabulary.	Written production of everyday language and subject-specific material.	Progress towards understanding of abstract concepts.	Possible background profile
A New to English	*Beginning* Tends to be silent and observing. May use own language for learning.	Repeating words and phrases to practise the sounds.	Copying words and phrases to become familiar with the patterns.	Starting to manage some of the patterns of basic everyday language. Needs a lot of EAL support.	A recently arrived refugee who is pre-literate or who has had intermittent L1 literacy development, with some English classes.
B Early acquisition. Becoming familiar with English	Everyday communication is *emerging* as the student starts to follow simple instructions.	Managing narratives with visual support. Some subject-specific vocabulary emerging. Useful to focus on pronunciation and spelling.	Managing some key words and phrases in reading and writing.	Familiar with some subject-specific vocabulary. Still needs significant EAL support – maybe 5 hours a week.	New to English learner after 1 year. OR learner with uninterrupted L1 literacy development and schooling. Studied English since primary school to variable levels depending on • education standards where they learned and • the difference between home language and English (Libya, Malawi, China).
C Developing competence Becoming a confident user of English	*Expanding* language knowledge participating with increasing independence.	Reasonable oral expression, but significant inaccuracies in the use of grammar and word choice.	Coping, but Literacy support still required to access text and write. Useful to focus on titles, headings and topic sentences.	Starting to follow some abstract concepts and more complex written English. Ongoing EAL support for full access to literacy – up to 2 hrs/week.	Good L1 literacy levels. Has been in UK mainstream system for 3–4 years (China, Poland).

D Being a Competent user of English in most social and learning contexts	*Successful engagement* in learning activities.	*Diversifying* with Oral English coming on, though it may lack complexity and contain occasional errors.	Can read and understand a wide variety of texts. Written English may lack complexity and contain occasional errors.	Needs some one-off diagnostic support sessions to access subtle nuances in meaning, refine English usage and develop abstract vocabulary.	Has been in English medium education at home, or in mainstream school in the UK for 5-6 years (Poland, Pakistan).
E Being a Fluent learner of English	Has *equivalent competence* to learner with English as a first language.	Competent oral English in a variety of everyday and subject-specific areas.	Competent reading and writing in a variety of everyday and subject-specific areas.	Can manage without EAL support. Will benefit from subject literacy support relevant to new content.	Second generation resident from another culture and language. Familiar with local culture. May use heritage language at home, but fluent in everyday spoken English. As familiar with academic uses of English as monolingual pupils at the same level (Pakistan).

Adapted from the Department of Education (2016:144).

The customary language support practices in a school

The support provision set out in the New Arrivals Excellence Programme (2007:3), http://dera.ioe.ac.uk/8393/7/newarrival_mangd_0004108_Redacted.pdf, mixes specialized language support with what we call 'immersion' so that language is learned in context as much as possible – the 'in at the deep end' approach. The amount of support available will vary according to numbers of EAL learners in the school and available resources.

The provision advocates a systematic approach based on 'Waves' or time-limited periods of tailored support that offer effective and appropriate provision for each learner. In Wave 1 a learner with no English may have 6 to 12 months English language and literacy plus intensive instruction in mainstream content areas, especially mathematics to familiarize the learner with the ways a subject teacher talks about knowledge in the classroom. At the same time the learner will spend time in the mainstream classroom for socializing purposes: to observe as much as to participate in what is going on.

Interestingly, data from the January 2017 School Census shows the majority of EAL learners in publicly funded Secondary schools in UK are at PiE level E 'Fluent' (55%) and very near to home learner competence. The lowest percentage (2.2%) is working at PiE level A 'New to English' (https://www.gov.uk/government/publications/pupil-nationality-country-of-birth-and-proficiency-in-english). So following the 'Waves' model outlined above, learners working at Level E (55%) will expect similar kinds of support as Home learners, while those working at Level A (2.2%) will have a significant language support plan.

Learners working at the three middle levels are the ones you need to take note of: PiE level B, 'Early acquisition' (4.6%), PiE level C, 'Becoming confident' (13.5%) and PiE level D, 'Being a competent user' (24.0%). They will be eligible for the subsequent 'Waves' of support which are based on assessed monitoring and will consist of a time-limited period of specialized support to meet particular needs identified. This might be 'in-class' support rather than 'withdrawal classes' during or after the school day. Homework clubs are sometimes used to offer a supportive space for feedback.

You can contribute to monitoring progress by noticing the learner's participation and language knowledge in the classroom. Ask yourself, 'Which PiE descriptors do they match?'

How do EAL specialists approach language support?

If you are lucky enough to have worked in partnership with an EAL teacher, you will have a good idea of what kind of support is beneficial to an EAL learner. EAL specialists are guided by policy that sets out provision for language support and guidance on inclusion, as mentioned above. But they also follow principles of how languages are learned based on the process that underpins learning the first language. This model is applied in a more structured format to learning a second language, and particularly, learning English as an Additional Language in a school setting is focused on learning the language for a specific purpose.

The learner needs to:

1) *Hear and see the words with associated meanings* through visuals, gesture and body language, bilingual and monolingual dictionaries, then match it to their own understandings of the language. Focus on a phrase with equivalent meaning rather than literal translation. For example,

    English: 'I am going home'
    German: 'Ich gehe nach Hause' ('I go after house').

    Many learners of Spanish are confused by how to use the two distinct forms of the verb 'to be'. It often helps to check understanding (and show interest in the other language) by asking, 'How do you say it in your language?'

2) *Notice the patterns and repeat the forms to achieve accuracy.* This is particularly true of spelling and grammar for the same reason that we repeat Maths tables to learn them. Listening (and repeating) is important for your EAL learner. The learner needs to go further than knowing the contents of 'a short phrase book' to learn IN English. Once the learner knows the grammar to support the meaning of the words, they can make a lot more sentences of their own.

3) *Try out the patterns and receive guided feedback* so that the number of words and patterns available increases over time and the learner is able to receive and respond to more complex patterns and meanings.

Teachers use the interactive approach set out in Communicative Language Teaching (CLT), developed in the 1970s when the European Union invested a lot of money in researching how to enable populations in member states to learn each other's languages and communicate confidently for the purposes of trade and having a mobile workforce. CLT has developed further as English language teaching has become a global phenomenon, but the main feature remains the interactive methodology devised at that time:

- *The aim is fluency rather than 100% accuracy, so the focus is on the meaning of the communication (word or phrase), followed by the form (or grammar structure) to support the meaning.*
- *The vocabulary taught is relevant to the area of communication, images are used a lot.*
- *The grammar structures to support that vocabulary are sequenced from simple to complex.*

Since the aim of the EAL specialists is to get the students communicating in areas needed for participating and studying in school, they will focus on relevant subject vocabulary with underlying grammatical accuracy for support. At the same time they will give guided practice to manage meaningful communication with some fluency and confidence.

So a typical lesson plan in language classes for EAL learners will consist of a series of stages that

- *model vocabulary meaning and grammar forms (supported by images),*
- *give 'repetitive' and then 'free' practice,*
- *give formative feedback.*

This approach is modified to match the type of EAL support to the PiE level of the learner, as set out in the outline of support provision above.

The practices recommended in this book complement the specialist approach to EAL language provision to support the development of literacy in the subject classroom.

How do EAL learners manage their languages in class?

What happens in practice is that the pragmatic EAL learner will make use of whatever linguistic, social and cultural resources they have from their previous contexts: their own languages and previous education, along with their emerging resources of English. For their English they will have been using translation, gesture, visuals, learning formal rules and imitating oral patterns they hear.

But they have to manage learning in English as well. Research on EAL learner language development in schools has shown that progress tends to occur in two interlinked areas of communication:

- Everyday – can be referred to as Basic Interpersonal Communication Skills (BICS);
- Language for subject literacy – can be referred to as Cognitive Academic Language Proficiency (CALP) (Cummins 1979).

Cummins developed these terms. His research in Bilingualism has underpinned EAL practice since the 1970s, see https://ealresources.bell-foundation.org.uk/eal-specialists/research-1970s-onwards-jim-cummins. See Baker (2011), for a wider view of working in more than one language in both international and UK contexts.

From this body of research, the main findings we draw on in this book are how we describe the two types of language knowledge (BICS and CALP) and how long it generally takes for this knowledge to develop. We start by looking at examples of what these two types of language knowledge might look like in your classroom.

The EAL learner's pragmatic skills: Basic Interpersonal Communication Skills (BICS)

As mentioned above, noticing and trying out language, along with getting feedback, are crucial to language learning. Not surprisingly, EAL learners with English around them every day in school make friends with peers and work out what goes on in class by observing and copying behavioural patterns. They tend to notice the most common words and phrases they hear and see around them and mix these with what they learn in formal language lessons. There is a lot of support from the context to support meaning and offer feedback on the success of the communication. So their everyday language skills comprise the following kinds of personal and social language, oral, visual and written:

- Signs for *directions, prohibitions*, etc.
- Basic vocabulary and limited structures. For example, the most useful verbs are often these: *be, have, give, put, do, make, take, get, go* ….
- The language of the playground: *'My name is ….' 'I have three brothers ….' 'I went home with … yesterday.'… 'I played'*.
- Classroom survival language, i.e. statements, negatives, questions:
    'I can't find my ….'; 'I don't understand ….'; 'Where is …?'; 'How do you say …?'
- Face to face and social media language for *greetings, farewells, requests*, words of appreciation with *positive and negative meanings (good/bad, kind/ unhelpful, necessary/unnecessary)*.

At the same time, they learn to follow the language of classroom organization:

- General directions and instructions to be understood for participation: *sit down, work with a partner, Today we are going to …. I want you to…. You need to…. etc.*
- General questioning words: *What? Who? Where? Why? How? When? Does …?* etc.
- Feedback: words with positive and negative meanings for praise and reprimand: e.g. *Well done …. Hurry up …. Listen …. We have to …. Can you sit down please.*

All this takes time. In the same way as in learning a first language, there is a stage known as the 'silent period' where comprehension of *input* is developing, before *output* is produced. Nonetheless, mastery of this type of everyday personal and social language is fairly speedy, so fairly efficient.

Research suggests that EAL learners can pick up enough everyday language knowledge in 2 to 3 years to match their monolingual peers (Cummins 1981).

An advantage of this kind of personal and social language knowledge is that the EAL learner is likely to meet it in other classrooms across the curriculum. We can match this kind of language knowledge to some of the register continuums we looked at in Chapter 1: *informal spoken language, playground slang, idioms and non-standard forms in both spoken and written formats* (see Teaching Resources, page 28). This can help you to make strategic choices about language to focus on and reinforce: to include in the classroom or reject.

To give you a general picture of EAL learners in daily routine in a school, here are some comments from a group of Science student teachers we worked with. We asked them to shadow an EAL learner for a day on one of their school placements. They sat in on classes, worked with EAL learners and spoke to teachers and EAL specialists. When they shared their thoughts, they were surprised by the range they found:

- They noted that most EAL learners felt supported and well settled in the classes. They had strategies in place for coping with communication: whether with language, signs, pictures or, in one case, music. They were making good progress and sometimes asking for the meaning of something when home students did not. Homework clubs were often useful places to support new study practices.
- In one case, there was an EAL learner who was not long in the school and, though his entry assessment showed his understanding of English to be quite good, he claimed he understood nothing in class. There appeared to be little differential provision offered in class, and he was unsettled still. Other EAL

learners, with mild learning difficulties in their own language and no evident differential provision for English in class, caused some disruption.
- When asked about points they would carry into their practice, they focused on the importance of learning names and supporting the meaning and form of new vocabulary.
  - They pointed out the challenge for EAL learners in our habit of using language in the non-literal/metaphorical sense (e.g. *Football teams have 'a fight' on their hands and companies 'fight' for market share, and minorities 'fight' for their rights*).
  - They noticed that teachers tend to use *idioms with reference to local heroes and events in areas like sport, acting and music* – mostly to establish common ground between themselves and the learners.
  - They also noted that specialist *words used in lessons can be hard to process and this can lead to confusion with EAL learners*.

We will carry this last point about vocabulary and specialist terminology that is *hard to process* over to the next section, as it is relevant to EAL subject literacy skills.

The EAL learner's subject literacy skills: Cognitive Academic Language Proficiency (CALP)

The EAL learner needs to be able to deal with the more abstract language of specialist terminology involved in the learning process. As the words 'Cognitive' and 'Academic' in CALP imply, this 'Language Proficiency' refers to an ability at a certain level to use language to articulate higher order thinking skills for processing, understanding and producing the more complex information. These more abstract language skills usually develop steadily through school stages as the learner encounters new concepts. But for a newcomer to the language and the education system, they may present a challenge due to the lack of a familiar context to support meaning found in the everyday language development referred to above.

We refer to the language examples set out on register continuums 4, 5 and 6 in Chapter 1: *from everyday to specialist, from speaking to writing and concrete to abstract* (Teaching Resources, page 28)

This implies a barrier to understanding. What exactly is the nature of *the words that can be hard to process* and possibly *lead to confusion in EAL learners*? What do we need to be aware of?

- When presenting subject content, the teacher uses language and notation as her cognitive tools, mixing everyday with specialist terms. And the EAL learner has to make the link. As one of our student teachers pointed out, for example, in History the concepts of 'revolution', 'democracy', 'bias', 'propaganda' and 'nationalism' are hard to explain simply. The teacher needs solid subject knowledge and experience to accumulate enough words and resources to do this.
- The EAL learner is required to receive and produce this language while learning in a new way, i.e. participating in pair work and using talk for collaborative learning of new material.

These are quite large demands. Let's look at two sets of examples of typical language involved with learning processes: *everyday words with specialist meanings* and *language for being precise (saying more in fewer words)*.

Everyday words with specialist meanings

We base these observations on the fact that

a) we may use different terminology to refer to procedures that might be the same, e.g. in Maths – 'subtract' means the same as 'calculate the difference'. Meanings are precise;
b) we use words in a non-literal sense, e.g. 'mouse' in ICT;
c) the same word can be used with different meanings (Table 2.2).

Table 2.2 Everyday Words with Specialist Meanings

| Word | Everyday meaning | Subject | | |
		Maths	Science	History
Power	n.physical ability, electricity supply	n.2^2 means '2 to the power of 2'	n.energy, force	n.power – authority or influence
Attraction	n.feeling between people to draw them together; feature of interest to tourists	n.(sub)traction = the opposite process of removing quantities	n.magnetic attraction	n.feature of historic, economic or political interest
Table	n.furniture	n.multiplication table	n.water table	vb.table a proposal for political discussion

Would these words be useful on a register continuum on your classroom wall? Can you think of particular everyday words that are used in your subject with specialized meanings? For more ideas see Nancarrow (2018).

Language for being precise, for saying more in fewer words

When we say more with fewer words, we choose specialist words as we saw in Chapter 1 (page 20), but we may also add extra words *before or after everyday words* to make the meaning more precise.

As we saw in the Frogs text in Chapter 1, it takes a lot of words to explain *amphibians* and *herpetologists*.

The examples below are *naming abstract or unfamiliar things* that are not obvious from the immediate surroundings (see register continuum 6, page 25):

Example 1: Nouns

Here is a sentence made up of everyday words from a Geography textbook (Maclean and Thompson 2009:109) showing how precise meaning is built up from a simple noun, 'Farming', *by adding more words and changing nouns to adjectives*. In the example in Table 2.3, we can see that *words are added after the subject noun 'Farming' (shaded) to make the subject more precise.*

Table 2.3 Extending the Subject to Include More Information

Subject (noun phrase)	Verb
Farming	has changed
The farming landscape	has changed
The farming landscape in Spain	has changed
The farming landscape in southeast Spain	has changed
The farming landscape in the coastal area of southeast Spain	has changed

The basic statement is 'Farming has changed', but as we add more detail, we can identify *what aspect of farming* has changed. We see that it is the 'landscape' that is the focus of the sentence – so 'farming' changes its role from a noun to an 'adjective' in front of the noun to identify *what kind of landscape*. When we add even more detail to identify the *location* of the landscape we add words *after the noun*, using 'in' before the country (*Spain*), the *general part* of the country (*southeast*) and then the *specific area* of the country (*coastal*).

⭐ This is a *long noun phrase* exemplifying a typical language feature of subject literacy that can be confusing unless the learner recognizes how all the parts fit together.

> ### Example 2: The Verb
>
> Here is a scientific definition where the verb 'diffuse' has been *nominalized*, i.e. changed to the noun 'diffusion', *to present a concept*. And the verb 'move' has also been changed to the noun 'movement', *to change an action to a process*.
>
> Diffusion is the movement of matter to fill all of the available space. (Mines, 2000:51)
>
> The writer also *adds words* after the noun 'movement' to provide more detail on the kind of process. The noun phrase 'movement of matter' names the process more precisely.

⭐ This example where a noun is used to name a phenomenon rather than a verb to report the process is preferred in academic language. Think back to how nouns and verbs were used at different stages of the Magnets lesson in Chapter 1 ('magnets attract' vs. 'magnetic attraction').

Changing the role of a noun to an adjective ('coast' to 'coastal') or a verb to a noun ('attract' to 'attraction') is called *word class shift*. This is simple everyday language put together in unfamiliar more abstract ways to give us specialist terminology to represent specific knowledge, moving from *concrete (what you can see)* to *abstract concepts (what you have to visualize)*. It is one of the ways we use to put more information into fewer words, and we call this 'information density'. Meanings can be harder to become familiar with and use.

⭐ Not surprisingly, research suggests that as the language and the ideas become more challenging and abstract, it can take an EAL learner between 5 and 8 years to develop to a level to match a monolingual peer, despite the learner being immersed in the learning context (Cummins 1981).

So the EAL learner needs as much support as you can offer for learning words and phrases to think and talk in your subject, as we shall see in the following chapters.

You may find the labels 'BICS' and 'CALP' conceptually useful to talk about different types of language you use in the classroom. On the other hand, you may prefer to think of teachers using a mix of everyday and subject-specific language. What is important to remember is that in the classroom these two kinds of language are interwoven. And for the EAL learner, the uptake of the simpler language is more straightforward and rapid than the more complex language carrying more complex ideas.

Based on this understanding of an EAL learner's language resources and how languages are learned, what does inclusive practice that pays attention to language needs look like?

An example of mixing everyday and specialist language productively in the classroom

To give you a picture of how everyday and specialized language can work together productively, here is a classroom extract from a Year 7/S1 Science class of twenty learners. In the class, thirteen out of twenty speak a language in addition to English: Arabic, Hindi, Punjabi, Urdu, Cantonese and Mandarin. The PiE levels vary, with a high proportion of 'competent' (Level D) and 'fluent' (Level E) EAL learners.

The transcript in the text box below is from a well-structured practical lesson on particle matter theory (heat transfer), where the teacher is demonstrating how heat travels along a copper rod covered with Vaseline on which a number of paperclips are fixed. Notice how the teacher selects and grades his everyday and specialized language to support the learning. The target is learning the process 'transfer of heat', and eventually the concept of 'conduction' (Figure 2.1).

> T: What dya reckon is goin to happen? .... It's going to melt. And it's going to fall down, right? So if you keep watching that for a bit of time ... Nusayba?
> Sanja: It's going to fall
> T: It's going to fall. This one's going to fall before that one's going to fall. Why?
> Sanja: cos that one's further away
> T: So?
> Sanja: It doesn't get as much heat
> T: It doesn't get as much heat. Exactly. So what is the hottest part of the rod at the moment? You can see quite obviously what the hottest part of the rod is. The end bit. OK? But heat will travel along the rod, won't it. And as it travels along the rod, the Vaseline melts, and the clips will fall .... So heat travels. *We call that the transfer of heat. There's a fancy name for it called 'conduction'.* So heat travels along solids in a straight line. It's called conduction. So these are conductors of heat.

Figure 2.1 Year 7/S1 Transfer of Heat Transcript (Research Data Zacharias 2018).

You may well be familiar with the content, but here we are interested in the teacher's language choices. We can see a mixture of *informal* (friendly, interpersonal) and the *pedagogic* content in scientific register. You may notice the skilful use of operational language: questioning, repetition, *'we call that …', that's a fancy name for …* 'and use of the logical linking word like *so*'.

The pedagogic content language highlights

- specific words: *'we call that the transfer of heat'* and
- a model of how to use those words in a meaningful context, i.e. *'So heat travels along solids in a straight line'*.

The teacher finally links this process to the abstract concept of 'conduction'. In this way he is making progress from the *action of* 'heat travelling' to the *process of the* 'transfer of heat'. The transcript shows how he is moving towards the target learning objective at the same time as offering the language support to reach it.

How does this background knowledge inform your strategies to support the EAL learner in the development of subject literacy?

Drawing together key areas of support for inclusive practice in the classroom

This chapter has looked at how a profile can be put together to learn about the cultural, educational and language resources the EAL learner brings. The school team will make this available to staff as a curriculum plan is put together for the learner. It is clear that the more familiar the teacher is with this information, the more relevant and inclusive the classroom practice can be. This knowledge also paves the way for a classroom culture where the EAL learner is valued as a contributor to the learning.

Background knowledge

We have identified the kinds of questions that can be asked to get a sense of the previous knowledge learners are likely to hold as knowledge schemas. Looking at the country profiles gives us an idea of possible world views that shape expectations of classroom processes. These show that views of the classroom roles of learner and teacher might be more traditional and that group work might be a new concept to be supported so that the learner can derive benefit.

Languages apart from English

The profile of the first of dominant language knowledge is key to establishing whether the learner is literate in their home language. Literacy means that the learner has the motor skills for writing and the mental image of receiving information in this mode. It also implies that the learner will have a sense that mastering language patterns is key to developing language knowledge in order to communicate effectively. Policy guidelines encourage the teacher to draw on their home language to support the learning when appropriate.

English language

The EAL descriptors for PiE reflect our approach to language learning that focuses on enabling the learner to communicate, with accuracy as a follow-up support. They outline what the teacher may expect in terms of class participation and language knowledge. They help the teacher appreciate that in the early stages of learning a language, or becoming accustomed to working in a different language, the learner may well need quite a bit of listening time. At the same time, the language support provision makes clear that a learner new to English will receive intensive language classes until they are considered ready to participate. During that time, the learner will come into class once or twice a week to become familiar with what happens in the classroom.

How EAL learners manage languages in class

We know from research that English language for social and everyday purposes develops more quickly than the more complex and abstract language used for learning. We saw that both kinds of language might occur in a lesson, but the examples of *everyday words with specialized meaning* and *language for being precise (using fewer words to say more)* identify two areas of potential challenge. Pragmatic learners will make use of their own languages, drawing, Google Translate, buddies – whatever resources they have available.

The Teaching Resources at the end of this chapter set out a series of strategies for classroom practice to support the learner. As we go through the book we look in more detail at the features of subject literacy we can support and give examples from a range of subjects that can be adapted and applied to your practice. We start in the next chapter by looking at describing how knowledge is presented and discussed in your subject.

Teaching resources

Three key strategies for EAL learner engagement

(1) Welcoming the learner to the classroom

- Familiarize yourself with the EAL learner profile: where the EAL learner is from (use an atlas?), how long she has been in the UK and what her general language and education profile look like.
- Identify a buddy to work with her.
- Names are important parts of identity, so show and earn respect by making an effort to remember and pronounce names correctly. If this is hard, ask the learner to teach you by sounding it out, spelling and writing it. This consolidates the learner's identity and models how you accept the newcomer for the class.
- Set up visual clues for communication in the classroom in the form of images of access and prohibition, written labels on equipment and translations.
- Back up this welcome through gesture, mime and body language. If there is a shared system of signs in your school to communicate basic ideas, encourage all learners to use it (*e.g. thumbs up, thumbs down, beckoning, gesture for 'sit down', 'think'*).

(2) Organizing group work and using the home language (L1)

- Exploit resources to support group work. If this is an unfamiliar way of working, help the learners become socialized into the idea by support, encouragement and success.
- Do not confuse language difficulty with learning difficulty.
- EAL learners will benefit from working with learners who can model the language for them to listen to. If EAL learner is confident, it would make good pedagogic sense to put her in a group with English speakers, at least one of which is a successful learner, to have the chance to produce English spontaneously and extend language skills in a supportive space.
- Alternatively, working in bilingual groups may be supportive at some points for understanding and discussion if the cognitive load is likely to be high. Thinking skills may still be difficult in a second language as PiE develops. Learners may find it helpful to translate and switch between languages. So you could put her in a group with a fellow EAL learner with the same language, or a learner working at a similar English level and a different language. If there is classroom support from a speaker of the EAL learner's language, take advantage of that. See Teaching Resources of this chapter, Access and Engagement on use of home language (page 59).

- Expecting output needs sensitivity. When EAL learners are being quiet it might mean they are busy listening and noticing. Let the EAL learner be silent and just copy, give them more thinking time to prepare an answer or think of other ways they can contribute with non-verbal language in a mode they are familiar with. Compare classroom behaviour with the EAL proficiency descriptors.
- Bear in mind that some EAL learners come from a culture where they will not answer unless they are sure they will be correct. Think back to the points about intercultural awareness of relationship issues with age and gender in the section with country profiles (pages 34–7). Nominate a learner to bring them into a discussion if you think they are ready. Give them that opportunity. Patience is important.

(3) Engagement in subject lessons

- Plan how to present your topic, e.g. for key words, make strategic use of realia, visuals or audio that will situate the topic in the learner's real-world experience. Label equipment.
- Back up with other resources such as images and diagrams, gesture, register continuums and word banks on the wall that can be added to; key word cards; tables, diagrams, charts, cycles and computer graphics. Use buddies. Label equipment.
- Make strategic use of translation when needed. Have both bilingual and monolingual dictionaries available in paper or digital form (Google Translate). Decide whether you want to give the EAL learner the new word (use a bilingual dictionary). Or remind them of the meaning they know (use a monolingual English dictionary). Note everyday words with specialist meanings and saying more with fewer words in long noun phrases with word class shift for precise meaning.
- Be consistent in modelling relevant language: give explicit attention to the form of a new/important word: enunciate it clearly to demonstrate how many syllables it has and sound it out for the spelling. Reinforce meaning by repeating words, saying the same thing in different ways, drawing explicit attention to the forms for a specific purpose and context.
- Make sure there are support materials. If appropriate, give learners a manageable word list to prepare before the class. In class ask learners to tick the words off as they hear you saying them.
- Display new language on a register continuum on the wall in the classroom showing the everyday/specialist distinction, or write it on the board.
- Offer practice with relevant sequencing and matching activities to help with consolidation: *match images with words* and *gap fills to complete sample sentences*.

- Demonstrate how to make meaning more precise. Start with a single specialist term and build up a sentence by adding more information, e.g. 'volume'. Demonstrate how to present the meaning, then model a statement to show how to define it. Finally add an explanation for 'how we measure it'.
- Beware of using too many idioms, analogies or metaphors that require local knowledge.
- Be aware of register changes for different contexts, purposes.
- Monitor use of key terms and point out cases where you say the same thing in a different way. Ask another learner to tell you what has been said in their words.
- Check understanding frequently. Make sure your learner can distinguish between the question words: What? Where? When? Why? How? etc., with a translation on the wall or in their book, for reference.

Planning lessons: A *language aware* teaching and learning cycle

This is a model of how to *integrate a language aware approach to supporting subject literacy* into the four-stage Kolb teaching and learning cycle. With this support for the EAL learner, the lesson can be cognitively challenging, using higher order thinking skills such as evaluating, inferring, generalizing and classifying.

Stage 1: drawing the students in and setting the context for the topic.

- Be familiar with the level at which the EAL learner is able to access curriculum context.
- Think about what the learner might bring to the task. Plan the language you think they might need. Select a realistic number of key words to focus on, with translated glossaries to hand. Plan opportunities for successful learning early in the lesson.
- Make clear the context for learning and relate to learner's prior cultural knowledge and experience. Use simple language and visual clues and pictures to help make meaning clear.
- Build in opportunities for EAL learners to hear models of language to use. Build in brief 'thinking time' to allow for processing the question before answering.

Stage 2: setting up tasks to model and deconstruct key ideas.

- Actively consider challenges that the learner will encounter and draw on flexible groupings, strategic buddies (L1 or L2 speakers for different pedagogic purposes) and appropriate staff resources where available.

Stage 3: drawing those ideas together to work with pupils to model construction of a product or outcome.

- Give explicit focus to target language words and forms (e.g. everyday and specialized) at certain stages in the lesson so that you can provide formative feedback on understanding and expression
- Actively encourage the EAL learner to produce language so that you have evidence of how progress is being made in learning in the additional language.

Stage 4: setting up tasks for pupils to manage their independent construction of a product or outcome.

- Encourage learner to become increasingly independent in their range of strategies. Make active use of the instruction – assessment – feedback cycle.

Policy documents and books for more detail on working with EAL learners

The work of Cummins, Gibbons and Schleppegrell underpins this book (see references). Here is a list of relevant policy documents, books and ideas for further reading, organized by title.

Access and engagement at KS3: teaching pupils for whom English is an additional language. Department for Education and Skills (2002) – National Strategy resources for twelve subject areas: Art, Design & Technology, English, Geography, History, ICT, Maths, MFL, Music, PE, RE, Science, http://wsh.wokingham.gov.uk/learning-and-teaching/mea/eal/eal-guidance/national-strategy/access-ks3/

Aiming High: guidance on the assessment of pupils learning English as an Additional Language. Department for Education and Skills (2005) https://www.naldic.org.uk/Resources/NALDIC/Teaching%20and%20Learning/5865-DfES-AimingHigh1469.pdf

CLIL (Content and Language Integrated Learning) – teaching a subject in a language other than English. https://www.teachingenglish.org.uk/article/content-language-integrated-learning

Connecting Classrooms – The British Council in partnership with the Department for International Development provide support for schools to connect and collaborate internationally. https://schoolsonline.britishcouncil.org/about-programmes/connecting-classrooms

Count us in: a sense of belonging: meeting the needs of children and young people newly arrived in Scotland. (2009) HM Inspectorate of Education Scotland. https://dera.ioe.ac.uk/10831/7/cuimnnus2_Redacted.pdf

Developing Language and Literacy in English across the Secondary School Curriculum: An Inclusive Approach. Urszula Clark (2019). London: Palgrave Macmillan.

EAL assessment framework for schools: secondary (Version 1.1) (2017) The Bell Foundation. https://www.bell-foundation.org.uk/eal-programme/teaching-resources/eal-assessment-framework/

eTwinning – a secure online platform to allow schools to collaborate across Europe. https://www.etwinning.net/en/pub/index.htm

Learning in 2(+) languages: ensuring effective inclusion for bilingual learners. Good practice for teachers, educational establishments, and local authorities. Education Scotland (2005) https://www.scilt.org.uk/ResourceView/tabid/1092/articleType/ArticleView/articleId/6548/Learning-in-2-languages.aspx

MOSAIC: the Centre for research on Multilingualism. https://www.birmingham.ac.uk/schools/education/research/mosaic/index.aspx

NALDIC – National Association for Language Development in the Curriculum (NALDIC), http://www.naldic.org.uk/. Numerous useful pointers about supporting EAL learners.

For NALDIC's pages on EAL and Initial Teacher Education see http://www.naldic.org.uk/eal-initial-teacher-education/ite-programmes

New Arrivals Excellence Programme (NAEP), National Strategies for Primary and Secondary Schools (2007) https://ealresources.bell-foundation.org.uk/sites/default/files/document-files/New%20Arrivals%20Guidance.pdf *You can also Google CPD programmes for implementing this NAEP guidance*

Newcomer guidelines for Schools Department for Education Northern Ireland (2010). https://www.education-ni.gov.uk/publications/newcomer-guidelines-schools

Planning for bilingual learners: an inclusive curriculum (2000) Maggie Gravelle (Ed). Stoke on Trent: Trentham Books.

School Education Gateway, developed and facilitated by EU Commission. https://www.schooleducationgateway.eu/en/pub/index.htm

Schools Online British Council – support from the British Council for developing international education and partnerships. https://schoolsonline.britishcouncil.org/global

SIOP *Sheltered Instruction Observation Protocol* http://www.cal.org/siop/about/ – the US equivalent of NALDIC.

The EAL Book: promoting success for multilingual learners. (2015) Jean Conteh. London: Sage Publications.

Voki – an educational tool that allows users to create their own talking character. It can be customized to look like historical figures, cartoons, animals and even yourself! https://blog.voki.com/2015/09/26/5-innovative-ways-to-use-voki-in-the-classroom-by-guest-blogger-tyler-hart/

3
How Is Language Used to Present and Discuss Knowledge in My Subject?

Chapter Outline

Starting points: Your subject-oriented lens	61
What you already know about communication purpose and text organization	64
Establishing types of communication purpose of texts	65
Identifying language patterns in sample text types: Lower Secondary Geography, Maths and History	67
Drawing together metalanguage for language patterns to support EAL learners	88
How challenging are these Geography, Maths and History texts for the EAL learner?	90
Teaching resources	93

- *What styles of language do you use to talk about your subject area?*
- *How can we systematically identify the key features of text-level and sentence-level language features involved?*
- *How can we apply this knowledge to support subject literacy development?*

Starting points: Your subject-oriented lens

Every subject area makes specific language choices to express specialist knowledge. As we saw in Chapter 1, learners may come from Primary level with basic understandings of text types and communication purpose such as *fictional narrative, non-fiction factual description* and learning to talk about *the properties of magnets*. In Chapter 2 we identified some of the language features of 'difficult words' for an EAL learner encountering subject language in English. We looked at *everyday words* with subject-specific meanings, *along with long noun phrases,* and *word class shift ('Farm (v.)'* to *'Farming (adj.)'* and *'Diffuse (vb.)'* to *'Diffusion (n.)')* to express subject meanings in precise detail.

We build on this and the underlying familiarity you have with how language is used to talk about knowledge in your subject area. You have accumulated these understandings through your participation in Secondary and Higher Education. This is like acquiring a set of habits, or particular ways of looking at and talking about things. As a subject specialist, you will look at something through *a subject-oriented lens*.

> Try out your subject lens. What do you see in your mind's eye when you hear the word 'salmon'? What interests you about it?

The word 'salmon' is likely to evoke particular mental images from your past experience, both as an individual (perhaps you like fishing or cooking) and as a subject specialist.

- Are you a geographer concerned with the relationship between nature and humans? Will you be thinking about fish populations, fishing policies and fish farms?
- Are you a painter concerned with visual representation? Will you be thinking of impressionistic flashes of colour, or technical drawings of scales?
- Are you a biologist concerned with the building blocks of life? Will you be thinking of the life cycle of a salmon?
- Are you a writer concerned with using language to entertain and move the audience? Will you be thinking of word images and poetry?
- Are you a mathematician concerned with algorithms? Will you be thinking of statistics of fish populations? Sizes and weights?
- Are you a musician concerned with notation and sound to capture this?
- Are you a dancer concerned with movement to evoke the salmon?
- Are you a scientist concerned with particles and atoms? Will you be thinking about features of a salmon's physiology that are suited to survival in challenging environments?
- Are you a linguist concerned with representation of knowledge in another language? Will you be thinking about how to tell us something about the salmon in Chinese? Or Spanish?

Each subject teacher will have their own focus for the construction of knowledge. How does the teacher support the learner with this new way of talking about knowledge?

Perhaps the first question is: 'How does the teacher learn how to present knowledge in the classroom in a clear way that the learners can follow?' This reflective question came up with the student Science teachers we worked with when they started their programme. They were asked to read Wilson and Mant's 2011 two studies investigating the question: 'What makes an exemplary Science teacher?' The findings represent the views of 5,044 twelve-year-olds and their respective teachers in England. The students then shared their responses on the VLE.

The main points the students picked out were that

- exemplary teachers will draw the students into a topic and relate it to their real-world experience and
- exemplary teachers give (clear) explanations that make sense to their learners.

But, they asked each other:

- How does a teacher acquire the skill of giving clear explanations? Is it intuitive? Or is it learned?

Some suggested that a teacher has to learn this skill, but that the starting point would be strong content knowledge. Then you could think about how to put that across in clear language. It is interesting to see that this reflection leads to an awareness of what Shulman (1986) terms 'content knowledge' (*knowledge of your subject*) and 'pedagogic knowledge' (*knowledge of the processes required to teach it and how best to represent it to their learners*).

This representation of knowledge to learners generally involves some kind of explanation, whatever the subject area, and apart from subject knowledge, every good teacher has an intuitive understanding of how language works in their subject. We can build on this idea because although the ways of looking and the primary concerns differ across subjects, there is an underlying similarity in the way we identify a communication purpose, select content and plan how to organize it.

We are taking written texts as a starting point because, regardless of the extent to which a teacher will draw directly on a text book in the classroom, a text book remains a point of reference for both the teacher and the student. A Physics teacher once said to me that writing was not relevant to his learners until they were at the Exam stage. However, he did agree that talking about diagrams, graphs and calculations is essential because this is how knowledge is represented in Physics. As mentioned in the Introduction, talking is part of learning to articulate ideas and communicate them. So having a clear communication purpose and pattern of organization is important for any text to communicate effectively, whether visual, oral or written.

To identify the key features of how knowledge is presented and discussed in a written explanation, we will deconstruct sample Lower Secondary teaching materials from Geography, Maths and History. Looking for specific features as you read the text will guide you to identify which aspects of language to focus on to prepare a lesson effectively. This way of looking at how knowledge is presented and discussed in your subject will offer you a metalanguage to talk about it and integrate it into your practice in the subject classroom. You can share this knowledge to scaffold EAL learners' understanding of both the content and organization of texts in all modes, so that when they come to create a text, or make a presentation, they can make 'effective language choices' (Schleppegrell 2010:26).

As we go through the samples, we show you how many of these features can be adapted and applied to other subjects.

> What we want to do in this chapter is wind back the clock from 'now' to when you were in transition from Primary to Secondary. What learner schemas of how to present and discuss knowledge of a subject can we build on at transition? What does the 'novice' (learner) know that you, 'the expert' (teacher), can build on?

This prepares you to consider how to frame your subject knowledge, supported by your *language aware pedagogic knowledge* to address some of the challenges in difficult words identified for the EAL learner.

We will look at:

- what you already know about communication purposes;
- what you already know about how texts are organized;
- patterns of communication purpose, text organization and language features in three sample Lower Secondary texts (Geography, Maths and History);
- how we apply these macro-level patterns and micro-level language features to other subjects.

What you already know about communication purpose and text organization

If we start with what you already know, you will probably be able to pick out a communication purpose from conventional patterns of text organization. For example, if you are given a jumbled text with sentence openings like the four below, what would you say is the 'right' or 'logical' order?

So….. Then….. First….. The result is…..

You will probably have chosen 'First' … 'Then' … 'So' … and selected 'The result is' … to stay in final position.

Which logical sequencing principles (or thinking skills) did you use to make your deduction?

i. Time,
ii. General to specific characteristics,
iii. Steps in a process or procedure,
iv. Cause and effect,
v. Comparison,
vi. Points for and against.

You probably chose 'iii. Steps in a procedure or process', but you might have wanted to add 'iv. Cause and effect' because of the word 'result'. That's fine. It illustrates the fact that you have a mental image or schema in your mind to which you can refer.

If we ask 'What was the basis on which you made that choice?' the answer is probably 'because that was what I was expecting'. We have expectations based on our knowledge of 'what is normally done'. Follow this principle when you are planning an explanation. Ask yourself: 'What is normally done in an explanation of X in my subject?' (Maths, Science, Languages, etc.).

None of these points will be a surprise to you because, as you have passed through stages of educational development, your knowledge has increased, along with the range of language available to you to articulate that knowledge in ever more sophisticated ways. How did you acquire these skills? It is likely that, apart from input from guided instruction and feedback, you will have worked out how to deconstruct a task or question to find a model of what is required for a particular type of answer to an essay or exam question. And your strategies must have been successful for you to be in your current career place.

Let's identify the components of these skills you have so that we can integrate them into our classroom practice to support learners.

Establishing types of communication purpose of texts

Research work has identified features of writing across the curriculum at Primary level (see Derewianka 1990), Secondary level (Rose 2006) and Tertiary level (Gardner and Nesi, 2012, Coffin and Donohue, 2014). The terminology used for each level varies, but the core communication purposes are:

- To describe, define, classify – what is it like?
- To narrate or record events over time – what happened?
- To outline stages in a process, to provide model steps for a procedure – what happens? How is it done?
- To provide logical reasons for cause and effect – to explain how and why?

The first three aims may be straightforward, but to answer further questions such as *Why?* and *How?* means looking at the contributing causes or effects. This involves the ability to reason and understand the relationships between the causes and effects, and to express these in an argument.

Consider this example: 'What is the best way to combat climate change at a local level?'

The explanation should not only demonstrate knowledge of the specific terminology used to refer to the concerns of climate change but also include an analysis and synthesis of the relationships between causes and effects to justify your point of view. Do you have the language to show your learners how to do this? This is a common question for learning teachers and a reflective point for any practising teacher when planning their teaching. Think about your own work.

What kind of explanation do you usually give in your subject area? What is the communication purpose?

We could go through examples from a few subject areas to work out communication purpose.

- In Geography: How do we explain variations in population density? Where does rain come from?
- In Maths: How did Archimedes find out about displacement theory? How do we solve x maths problem?
- In Chemistry: What's the difference between a gas, a liquid and a solid? Explain what you did in this experiment.
- In History: Where did that castle come from? Why is it there?

To describe the structures and patterns of these explanations, we can refer to the work of Derewianka and Jones (2016:195), who suggest that there are two kinds we can use: *simple* and *complex*.

1) A *simple sequence* is used to answer questions such as
   - What is it like? i.e. Description

- How is it done? i.e. Procedure
- How does it happen? i.e. Process – linear or cyclical

2) A *more complex sequence* is used to answer questions such as:

- Why does something happen? or
- Why and how did it happen in the past?

The *complexity* comes from a focus on

- factors that are causes of something,
- consequences that are the result of something or
- a mixture of both causes and effects.

This discussion shows that despite the fact that there will be specific terminology to reflect the concerns of the discipline, whatever the areas of investigation for a subject area, there are likely be similarities in communication purpose. And, as mentioned above, a focus on contributing factors to explain *why* and *how* can involve sorting out complex and possibly abstract relationships between the causes and effects.

In summary, we are looking to identify language patterns of how subject knowledge is discussed and presented. At macro-level, this will be identifying *the communication purpose and text organization of an explanation for a particular concept*. At the micro-level of sentences and words we can refer to types of sentence structures, as identified in previous chapters, where we looked at the way noun phrases are used to carry additional detail to give precise subject knowledge. We want to extend this focus to identify *what kinds of micro-level language features are used for a particular purpose*. Bear in mind that this representation of knowledge may also draw on visuals and analogies to support conceptual learning.

Identifying language patterns in sample text types: Lower Secondary Geography, Maths and History

The samples of Lower Secondary text types from Geography, Maths and History we have selected may be far too difficult for many EAL learners, but knowing how to identify the language patterns set out above can help the teacher read a text more efficiently herself and select what she needs to focus on with the learners. At the same time, we have to bear in mind the points made in the Introduction about awareness of cross-cultural variation in existing knowledge schemas and world views. The patterns we are looking at as we deconstruct these text types have been developed in a cultural context that might well vary from the one the EAL learners are familiar with.

Some languages organize these patterns slightly differently, so a cross-cultural awareness will help us make explicit reference to the patterns in your subject area to support EAL learners in their subject literacy development.

We will take the discussion of each sample in three stages:

(1) Macro-level: concept and key words plus communication purpose
(2) Macro-level: how it is organized
(3) Micro-level: language features for particular purposes

Following discussion of each sample at macro- and micro-level, we give examples of how the patterns can be applied to other subject areas. We do this with samples discussed in subsequent chapters too, as we look at *supporting engagement with knowledge* in Chapter 4, and *supporting output* in Chapter 5.

Geography: The formation of volcanoes

The concerns of Geography are with the Earth, its physical features, their formation, changes and their effects and how humans interact with them, with both benefits and risks. Let's see how these concerns are presented and discussed in an explanation text about the formation of volcanoes below, adapted from a chapter called 'Earth Movements' (Maclean and Thomson 2009).

We discuss the text in three stages of deconstruction. As you read, use these questions to help you note down what strikes you.

Stage 1:
- What are the concept and key words?
- What communication purpose does the writer choose?
  - Description: What is it like?
  - Procedure: How is it done?
  - Process: How does it happen? Linear or cyclical?
- Does the explanation include the added complexities of *why?* and *how?*

Stage 2: How is it organized?

Stage 3: What are the language features for particular purposes?

The Formation of Volcanoes

[Process of volcano formation and key terms involved] → Volcanoes are formed from molten material called magma which lies beneath the earth's crust in the layer known as the mantle. The *magma* is forced through an opening in the crust called a vent. When the *magma* comes out of the ground, it is called lava.

[General classification] → There are three types of volcanoes: composite, shield and dome.

[Specific example of Composite] → An example of a Composite volcano is Galeras in the Andes of SW Colombia.

[Specific classification & description of features] → This type of volcano has the following main features:

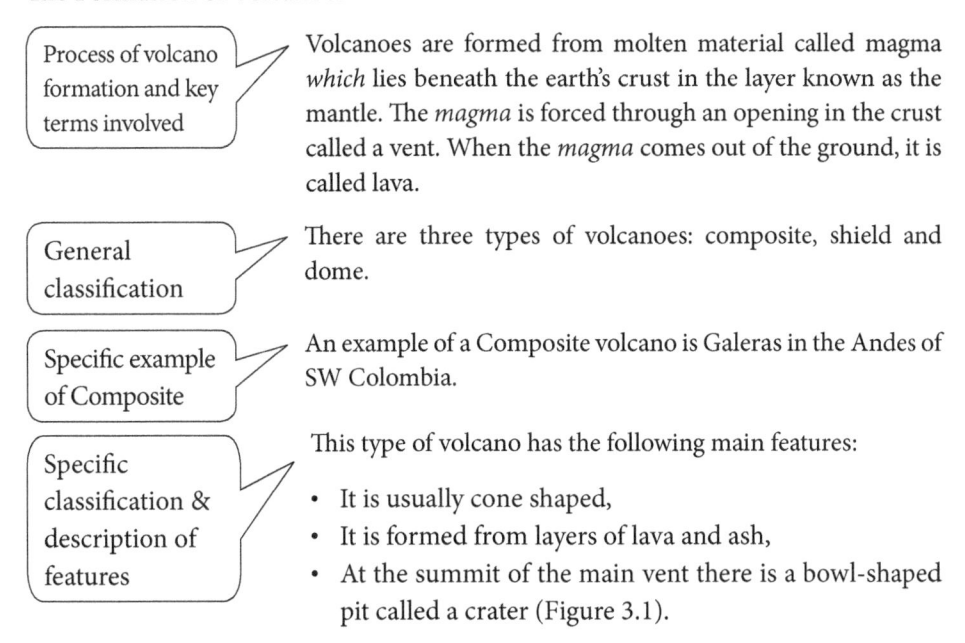

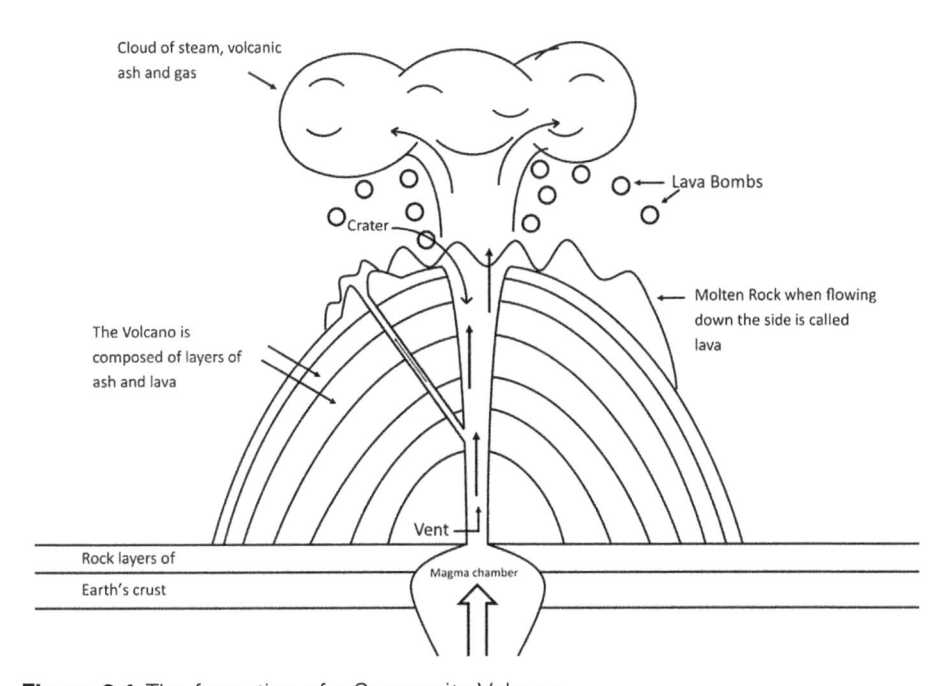

- It is usually cone shaped,
- It is formed from layers of lava and ash,
- At the summit of the main vent there is a bowl-shaped pit called a crater (Figure 3.1).

Figure 3.1 The formation of a Composite Volcano.

[Specific classification, formation & description of general features] → Shield volcanoes are formed from lava that is thin and runny. Gentle lava flows spread from the main vent. They are only a few metres thick and are formed from basalt.

[Example and description of features] → An example of this kind of volcano is the Mauna Loa, the world's largest volcano on the island of Hawaii. The whole structure rises from the floor of the Pacific Ocean and is almost 10,000 metres high – even taller than Mount Everest. The contour map on the next page shows how gentle the slopes are.

[Formation & description of specific features] → Dome volcanoes are formed from lava so thick that it can hardly flow. It quickly cools and hardens into a steep-sided mass of rock. The lava in the vent frequently hardens and forms a plug. This traps gases and magma under great pressure until a giant explosion occurs.

[Example of dome volcano & process of eruption with results] → One of the best examples is Mount St Helens. In 1980 its northern side started swelling until, on 18 May 1980, a powerful earthquake triggered a landslide which released the pressurized gas and steam. The blast blew sideways and removed a massive chunk of the mountain top.

Deconstruction stages of the Geography text: What did you notice?

Stage 1: What are the concept and key words and what communication purpose does the writer choose?

- Concept and key words:
    Volcano formation: pressure, molten magma, earth's crust, lava, ash
- Communication purpose:
    - The process of how the formation happens and the key physical phenomena involved;
    - A description of the three different types of volcano to classify them.
- The added complexities: the causative factors are included in to answer the question 'Why does it happen?'
    - location on a fault line,
    - pressure building up from the core leading to the explosion.

Stage 2: How is it organized?
For each type of volcano the formation and description move from general to specific. We have

i) stages of the formation process,
ii) definition of the specialized terms and
iii) description of physical features to classify them using words, diagrams and, in the original text, photos and maps.

This is a fairly typical process explanation structure. Each purpose tends to have a predictable structure, which helps you read more quickly.

Ask yourself questions to identify the concept, key words, communication purpose and organization of a text you might use for teaching your own subject.

Stages 1 and 2 have identified general features of the whole text (at macro-level). Now we move on to micro-level: words and sentence structures.

Stage 3: What are the language features for particular purposes at micro-level in the Geography explanation?
In this section we identify the micro-level language features for particular purposes in the Geography explanation. They present the stages, the definitions and the description. We see further examples of the language features already identified in Chapters 1 and 2. They show the way in which everyday and subject specialist language differs in terms of how precise it can be because the academic register likes to say more in fewer words. This text has a significant number of 'new' or specialist words that exemplify this feature of subject literacy.

We will deal in more detail with finding the meaning of new words in Chapter 4, but for this chapter we are extending our focus on the metalanguage for talking about the grammar of a sentence.

Meaning is often supported by groups of words for a particular communication purpose, e.g.

- to add detail in *noun phrases* for definitions, or
- for description in an *adjective phrase*,
- for events and descriptions in a *verb phrase*,
- for location in a *preposition phrase* and
- for 'time' and 'manner' in an *adverb phrase*.

Looking at language in this way will help you to think more specifically about the type of language patterns chosen. Let's look a bit more closely at how the patterns of language work to make meaning more precise.

(i) **Definitions: noun phrases and multi-clause sentences**

- *Noun phrases* (shaded in Table 3.1) are used to introduce the key physical features: Volcanoes, Molten magma, Lava.
- Some of these words, as we saw in Chapter 2 (page 50), are everyday words used here with a specialized meaning: 'Crust, Mantle and Vent'. Of these, 'crust' is key to understanding *how the eruptions can occur*.
- At an earlier stage in the chapter there is a diagram of the earth, with the 'mantle' likened to a cracked egg shell. This background understanding is key to understanding the causative factors.
- *Noun phrase* sentence starters to introduce items to be defined and exemplified are:
  - There are … and
  - An example of this kind of volcano is ….
- *Noun phrases joined together in multi-clause sentences*, i.e. sentences with more than one idea. To demonstrate this, the example in (Table 3.1) is set out as four separate ideas to show you how they have been joined together. The noun phrases are shaded. The words in brackets show what the sophisticated user of language has omitted (crossed out) and added ('which') in order to join the four statements.

Table 3.1 Making Four Simple Sentences into a Multi-clause Sentence

1		'Volcanoes are formed from molten material
2	(it is)	called magma
3	(it)	(which) lies beneath the earth's crust
4	(it is)	in the layer (which is) known as the mantle'

You will see that the writer has avoided using 'and' as a coordinating word. By using 'which', or 'that', or 'who' to introduce the additional statement about 'magma', the writer makes it into a *subordinate (less important)* clause. This is an important change, because 'which lies beneath the earth's crust' no longer makes sense on its own. It has become a subordinate clause. To be grammatical, it needs to join onto the *first part of the sentence (the main clause)*.

(ii) **The process of volcano formation: verb phrases, adverb and preposition phrases**

Verb phrases: In a subject text like this one we are interested in *tense* and *voice* (*active or passive*) in the verb.

- The verb choices are words with two kinds of meaning:

  either 'action/doing' – for events and processes *or*
  'being/having' – for describing.

- The present tense is what we would expect because the text is about what is *generally true all the time*. Mostly the present tense is used here with a mix of
  ○ active voice: *is, has, hardens, lies* and
  ○ passive voice: *are formed, is called, known as.*
- Writers in subject texts *mix active and passive voice for variety*. As we noted in the Introduction, it is not essential to use the passive unless you want to focus on the agent or cause of the event, e.g. 'formed from molten material'.
- Notice there are no verbs for *mental processes* in this text. These are verb phrases for *thinking, feeling* and *remembering* that tend to be used to express opinions or emotions. You would likely find them in an 'eye-witness' account of a volcanic eruption. With that text purpose, you might also get some verbs expressing *verbal actions* (*saying, telling, asking*). Verbs with this type of meaning tend to report evidence (*state*) or tell personal stories (*said, asked*).

Adverb phrases and clauses: single adverbs, multi-word adverb phrases and clauses with following examples are used to add information. They make the meaning of the verb phrase more precise by telling us *how, when or where something happens.*

- Single adverb: *usually* (how often?), *frequently* (how often?), *quickly* (in what manner?), *forwards* (which direction?)
- Adverb phrases in this text are mainly introduced by a preposition (shaded below) and end with a noun to show the position of one thing in relation to another. In this case they *help the verb to connect one noun (subject) to another key feature (object)* to make the meaning more precise.

In these examples we have included a question (in brackets) to show what question the adverb phrase is answering:

i. Magma which lies beneath *the earth's crust* (where does magma lie?);
ii. The magma is forced through *an opening* (where is it forced?) in *the crust* (where is the opening?);
iii. It is formed from *layers of lava and ash* (what is it formed from?);

iv. The whole structure rises *from* the floor of the Pacific Ocean (where does it rise?);
v. This (plug) traps gases and magma *under* great pressure (how does it trap the gases and magma?)

(See Teaching Resources for this chapter for more on the use of prepositions (page 95).)

- Adverb clause: an adverb phrase with a verb in it, e.g. '*until* a giant explosion occurs' (how long are the gases and magma trapped?).

(iii) The description of the physical features – adjective phrases

These examples of adjective phrases (shaded below) show that Geography is concerned with descriptions of 'physical shape and height', and also with the 'thickness and consistency of the lava' as it changes state from liquid to solid,

- … cone shaped,
- … bowl-shaped pit,
- … lava so thick that it can hardly flow …,
- … how gentle its slopes are,
- … bigger than Everest,
- … the largest in the world.

Notice that the writer uses a range of ways to express description.

Apart from the reference to physical characteristics, the writer uses comparison to give an idea of size, e.g. 'bigger than', 'the largest', and one example tells us the effect of the consistency: 'so thick that it can hardly flow'.

Description is an important function and the more words and phrases the learner has available for expressing it the better.

Putting together a Geography key word hunt

This process of searching for key or principal content words is helpful practice for tackling a text to build meaning and to become familiar with the form and use of the words in context.

To help learners focus their attention on the key words of the text, the teacher could ask, 'How many words for volcano can you find in the Geography text?' The answer will be 7, or 8 if you include the word 'structure'.

What other key words occur more than once? *Magma* 4 times; *Vent* 4 times; *Lava* 6 times. The frequency of these words in such a short text shows how important they are to talking about the topic.

We develop this process of focusing on the meaning of key words in context in Chapter 4 when we look at supporting engagement with knowledge.

Typical features of how knowledge is presented and discussed in Geography

This text includes a cross-sectional diagram with directional arrows to support the meaning of the written text, exemplifying how the description of a process might be presented in a multimodal way in a Geography text.

Usefully for the EAL learner, Geographers record information about the natural world: through survey and measurement, so communication is not just in words.

In other parts of the same chapter, photos of a volcanic eruption are used; moving images and sound are available online; locations and shapes are presented in maps and contour lines.

But beware of making cross-cultural assumptions. How are your EAL learners' visual literacies? Are they familiar with a cross section? Think of a Maasai student: Is his image of a typical house the same as yours?

Apply these language patterns for *change and description* to other subject areas

We can apply this explanation pattern to other subject areas where a process of change and description of features or characteristics needs to be set out. We support the EAL learner with sample *verbs* and *adjective phrases* as shown for other subject areas in Table 3.2.

The defining characteristics will reflect the concerns of the subject area.
Has this helped you evolve a definition for your own subject area?
Can you produce one that would be clear to an EAL learner?

Table 3.2 Apply Language Patterns for 'Change' and 'Description' to Other Subject Areas

Subject area	Topic area	Examples of verb/adverb phrases for a process of change	Examples of adjective phrases for characteristics / features
English	Changes in characters in the course of a story, novel, play, film	started moving more slowly decided to	with snow white hair
Physics	Heat transfer theories. Observations and results of experiment, theories	cause, lead to	It is like ... (colour? texture? shape?)
Biology	Growth of a plant from seed to fruit bearing	extend, develop, grow	composed of ... long, soft, strong ...
History	Development of new trade route, or machinery & manufacturing processes	establish, build up, emerge, supply	includes ... made of, manufactured, companies that ... vpeople who ...
PE	Positions of limbs and how they change when throwing, catching, stretching etc.	changes from X to Y straightens, bends	forms a right angle, makes an arc, extends straight up
Maths	Following an algorithm with commentary on what is found at of each step	when we calculate, we find	multiple, accurate
Add yours?	Think about your own subject area? How would these categories be expressed to reflect its concerns?		

Maths: Squares and cubes

The concerns of Maths are recording experience of the world in terms of number, algebra, geometry and statistics. We have chosen to look at Maths next because, significantly for the EAL learner, apart from the use of words, the notation systems used for each of these concerns tend to be used internationally (Rose 2006). So they may well be known to them.

The text types of Maths are the algorithms or operations that use step-by-step methods for solving a problem. This text is from the start of a chapter on Squares and Cubes from Brown et al. (2002: 6).

Use the same strategy with this text as you did with Geography. Here are the question prompts again to help you note down what strikes you.

Stage 1:
- What are the concept and key words?
- What communication purpose does the writer choose?
  - Description: What is it like?
  - Procedure: How is it done?
  - Process: How does it happen? Linear or cyclical?
- Does the explanation include the added complexities of *why?* and *how?*

Stage 2: How is it organized?

Stage 3: What are the languages features for particular purposes?

Squares and Cubes

Definition of 'to square' → When we multiply a number by itself, we are said to square the number

Examples Square 3 and we get $3 \times 3 = 9$ *Demonstration of procedure*
Square 5 and we get $5 \times 5 = 25$

Notation & how to express it in words → We write $3^2 = 3 \times 3 = 9$ and we say '3 squared equals 9'
$5^2 = 5 \times 5 = 25$ and we say '5 squared equals 25'

Notation & how to express it in words → The small number is often referred to as a power or index.

We can say 3^2 is '3 to the power 2' (or '3 squared')   *Definition*
5^2 is '5 to the power 2'

Extending to include 'to cube' with algebraic notation & how to express it words

For any number a, $a^2 = a \times a$ (a^2 is the second power of a)
Similarly $a^3 = a \times a \times a$ (a^3 is the third power of a)
a^3 is read as 'a cubed' or 'a to the power 3'

Examples $2^3 = 2 \times 2 \times 2 = 8$ $5^3 = 5 \times 5 \times 5 = 125$ *Demonstration of procedure*

3 tasks to practise notation & express answers in words

Exercise 4.1 No calculators unless the question asks you to use one

1. Calculate:

   a. 4^2 b. 3^3 c. 6^2 d. 7^3 e. 8^2
   f. 10^3 g. 100^2 h. $(5 - 3)^3$ i. $9^2 - 7^2$ j. $(1^3 + 3^2)^3$

2. Find the value of each expression when $a = 2$ and $b = 4$:

   a. $a^2 + b^2$ b. $b^3 - b^2$ c. $(ab)^2$ d. a^2b^2 e. $2b^3$
   f. $(a + b)^2$ g. $5a^3b^2$ h. $3a^3b$ i. $(a + b)^3$ j. $a^3 + b^3$

3. (a) For a square of side L cm, what does L^2 cm^2 represent?

    (b) For a cube of side L cm, what does L^3 cm^3 represent?

Deconstruction stages of Maths text: What did you notice?

Stage 1:

- Concept and key words:
    Squares and cubes: expression, number, power
- Communication purpose: it is presented as *a Procedure*: How is it done?
- There are no added complexities. It is a simple explanation of procedure.

Stage 2: How is it organized?

It consists of

- *a statement or claim* to define the algorithm followed by
- *demonstration* of the multiplication operations to be followed to square a number,
- *examples to practise*: *practice* in applying the algorithm with the correct notation.

Try this set of headings for a procedure text in your subject area that you might use for teaching.

Stage 3: What are the language features used for particular purposes in Maths explanation?

The patterns of language used for the procedure make a claim, command the operations, show notations and encourage talking about carrying out the procedure. We have multi-clause statements and commands that directly address the reader to give an oral demonstration.

(i) **Multi-clause statements or claims**

› The style of the definition is very formal. It is framed in a multi-clause sentence giving *the condition*, 'When we multiply a number by itself' which is required for the procedure to take place. It is followed by the definition, 'we are said to square the number'.

› The second part of the demonstration is also framed by a condition, 'For any number *a*' which is followed by the sample notation.

(ii) **Commands to demonstrate operations**
   ➢ The *verb forms* for the operations are *commands* such as 'square'.

Notice the shift of word class. 'Square' is not the noun for a shape, but a verb with a specialized mathematical meaning (see Chapter 1: a verb shifts to a noun form: 'attract'/ 'attraction', and in Chapter 2: a noun shifts to an adjective: 'farming').

   ➢ Commands with specialized meanings occur in the first two exercise tasks: 'calculate' and 'find'.

(iii) **Notation giving examples of conventions to be followed** – e.g. what 'we write', what 'we say' and how 'we refer' to a squared number.

Notice that the use of 'we' is *inclusive* for the reader who is implicitly part of the community of mathematicians. The habits of the community are being displayed by the statements 'we write', 'we say', 'is often referred to as' and the notation prescribed to represent the knowledge.

Putting together a Maths key word hunt

A word hunt for the Maths text will be useful for understanding and talking about the topic. The teacher could ask, *How many repetitions of the word 'square' and 'power' can you find?* The answer will be 5 and 6 respectively.

Typical features of how knowledge is presented and discussed in Maths

(a) **Layout and notation**
   ➢ Visually there is a lot of white space in the layout. This is an important convention which helps to separate the ideas, in the same way as paragraphs do in written texts.
   ➢ But at the same time, there is of a mix of notation and words to express numbers.

(b) **Oral style**
   It is important to note the formal, commanding oral style used to explain the operations and required notation of the 'squaring' procedure. Remembering the procedure is hard, particularly if the memory of what to do comes from watching a spontaneous oral presentation by a teacher or reading the book.

(c) **Fluency**
Some recommend that steps are best learned by talking oneself through them until the patterns become 'fluent', as you would when learning a language.

Does the wise learner follow the examples by 'speaking' the problem to keep the link clear between words and the notation? Does she work it through, using the notation and expressing it in words at the same time?

The concept of 'fluency' as a skill is based on the idea that there is generally more than one way to come to a solution. This meaning of 'fluency' is a goal set out in the Maths curriculum so that a learner can move from one algorithm to another without difficulty. In the example above, the third task requires the learner to apply the procedure to working with shapes. Thus 'fluency' can provide practice in applying simple algorithms of addition, subtraction, multiplication and division to other contexts.

Apply these language patterns for *presenting procedures* to other subject areas

Any subject teacher may find it useful to take up this notion of 'fluency' to represent the application of knowledge to other contexts. For example, a language teacher may think of fluency in terms of the ability to apply learned patterns of language to real communication. That probably means the use of planned repetition and reinforcement through interaction which may assist learners in acquiring the specialist language in the classroom, making the actual construction of new knowledge easier.

What would the components of 'fluency' in your subject look like?

Each discipline uses an everyday language along with specialized terms or 'notation' that their subject community uses.

Do you hear yourself saying phrases like 'we write' and 'we say' when you are explaining something to others in your subject area?

Think about supporting the EAL learner by offering the words for commands, equipment, sequence of instructions and the mode of recording or notation to be used, shown in Table 3.3.

This gets you started to cover the supporting language that an EAL learner needs for procedure in your subject. Can you think of any additional language features that would be useful?

Table 3.3 Apply Language Patterns for Presenting Procedures to Other Subject Areas

Subject area	Demonstrating a procedure	Commands, equipment and sequence of instructions	Mode of recording or notation
English	Analysis of plot structure in a narrative	start with, identify	insert a table with the number of rows for stages
Geography	Conducting a land or population survey	notice, look for	sketch, map references, compass points, contour map
Chemistry	Demonstrating the principle of distillation (hypothesis and expected result)	(1) set up the apparatus as shown in Figure x, (2) observe, (3) note	does the colourless liquid contain only water? Check boiling point is exactly 100°C at 1 atmosphere pressure
Biology	Carrying out a dissection procedure	make sure, set out, prepare	measure, draw, outline
History	Using CAD to reconstruct a Motte and Bailey from archaeological evidence	use, check	select an appropriate scale
PE	Following an exercise regime to achieve a level of fitness	warm up, stretch	count, time, stretching exercises
Add yours?	What procedures do you use in your subject? What language features would you offer to support the EAL learner?		

History: The Norman Conquest

The concerns of History are events in the past influenced by social structures such as power and trade. History tries to determine objectively the patterns of cause and effect that lead to events, while at the same time acknowledging the role of interpretation of evidence and the fact that therre may be more than one perspective. Based on these concerns, how is knowledge presented and discussed in the text below? The text is adapted from Chandler (1998).

Here are the question prompts once more to help you note down what strikes you.

Stage 1:
- What are the concept and key words?
- What communication purpose does the writer choose?
  ○ Description: What is it like?

- Procedure: How is it done?
- Process: How does it happen? Linear or cyclical?
• Does the explanation include the added complexities of *why?* and *how?*

Stage 2: How is it organized?

Stage 3: What are the languages features for particular purposes?

The Norman Conquest

[When, event, consequence & further problem]
When Edward the Confessor died in January 1066 he had no children. But there were several contenders for the crown.

[Contender 1 & reason for selection]
The English nobles chose the most powerful among them to be king: Harold Godwinson.

[Reason for claim] [Contender 2]
Harald Hardrada, King of Norway, thought he had a good claim because his ancestor, King Cnut, had ruled England thirty years before that (1016-35). So he landed in Yorkshire in September 1066 with the help of Harold Godwinson's brother, Tostig. But Harold

[Consequence and result]
defeated the invaders at the Battle of Stamford Bridge on 25 September.

[Contender 3 & reason for claim]
The third contender was William, Duke of Normandy, from northern France. He claimed Harold had sworn an oath to help him become the king of England when he was shipwrecked on the coast of France in 1064. He had the support of the pope.

[Consequence & result]
William and his army landed on the south coast of England at about the same time as Harold was fighting in the North. So Harold's soldiers had to march 500 miles south for a second battle within two weeks at Hastings on 14 October. Harold was killed and William became the king.

[Evidence]
Evidence of the battle is depicted in the Bayeux Tapestry – a very long embroidery panel made at the time to record the events. The tapestry also shows us the kinds of clothes, boats and armour the Normans had.

[Results of invasion]
After the battle William the Conqueror used several strategies to gain control over the country.

[General actions for control]

How Is Language Used to Present and Discuss Knowledge in My Subject? 83

> **Specific actions for control**

1. He rewarded the Norman Barons who had helped him win the Battle of Hastings by giving them 50% of the land seized from Anglo-Saxon owners.
2. He organized these Barons to build around 70 stone castles for defence including Windsor Castle and the Tower of London, which are still standing today.
3. He rewarded the Church because his invasion had been backed by the pope. He appointed Normans to the most senior church posts and gave them 25% of the land for building monasteries and abbeys.
4. To control the people, he established the feudal system, which put everyone into ranks. At the top was the king, followed by the barons, then the knights, with the serfs at the bottom. Land was rented out to each rank in exchange for taxes and manpower if the king needed fighters.

> **Evidence**

Supporting evidence for much of this comes from the Domesday Book. This document was made by William the Conqueror to record how many people lived in England, and what they owned. He used this to work out how much tax people owed him. Today, we use the Domesday Book to learn more about the people who lived in Norman times.

Deconstruction stages of the History text: What did you notice?

Stage 1:

- Concept and key words:
   Conquest, power and control: kings, battles, systems of control, evidence
- Communication purpose:
   ➢ This is a process (*how did it happen?*) set out as a series of events like a story.
   ➢ It explains *why* and *how* these events happened and supports the information with evidence (*the Bayeux Tapestry, and the Domesday Book*).
- Added complexities: this is a complex explanation involving multiple actors and contributing factors.

Stage 2: How is it organized?
It is organized to build the parts of an 'argument' with the pattern 'situation, problem, solution and evaluation'. It follows a *chronological sequence (time)* with each *causative*

factor expressing the *result of the previous outcome*, thus creating a *chain of events*. This chain analogy suits the linked organization of this text, as can be seen in the following:

- The situation or setting – This sequence of events took place in the 11th century in England which had close links with France and Norway.
- A problem – The king died with no heir, and the system for succession was not well established. The role of the king went to the person who could establish power through persuasion and influence.
- Three possible solutions – There were three contenders who took action.
- Resulting actions and outcomes – There was no voting system, so practices for resolving conflicts were based on the personal leadership skills of the three contenders and their ability to gather supporters and lead an army to victory. Three outcomes and a further resulting action in the form of William the Conqueror's strategies for government.

Key to this text is the interplay of 'time', 'place', 'circumstance', 'actors' and 'actions' (*Who? What? When? Where*).

Try this set of headings to help deconstruct a complex explanation text in your subject area that you might use for teaching.

- The situation or setting – *Who? What? When? Where?*
- A problem
- Possible solutions
- Resulting outcomes/actions

The mode of presentation would be helped by a flow chart of graphics to display the sequence. Sometimes History revision texts use timelines to set out events in a way that highlights the concept, key words and organization.

How important to your subject is visual representation? How important is evidence?

Stage 3: What are the language features used for particular purposes in the History explanation?

History is concerned with concepts and factors, so the specialized language in this text uses both abstract words and multi-clause sentence structures outlining *Who? What? How? When? Where? Why?*

Table 3.4 Key Concepts in the History Text

Key concepts	Vocabulary
Contenders for the crown	*powerful, claim, ruled, support*
Conquest	*invaders/invasion, battle, defeat*
Supporting evidence	*record, depict, show*
Strategies to maintain control	*reward, seize, organize, defence, feudal system, rent, tax, own, manpower*

(i) **Abstract words that refer to key concepts**:

Table 3.4 shows the abstract words taken from the text. The conceptual challenge is to transfer images of power struggles we have encountered in films and historical novels to the image of real political power and associated struggles represented in abstract processes like *invasion, conquest*.

(ii) **Key factors involved**: Table 3.5 shows 'the time', 'place', 'causes', 'actors' and 'actions'. The term 'cause' refers to a previous event that contributes to the current sequence of events and outcomes.

This deconstruction shows what a lot was going on, and the sentence structures to carry the meaning are complex too, as we see in the next section.

Table 3.5 Key Factors Involved in the History Text

	Vocabulary expressing key factors involved in the History text
Time	*January 1066, 25 September 1066, 14 October 1066, After the battle, Norman times*
Place	*England, Norway, Yorkshire, Stamford Bridge, Normandy northern France, South coast of England, Hastings, Windsor Castle, the Tower of London*
Causes	○ *When Edward the Confessor died ....* ○ *... his (Harald's) ancestor ... had ruled England ....* ○ *Harold had sworn an oath ... when he was shipwrecked off France in 1064. He (William) had the support of the Pope.* ○ *At about the same time as Harold was fighting in the North ....* ○ *... second battle within two weeks.*
Actors	*Harold, English nobles, Harald of Norway, King Knut, Harold Godwinson's brother, Tostig; William, Duke of Normandy, the Pope, Harold's soldiers, the Norman Barons, Anglo-Saxon owners, knights, serfs*
Actions	○ *Chose, the help of ... Tostig, landed, defeated, claimed, landed, had to march, killed, became King.* ○ *Bayeux Tapestry made to depict, show ....* ○ *Strategies to gain and maintain control, reward, give, seize, organize, build, appoint, establish.* ○ *Domesday Book made to record ....*

(iii) Multi-clause sentences for setting the scene in a sequence of events

The first two multi-clause sentences used in this text present *the time, the problem and the complicating problem*. Have a look at Table 3.6, where you will find the text in the left hand column and a comment identifying the language purpose of the information in the right hand column.

Table 3.6 Types of Information to Set Up the Text Introduction

Sentences 1 and 2	Language purpose of information
1) When Edward the Confessor died in January 1066	setting of the sequence of events (time and action)
he had no children.	reason why there was a problem.
2) But	indicates something different is coming – a solution? Or another problem?
there were several contenders for the crown.	introduction of a solution, which also holds a problem because there is more than one claimant/contender.

The two sentences in Table 3.6 tell us *a lot in a few words*. In the first, starting with a 'When' subordinate clause means the emphasis of the sentence falls on the *main clause at the end of the sentence*: 'he had no children'. This is the important information in the sentence to identify the problem.

The second sentence is linked by the word 'But', indicating a further problem. The information is introduced with the phrase 'there were'. As we saw in the Geography text, the word 'there' is a very useful text component in English to introduce something (*there is*) or many things (*there are*).

★ The sentence structures and linking words exemplified here show us how to organize 'the contributing factors' that need to be mentioned. Such patterns can be applied to introductions in a text in any subject with the 'situation, problem, solution and evaluation' structure.

Putting together a History key words hunt

Again, the teacher could challenge the learners to a word hunt in the text to establish the main concerns, evident from the most frequent words.

This time the question could be: *How many times are words associated with fighting used in the History text?* The answer will be 11: 'defeated the invaders', 'battle', 'fighting', 'second battle', 'killed', 'evidence of the battle', 'armour', 'after the battle', 'win the battle', 'defence', 'invasion', 'fighters'. It gives the reader a clear idea of the source of *power*.

Apart from the numerous actors involved, there are wide ranging actions and reasons for them (causes). This breadth demonstrates the complexity of *power*: where it comes from, how it is gained and kept.

Repetition of words indicates the relative importance of the numerous causes, actors and actions, and helps to remember the concepts.

Typical features of how knowledge is discussed and presented in History

This History text offers a useful model of how to sequence and link a complex explanation such as may occur in the History curriculum at Upper Secondary levels. Learners can practise identifying purpose, structure and language patterns, and build on these skills as they move through the school.

The deconstruction will help your reading become more efficient and offer a useful model for preparing a written explanation. As mentioned earlier, dealing with the questions of *why* and *how* can be complex, so scaffolded practice is recommended. A text jigsaw activity could serve to draw attention to the words selected for linking. Cut up the printed text into paragraphs and ask the learners to put them in order.

Looking at the text in this *language aware* way will support your understanding of further aspects of subject literacy.

Apply this strategy for identifying key concepts and factors to other subject areas

Think about your own subject area, where a sequence of events in the past is a typical style of explanation. Examples of useful language and sentence structures for other subject areas are set out in Table 3.7.

This table will get you started with key concepts and key factors in an explanation. What sentence structures could you offer to integrate causes into the opening sentences? Can you think of any additional language features that would be useful?

Table 3.7 Apply this Strategy for Identifying Key Concepts and Factors to Other Subject Areas

Subject area	A sequence of events in the past	Key concepts	Key factors
English	Plot events of a story, novel, play, film, biography, autobiography	structure, narrative voice	Examples to adapt

time, place, causes, actors and actions |
Science	Reporting discovery or principles in experiment	vaccination	
Geography	Account of prehistoric geological developments	pressure, erosion	
PE	Development of the PE curriculum in schools	competitive sport	
Add yours?	What sequence of events and key concepts could you use for a sequence of events I the past for your area?		

Drawing together metalanguage for language patterns to support EAL learners

The metalanguage developed in this chapter for language patterns in subject texts has built on what you already know about communication purposes and organization of texts. It has further developed your understandings of the language styles used in subject literacy to set up an approach for deconstructing texts at both macro- and micro-level.

At macro-level, the process enables the teacher to keep in mind

(a) what to look for in a text to read it efficiently and
(b) how to think through these ideas for planning an explanation in a *language aware* way to support EAL learners.

The question prompts for preparation are generic: 'What concepts are involved in this topic?' 'What are the key factors?' and 'How do they all fit together?' (see Teaching Resources, page 93).

In any subject area the teacher has to have *clear questions to find answers* to before starting to read efficiently. At the same time, the teacher has to have *clear answers to these questions* before starting to plan an effective explanation.

Identifying the cognitive operations that the learners will have to carry out in thinking and talking about the concept is key to choosing the communication purpose for each section of the explanation. The texts we have chosen represent only samples of the whole range of texts that the learners will encounter. But the process of deconstruction has allowed us to extrapolate similar communication purposes, patterns of organization and language features across subject areas, while at the same time acknowledging the particular concerns of the respective knowledge cultures.

These are starting points. You will find others. Communication purposes are not just expressed in words. There will be maps, maths notations, historical timelines, etc.

Your subject area may use demonstration of

- an experiment,
- a technique in PE,
- a computer application in technical design or
- a particular musical rhythm.

Once you have identified the cognitive operations, you will recognize the explanation type you need to use, i.e. how the text is organized and the appropriate language features used for particular purposes.

The templates for organization we have offered can be used as note frames, or writing frames as long as they are withdrawn when the scaffold is no longer needed (see Teaching Resources, page 93). Alternatively, the teacher can use the question prompts with the EAL learners themselves to help them to identify the communication purpose and organization.

At micro-level, there are two points:

(1) We have established the idea that the key words in a text are the ones that will occur most frequently and indicate the main concerns of the concept or topic. This point is relevant to strategies for engaging with new knowledge. We take it up again, along with focus on learning new vocabulary in context in Chapter 4.

(2) We have built on the awareness set up in previous chapters, that academic language in the classroom and in subject texts often uses fewer words to say more in a more precise way. For each of the three text types discussed in this chapter we have shown how the patterns of language used for particular functions can be extrapolated to other subject texts: *definition, description, process of change, maths operations, multi-clause sentences to join a series of simple ideas showing the complex relations* (see Teaching Resources, pages 94–6).

The deconstruction of these subject texts has also illustrated how the respective *knowledge cultures* of Geography, Maths and History favour their own modes of recording and presenting information based on the concerns of the discipline. This knowledge culture is most clearly expressed in the Maths example, with the use of 'we say', 'we write' to generate a sense of the Maths community and notation that appears to be based on an oral approach to recording knowledge. Equally there is a sense of *ownership of knowledge* in the visual system of recording information in Geography in maps, diagrams, surveys and the use of primary sources of evidence in History, that may be visual as well as written. These are habits that the teacher can make explicit to the EAL learners, so that they too can get a sense of the distinguishing features of that discipline.

Based on the idea of *what is usually done* in subject texts, in this chapter we have used questions to develop a *language aware* view of what constitutes a clear explanation.

The metalanguage for the patterns of organization and language features of subject texts will offer tools for the teacher to model for learners *how to talk about their subject knowledge*. Those learners can also participate in some of the deconstruction to become aware of how to look at a text as a vehicle for information.

There remains one question for this chapter.

How challenging are these Geography, Maths and History texts for the EAL learner?

As we set out in the Introduction, developing language for learning is not just a matter of words and grammar structures. Meaning is mentally constructed. What thinking skills are involved in understanding the knowledge in our sample texts? What are the cognitive challenges?

When you are planning to work with these sorts of explanations it is helpful to think of the relationship between the resources the learners have available to deal with complex language and the type of thinking skills involved. Cummins (1984: 139) developed a model to conceptualize the language proficiency for bilingual language learners with two dimensions to represent the relationship between the cognitive demand and the amount of support available from the context: *everyday versus unfamiliar and abstract*. The resulting quadrant or matrix offers a useful model for us to adapt to illustrate the level of challenge for the EAL learners to be found in our texts (see Figure 3.2).

The two dimensions of our matrix represent:

- the kinds of *thinking skills* involved in our sample texts (lower order/higher order?) and
- the extent of *topic familiarity* (are there any mental 'hooks' to trigger previous knowledge?).

Have a look at this matrix with your 'lesson-planning' hat on to see the extent to which you agree with the locations in the intersecting boxes allocated to the different aspects of the three explanations from this chapter. All three texts are culturally coded and contain many assumptions about previous knowledge.

Which aspects of the text do you think are straightforward and which are challenging?

The matrix illustrates the view that meaning is cognitively constructed between language and experience and offers clues as to where links with previous knowledge might lie. So engaging with and processing the knowledge will depend on the relative proximity of the new information to everyday experience and the relative mental complexity of the subject matter, along with the complexity of the language patterns used to express it.

In this chapter we have looked at how to talk about the type and structure of an explanation and the language patterns used for particular functions (description, definition, etc. see Teaching Resources, pages 93–6). Identifying these features will enable effective lesson planning for the teacher and allow you to develop *a language aware pedagogy* to support subject literacy development. However, these patterns of subject literacy constitute a social construction into which you, as a subject specialist, are socialized in your respective knowledge cultures. The business of a teacher is supporting the EAL learner in engaging with this knowledge. We will consider the challenges we are setting out for the learner in Chapter 4 where we look at supporting engagement with new knowledge.

92 Subject Literacy in Culturally Diverse Secondary Schools

Lower order thinking skills

Your experience of the text	*Your memory of something not present*
• Hear new words • Describe what you can see in the visual of the volcano • See mathematical notation that is known and new • Talk about these things	• Talk about existing knowledge you have of expressions for calculating numbers, shapes (globe, cone) your times tables • Stories of kings and power from films • Films you have seen of erupting volcanoes
Work with what you know	*Think about the possible*
• Describe a volcanic landscape • Compare and contrast the three different types of volcano, their features, and their locations • Summarize the events of the Norman conquest • Recall and review the algorithm for squaring and cubing that is now added to your knowledge of mathematical notation	• Evaluate and analyse critically the interaction of circumstances, people and their actions to consider the outcome and new system of control • Interpret evidence • Consider the implications of volcanoes for the life of humans • Apply maths algorithm to new problem area

Everyday/familiar ←→ Specialist/unfamiliar/abstract

Higher order thinking skills

Figure 3.2 Matrix of activities in the three text types showing intersection of *thinking skill challenge* and *topic familiarity* (adapted from Cummins 1984:139).

Teaching resources

Macro-level – Questions and answers for planning the explanation

Questions to ask the text before reading, or answers to have in the teacher's head when planning an explanation.

What is the concept?	
What are the key words?	
What communication purpose is chosen to explain the topic? *Description? Procedure? Process?*	
Does it include the complexities of *Why?* and *How?*	

Macro-level – How is it organized? Note-taking and writing templates for three types of explanation

A note-taking/writing frame for process descriptions

The process or activity	
The key terms with definitions	
The stages in the process – including (a) the circumstances or conditions that caused this to happen (b) classification of general class and specific types (c) specific features selected for the description in words and visuals (d) examples to make it relevant and provide evidence	
The result	

A note-taking/writing frame for procedures/experiments/demonstrations

A statement or claim to define the algorithm/theory/hypothesis/design target	
Demonstration of the operations to be followed	
Examples to practise/a report on applying the operations	

📝 A note-taking/writing frame for a sequence of events with contributing factors

The situation or setting – Who? What? When? Where?	
A problem	
Possible solutions	
Resulting outcomes/actions	

Micro-level – Language patterns for particular purposes

Nouns: Adding detail for precise definitions, actors, actions, concepts, factors

Noun phrases:
Made up of a <u>single noun</u> plus detail before and/or after it
- ... a *better nutritional* <u>balance</u>.
- ... <u>the DNA</u> *of your skin an eye cells*.
- <u>A slice</u> *through the narrowed air tube in the lungs of an asthma patient* ....
- Diffusion means/<u>*the movement*</u> *of molecules to fill all available space*.

Noun clauses:
Made up of a <u>single noun</u> followed by an identifying clause often introduced by 'that', 'who' 'which', 'where', 'when' (use NO comma!)
- The particles/<u>*(that)*</u> *are near the end of the rod*/become warm.
- The leader <u>*who*</u> *made the most impact on World peace in the 19th Century*/was ....
- Written music shows/groups of notes in bars <u>*which*</u> *are separated by barlines*.
- Most local anaesthetics are injected at/a place <u>*where*</u> *they can reach the finely branching nerves of the pain receptors*.

Verbs: To express 'action' (doing, happening); to express 'being'/'having' (characteristics)

- Action: The thinnest string on guitar *produces* the highest notes.
  Excessive rainfall *floods* rivers.
- Being: There *are* many kinds of musical instrument.
  Polar bears *live* at the North Pole.
- Having: Zithers *have* strings stretched across a sound box.
  This genus *includes* more than one species.

Adjective phrase: Adding detail before or after noun to describe key characteristics

- The flute produces *a more mellow* sound than the violin,/*with only a touch of brightness*.
- *A more mellow sounding* instrument/is the flute

How Is Language Used to Present and Discuss Knowledge in My Subject?

Adverb phrase: Adding detail to describe key characteristics
Adverb phrases, often starting with a preposition, can go at the <u>start</u> or the <u>end</u> of the sentence. • Use a comma when the phrase is at the start of the sentence. • NO comma needed when the phrase is at the end of the sentence. • Teach the punctuation rule at the same time as the phrase.
<u>At the start</u> • *In his orchestral piece La Mer,*/Debussy used subtle rhythms and unusual scales (where) • *In cases of food poisoning,*/the cause is frequently poor hygiene (condition) • *In winter in Norway,*/there are few hours of daylight (when) • *As shown on the map,*/the Vikings took the shortest route from Europe to America (how) <u>At the end</u> • Rocks have weathered/*over the years (when)* • Beethoven composed his music/*slowly and thoughtfully (how)* • Rhythm indicates the regular beat/*in a bar of music (where)* • Some people follow a vegetarian diet/*for health reasons (why)* • Cassava can grow/*in spite of lack of rain (concession)*

Adverbial clauses adding detail of when, where, condition, contrast, concession, reason, purpose, result
Adverbial clauses can go at the <u>start</u> or the <u>end</u> of the sentence. • Use a comma when the phrase is at the start of the sentence. • NO comma needed when the phrase is at the end of the sentence. • Teach the punctuation rule at the same time as the phrase.

To **set the time** 'when', 'after', 'once', 'before', 'while' • *Once the land has been ploughed,*/the farmer sows the crop.

To **set the place** 'where', 'wherever' • Farmers settle/*where they can find fertile land.* • *Wherever they go,*/nomadic groups find water for their cattle.

To **outline a condition** 'if', 'as long as', 'in case', 'in the event that' • Over half the people who get cancer can be cured,/especially *if the cancer is found before it has spread around the body.*

To **show a contrast or a problem** 'but', 'however', 'while', 'whereas', etc. • The sound waves are small,/*but they cause rapid changes in air pressure at the same rate as the vibration of the instrument.*

To **set out a concession** (contrasting expectations) 'although', 'however', 'even though'
- *Although mining yielded much wealth,*/Latin America's chief resource for colonists was its farmland.
- Early seafarers made great discoveries/*even though conditions were harsh.*

To **give a reason** 'as', 'because', 'since', 'as'
- People might not eat certain foods/*because they are allergic to them.*
- *As the map was out of date,*/we missed the turning.

To **show an aim or purpose** 'in order to', 'so that'
- *In order to survive,*/fish get oxygen from the water.
- The drums are carried in a sling round the body/*so that the drummer can walk.*

To **show result/consequence** 'so', 'therefore'
- Tractors reduced the need for work horses on farms,/*so fewer were bred.*

Sentence starters: Expanding vocabulary for particular purposes			
Describe, explain, classify	This	explains shows demonstrates	X Y Z
Introduce purpose, aim	Your essay will	investigate explore look at	X Y Z
Presenting processes, causes and effects	The	effect cause reason change problem	is that …
What is it like? What is it made of?	The	components texture materials colour	include … are …
Compare quality	They are	large/larger/the largest	X
Compare quantity	There are	more than less than fewer than the same … as	X Y Z P
Compare one entity or process with another	This process	more efficient than quicker than	X Y
Present choices or preferences	They chose to plant rice	rather than in preference to	corn

4

How Can I Support EAL Learners to Engage with New Knowledge in Challenging Texts?

Chapter Outline

Starting points: Identifying challenges	97
How did your receptive skills develop?	100
How do fluent language users approach a topic using prediction?	101
Supporting the EAL learner with hearing new words	105
Supporting the EAL learner with reading new words	108
How many words do EAL learners need to know?	109
Dealing with the challenges of complex language	113
Apply these strategies systematically to engaging with challenging texts	118
Teaching resources	132

- *What are the likely challenges for EAL learners in different kinds of texts?*
- *What do we know about how receptive skills develop?*
- *What strategies can we use to support ways into difficult language and building meaning?*

Starting points: Identifying challenges

In this chapter we explore how the teacher can support EAL learners to engage with new knowledge. What is important for the EAL learner is that input is *comprehensible*. When it comes to engaging with texts, research suggests that the significant factors affecting comprehension are

- familiarity with topic,
- recognition of words,
- the ability to manage the language complexity, and
- ease of dealing with layout and typography.

(Carrell, 1987, Dyson 2004)

These are the challenges we want to explore in this chapter in order to outline a *language aware pedagogy* for supporting engagement with new knowledge and development of subject literacy. Since our view of learning is that there will be a place in our existing bundles of knowledge or schemas that we can use as a 'hook' to link to the topic, the challenge is to find an appropriate *hook* for the EAL learners to trigger their existing mental representations so that they can listen, look, read and build new knowledge.

Approaching subject content may involve listening to the voice or to music, looking at visual images with and without sound, using photos, video and films. Importantly, these are modes that are likely to be more in line with learners' everyday experiences.

Dealing with new words and making sense of the message can be well supported in a collaborative classroom with an ethos of *purposeful talk*. As we saw in Chapter 3, different subject areas will have different ways of talking about the material of their subject. Asking questions about language in a text helps us recognize patterns at macro-level and micro-level and shows us what features to make clear to learners. At the same time, we acknowledge the level of challenge there is in text activities and the multiple interpretations the EAL learners may have of their classroom experience.

To guide our planning we make use of a matrix adapted from Gibbons (2015: 17), where the intersecting axes reflect *the level of challenge and level of support available to the learner*. Four possible outcomes from these intersections are set out below (Figure 4.1).

	High level of challenge	
High level of support	• Stimulation • Participation • Engagement in learning	• Frustration • Anxiety • Feeling of failure
	• Comfort zone • Status quo	• Non-participation • Lack of engagement • Boredom	Low level of support
	Low level of challenge	

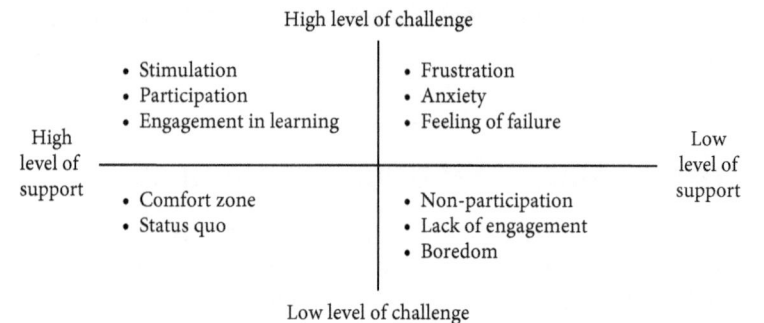

Figure 4.1 Matrix showing the intersection of challenge and support.

Ideally, the teacher will aim for the 'high level of challenge/high level of support' sector. If you achieve that, learners are stimulated and have little choice in whether to participate or not. Implicit in the collaborative model for the classroom you have chosen, there is an unspoken contract of shared purpose between teacher and learners. As we know, learners tend to choose for themselves to work in the environments that match their preferred level of cognitive functioning.

At the same time, your awareness of learner need will guide you to vary the levels of challenge in the activities to encourage learners to participate at their level, especially if they lack confidence in their language in the early stages. When we plan an activity with a challenging text with the class, we note the aspects of subject-related language discussed in Chapter 3 to give us a starting point for how to look for meaning in a text, i.e.

- key words in a text (to identify topic)
- text purpose (to identify logical organization)
- language features (to identify language for particular purposes)

We integrate this language knowledge into the pedagogy so that EAL learners are guided to identify topic, text purpose and so on, whether in a written text or in other modes, such as looking and listening.

This kind of approach will support EAL learners to build on previous knowledge, build meaning, ask their own questions and become more independent readers/listeners/visualizers.

As with any challenge, it is wise to break down the task of tackling a text into smaller stages. Many Primary schools use DARTS (Directed Activities Related to Texts, Lunzer and Gardner (1984)), where learners are offered supported tasks to approach a text and focus on the information they need. At the same time they are encouraged to check understanding at each stage to repair any problems. This model helps to cast the reading process as a structured and collaborative event with some kind of production as the goal.

This kind of activity pattern is gradually extended through Primary school, so that the learner can become a 'proficient' reader. This implies being able to

- read complex children's literature and straightforward informational texts;
- consult reference materials to source information;
- have basic familiarity with visual information such as charts, graphs, and tables to retrieve information with guidance.

The learner coming from Primary school will be familiar with finding a word in a dictionary to check spelling and meaning. She has been encouraged to read between the lines in literature and to provide reasons and examples in discussions. So when the learner transfers to Lower Secondary school, she is on course to start evaluating, interpreting and analysing subject content.

With awareness of challenges and our existing resources as starting points, in this chapter we explore the components of the challenges systematically to guide our approach to supporting engagement with new knowledge. What strategies do good listeners and readers use to build meaning? To find out how to supplement these in a *language aware* way, we need an understanding of

- the basic processes involved in using receptive skills to interpret the message and
- the challenges posed by unfamiliar topic, new words and complex language.

As we go through the chapter, we offer activities for the teacher to guide learners to interact with the text and interpret the new knowledge for themselves.

How did your receptive skills develop?

Finding ways into new knowledge can be a complex business, as any one embarking on a new topic, or course of study, or new job will testify. How does your brain make sense of what you hear, see and touch? And what are the skills for making meaning of new messages? How do competent language users do this?

As you were exposed to language as a child and started to associate it with meaning, you became accustomed to the patterns and realized that you could make sense of separate bits of language by using contextual clues and then joining them together. As discussed in Chapter 2, the EAL learner has similar skills, but she is seeing and hearing with the images and sounds of her own language, as well as what she knows of English.

As we saw in previous chapters, our schemas are essential for learning to take place. They consist of the experiences we have had. Some learners will have more background knowledge about specific situations and phenomena available to interpret a text than others (Emmott and Alexander 2014: 757). When recognizing and interpreting spoken and written texts, the schemas enable them to fill in the gaps because they supply the missing information that a text itself does not give.

Reading, like listening and looking, is essentially an interactive process (Nuttall 2005). The reader engages with a text produced by the author and meaning is built through the interaction between the content of the author's message and the reader's prior knowledge i.e. the act of reading and how a reader connects the content and structures of the text to her own experience (Iser 1972, Langer and Alexander 1990).

So, to make meaning the *reader* draws on what she already knows to link the form of the words to make a meaningful sentence, a paragraph and then a structure to build a whole story, continually checking the sense of her interpretation as she goes along. The challenges presented by the conventions of subject literacy, as seen in Chapter 3, might lie in *schematic representations* like maps and diagrams, signs and symbols. The interactive meaning making processes of *reading* and *listening* are best supported by activities involving *purposeful talk* in the classroom to build meaning and knowledge.

Learners need a hook to trigger their existing mental schemas so that they are ready to explore new knowledge. Learning a new concept, like learning a new word or phrase, is a matter of encountering and using that concept in many different ways until it is settled.

We first look at strategies for coping with topic, then new words and finally language complexity.

How do fluent language users approach a topic using prediction?

We rely on prediction to the extent that we might all recognize a situation where we mishear or misread a sign or text that is in front of us. We tend to rely on what we expect to hear, see and read. We know that it takes a few seconds to recognize a piece of music or a song, and that we need to hear it several times before we become familiar with it. The same is true of an unfamiliar accent: it takes a while to get used to different sounds, to add them to our schemas.

Let's look at how we approach topic knowledge to find something familiar: through visuals, through listening and through reading. Visuals first.

Approaching a topic through visuals

Have a look at these two images (Figures 4.2 and 4.3). Which one do you find easier to recognize and make sense of? Why do you think that is?

Which one did you spend less time on to work out what it was?

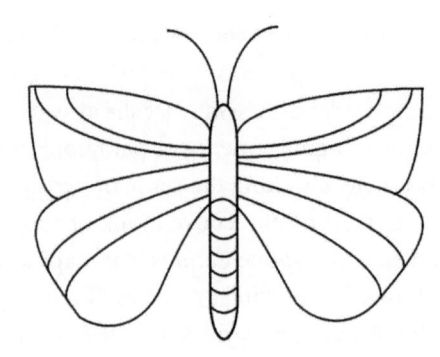

Figure 4.2 Butterfly.

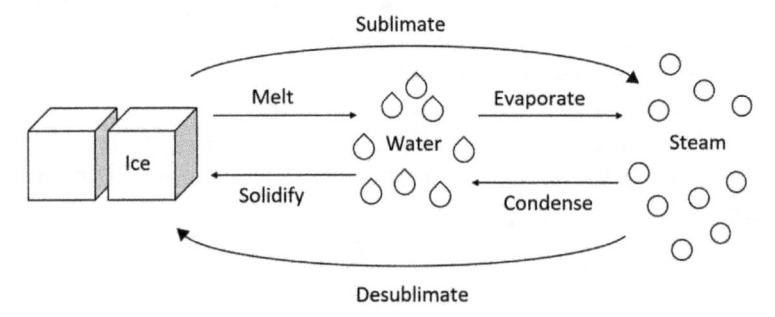

Figure 4.3 Change of state: Solid, liquid, gas.

We would expect that the Butterfly image is easier than the Change of state because

- the title has quite a general reference. It names an image that is easy to associate with the one already in your brain of a typical shape and pattern of design.
- it may appeal to aesthetic as well as scientific eyes. It could equally well be selected for teaching by an Art teacher or a Biology teacher.

It all depends on how specialized your expectations are. Some might question the anatomical accuracy of the butterfly image, arguing that it looks more like a dragonfly.

On this basis, we would expect that, unless the Change of state image is familiar to you as a scientist, it takes more processing time.

- The title implies a process of change, as illustrated by the arrows and labels. We tend to read such an image from left to right and from the general to the particular, looking for 'the story' (Kress and van Leeuwen, 2006).
- Aesthetically the image appeals to us for the clarity and balance of the design.
- The visual contains significant factual information on the relationship between ice, water and steam. As Mohan (1986) points out, a visual can contain a lot of information, giving it pedagogical value, which may be

- to increase content understanding,
- to stimulate exploratory talk and
- to help assess what is being understood.
• The amount of information is hard to remember unless you are a specialist, in which case you may perceive it as a single integrated image, in a similar way to how you, as a specialist, might look at the composite volcano diagram (Chapter 3, page 69).
• Although we might have everyday knowledge of what ice, steam and water look like, the abstract processes that make one substance different from the other require a different kind of knowledge. In a school context, this image might be a summary at the end point of a revision lesson, rather than a starter.

So recognition of how the information is presented is generally necessary for us to find a link with previous knowledge.

But be careful! The style of these images is culturally coded. You might anticipate that the EAL learner has seen a butterfly. What about ice? Encounters with ice might be limited to what is inside a freezer, not necessarily represented as a cube.

With these thoughts in mind, let's consider how we approach a topic in listening and then reading.

Approaching a topic in Listening

What clues for meaning do we have when we listen? Visible context, words, gesture, facial expression, expression in the voice (intonation, pitch, stress,) and accent (Lynch 2009). What information is available in the words? And what is missing?

We noted differences in Chapter 1 between expectations of a speaker and writer as to the needs of the receiver. It is often the case that speakers have shared background knowledge of the topic, so detail is omitted. This example from an encounter between two strangers in a supermarket shows how the Speaker 'A' relies on the prediction skills of the Listener 'B'.

A. Where's the gravy?
B. Sorry, I'm a cyclist.

Person 'A' is a shopper who saw a Person 'B' in a 'high vis' jacket and made an assumption about his knowledge! (Joan Cutting, personal communication). In this case the schematic prediction goes wrong. As Brown and Yule (1983) point out, context plays an important role in interpretation of meaning.

The example illustrates our tendency to speak in incomplete sentences in informal speech. Now we know more about the two speakers, we can imagine how the exchange would go if everyone spoke in complete sentences. The extra information is added in brackets.

- A. (Excuse me, I wonder if you can help?) Where's the gravy?
- B. (I'm) Sorry, (but I can't help you. I don't work here.) I'm a cyclist. (I've come to get some bread.)

Fluent users of English become accustomed to what is left out because we rely on breaking up what we hear into phrases and locating key words to build the meaning of the topic.

But remember the EAL learner – if she is in early stages of English, she might need the complete message. She has not got enough language yet to fill in what is left out.

Approaching a topic in Reading

As with the listening example above, 'what you already know about a topic is a key resource for reading' (Gibbons 2015: 139). As with a film of piece of music, the main resource for identifying the topic is the title. That will also help with the communication purpose.

To demonstrate this idea, this text box shows you a text with no title. It is based on a psychology experiment that tested how much readers could recall of a text, with and without a title (Bransford and Johnson 1972, cited in Brown and Yule, 1983: 72).

Can you work out the topic by focusing on key words? The shaded words give you a clue.

> Although the process is common in everyday life, it is time consuming in your professional context because it requires attention to detail. It must be done in advance of the event and requires visualization of what is going to happen at each stage. It is important to build in contingencies to meet the needs of those involved. For the novice, the documentation is especially challenging because it will be checked by others. Fortunately, the whole process becomes easier with experience, as practitioners become more systematic in how they approach the task. They rely on key questions to prompt them and keep them on track. Nevertheless, the old wives' adage remains true, even for those whose practice extends to more than forty years. If you fail to do this, you must be prepared to fail!

You have probably guessed that it is a something to do with teaching. You can check your answer in the Teaching Resources at the end of this chapter (page 134).

A text with no title is hard. You will have looked for key words that fit a scenario from your previous experience. What questions did you ask yourself as you read it? Did you get clues from words like 'process', 'documentation' and 'task'?

This example shows how schemas support *ease of reading, or readability*, with reference not only to text-based factors but also to reader-based ones. It implies that ease or difficulty of a text is determined by the interaction between reader and text (Meyer, Marsiske and Wills 1993). The reader response theory, about which these researchers write, emphasizes the importance of the transactional process in interpreting a given text. It is an active process of meaning construction.

What the learner already knows will include predicting what the text will tell her by looking at the title and predicting what it is about. The ease of constructing meaning will be related to the familiarity of topic, the words and the level of language complexity.

Supporting the EAL learner with hearing new words

How do you deal with hearing new words? If you hear an unknown word, does it help you to see an image of what it represents or see it written down? How do you manage reading in a foreign language?

One of the main strategies we use in listening is to break up the stream of language or sound (with music) into units of meaning using pauses and intonation (or musical key changes). In spoken language, a falling tone generally indicates the end of a sentence or section, a rising tone indicates a question. Although, you may have noticed that international English has affected this pattern. For example, you may hear an Australian feature, where a rising intonation might be used at the end of a statement to indicate friendliness.

A Chinese speaker of English finds English intonation hard to master as Chinese is a tonal language, where rising, falling and level intonation distinguishes one word from another.

An example where two words share the same Chinese character but have different meanings depending on the tone used is '好', which means 'good' when pronounced 'hǎo' (fall-rise tone) and 'like' when pronounced 'hào' (falling tone) (with thanks to Peiyue Xu).

In English, the stream of words is then segmented into meaningful phrases, using main syllable stress to identify the key word in a phrase. If you look at how the sentence below is divided with '/', you could use the key words for a text message.

e.g. It is /NE-ce-ssar-y to /CLOSE /the SHUTT-ers when a /HURR-i-cane is /COM-ing to /KEEP /E-ver-y-one /SAFE.

> For more on patterns of syllable or word stress, check out the four key rules that the EAL learners might find useful in the Teaching Resources for this chapter (page 134).

The disadvantage of this reliance on syllable stress for an EAL learner trying to make sense of unfamiliar language is that in fast speech, unstressed syllables and gaps between words sometimes merge together (Lynch 2009). We tend to join words together and sounds of vowels and consonants get lost. Where does one word end and the next word start? Here are some examples:

(1) Vowels in little words tend to be shortened to an *uh* sound, e.g. *a cup of tea* becomes *uh cup'uv tea*.
(2) A vowel at the beginning or end of a word means we might join the two words together, e.g. *his own* becomes *hizown* and *it is time for lunch* gets shortened to '*it's time f'lunch*'.
(3) We leave out consonants in everyday speech, so *Thank you* can become *thanQ*, or *good morning* loses its *d* and becomes *goo'mornin*.

> The challenge for the EAL learner is that the sounds that she hears in everyday informal speech might bear little relation to the individual de-contextualized words she finds in a dictionary or grammar book!

> Fortunately for the EAL learner, in the classroom context, the rate of speech from the teacher presenting and guiding is likely to be slower than in informal conversation between mates. Clear articulation and complete sentences are more likely to occur.

To give you an example of this, here is a lesson transcript where some Year 6 EAL learners are coping with new words. They are discussing *The Silver Sword*: a novel with twelve and thirteen-year-old protagonists who are struggling to survive in a war time context. The group task is to match up new content words to describe the main character with everyday meanings. The words are 'inspirational', 'encouraging' and 'calculating'. In the examples below, the teacher is encouraging the learners' attempts.

Sophia: (reading a card) In … in … springing.
Teacher: Insp … Inspiring, or encouraging.
Jamila: Is it couraging?
Teacher: Yes, inspiring, … or inspirational.

(NALDIC, 2009: Transcript 300509)

Sophia's 'in-springing' and Jamila's 'couraging' show they have difficulties with the consonants '*nspr*' and the prefix '*en*'. However, Jamila does get the prefix for 'inspirational' because later in the lesson she produces her own form – 'inspation'.

To help the learner with the form of the new word as well as the pronunciation, the teacher can respond with feedback to set the learners on the right track, for example,

Teacher: Yes! Good try. 'in-spir-A-tion' (writes word on the board).

Here the teacher accepts and praises the attempt, at the same time as reformulating it orally by articulating the stress pattern of the four syllables and then writing it on the board so that the learner can see the spelling.

This *language aware* approach, directing explicit attention to the language *in the moment* when the language is being used in the interaction, will help EAL learners to *hear the sound pattern as well as see the letter pattern of the word*.

Can you think of any key content words in your subject area that deserve the same attention? Do you use this type of language focus in your normal practice?

Apart from *key content words* it is important to pay attention to what we call *word frequency*. The questions to ask yourself are

- How often is the learner likely to encounter this particular word on a day to day basis?
- How often does the learner need to use this in subject literacy?

The answer will guide you as to the amount of attention you give to its form and meaning. There is an important distinction between *high frequency every day* and *low frequency subject words*. A basic 2,000 word vocabulary of *high-frequency* items comes first (Cameron 2002).

There is a strong link between listening and knowing a word: a child needs to engage with a word several times before the auditory memory retains it. There is a link between the ability to segment a word into sounds and reading, and the ability to segment a word into syllables and spelling. Despite these challenges, a learner gradually learns to listen for ideas, not just words. And it is a similar case with reading.

We will turn our attention to how we support ways into words and phrases to build meaning in reading in the next section.

Supporting the EAL learner with reading new words

When it comes to written text the reader also segments the text into meaningful units of words. This time by making use of layout, left to right, scanning for key words, spaces, sentence punctuation and paragraphing. The knowledge of the world (schema) is the starting point for working out meanings.

Can you remember in your early days of reading what you did with unknown words? Guess? Look them up in a dictionary? Ask an adult? A friend? Most of us guessed, sometimes erroneously and discovered the actual meaning later. It often depended on how essential that word was to the message.

The most common strategies teachers use for encounters with new words in text are through active engagement in reading and listening. Activities that engage with text and exploratory talk will support productive interaction to build meaning.

As in listening, so in reading, once the new reader has started to recognize words, she needs to engage with a word between 4 and 14 times in different contexts to recognize it automatically (Sökmen 1997). And the more a learner can read a text at their level, the easier it will become (Nuttall 2005).

The reader and listener need a reason to be actively engaged in reading or listening. In the early stages of listening in class or learning to read, unless the child is interested in the content, she will 'decode' only, i.e. read only the words. As we saw with DARTS, the strategy for extending receptive skills is to set 'focusing tasks' which ask the learner to listen for key points, or to talk to another learner about what they heard or read using questioning.

The teacher will also use questioning in exploratory talk. In the extract below the teacher is not using another language, or a dictionary. She is using literal and inferential language with extending questions to build meanings with the same Year 6 EAL learner group we met in the previous section.

The teacher picks up a card with 'clever, able and sharp' written on it. One of the learners chooses the card with 'calculating' on it to match the meanings. We come in on the teacher's response. Notice how she extends Sophia's one word answer with an open question to build on previous knowledge and elicit ideas about word meaning.

> T: 'Calculating'. Yes then you are calculating. Do you know what a calculation is?
> Sophia: Yes.
> T: What is it?
> Jamila: It's like in maths, you calculate something.

T: Yes. So if you're a calculating person what would you do?
Sophia: You do too much maths.
All: No!
Jamila: You'll be like, you'll be, you'll do, you'll be like able to do anything and sharp. You'll be sharp like clever.
T: What will you do with your mind? Yes, you would be ….
All: Always use it.

(NALDIC, 2009: Transcript 300509)

The group is not able to complete the teacher's last statement grammatically, but they have the meaning. Jamila extrapolates the meaning of 'calculating' when it is linked with maths. She can see that it belongs to the same word root, 'calculate'. Sophia is working hard to guess meaning from context, but in this case the word 'calculating' shifts meaning across contexts. Her guess misfires and she ends up making a joke, which the whole group recognizes! Jamila takes the opportunity to try out her language, and although she makes several false starts, she eventually finds the right one to carry her message: 'able to do anything ….'

These examples show learners trying out new language to make it their own. A similar approach could be taken when an EAL learner asks for clarification or says, 'I don't know.' A common strategy is to call on the class 'Who can tell/remind us what xxxxxx means?'

This way of building knowledge, by listening, sharing and discussing ideas and coming up with an opinion helps the learner take ownership of the ideas (Mercer 1995).

How many words do EAL learners need to know?

Have you ever wondered how many words you know? Apparently, the average educated speaker of English has a vocabulary of 20,000 words (Nation 2006).
Of that vocabulary,

- 40% of words in English have more than one meaning.
- 60% have only one meaning (Nagy, Anderson and Herman (1987)).

EAL learners need to know 95% of the words in a text to manage comprehension comfortably (Nation 2001). The EAL service in your school may have graded reader texts available with vocabulary levels as low as 300 words to help learners get used to reading text fluently at an early stage of language learning. This 300 word vocabulary is based on The General Service List of 2,284 commonest words in English (West 1953, updated Bauman and Culligan 1995). Although it has historical origins, its principles are still used as a guide on which to base the selection of words for different levels of readers for language learners. You may remember that Jose Mourinho, a Man U football manager, boasted that he could do his job with a vocabulary of 300 words!

What kinds of words are we dealing with in an academic text such as our EAL learners might encounter at school?

The Academic Word List, developed by Coxhead in 2000, gives us 570 'word families' that occur more often in academic discourse than in general use. These are words with the same *root*, e.g. *calculate/calculated/calculator/calculating/calculation*.

Coxhead (2000) groups the words into three categories based on *frequency* (how often they are used): *basic* (everyday), *general academic* (used across different subject areas) and *subject specific*.

The percentages are as follows:

- 80% are likely to belong to a basic 2,000 word vocabulary of high-frequency items.
- 10% are general academic words useful across other subjects.
- 10% of the words are subject-specific words. This is a relatively small number. For example, the 'volcano' text used in Chapter 3 has 300 words. In that text, we find around 20 subject-specific words like 'magma', 'lava', 'basalt', 'crater' and so on, which is 6.6%.

This gives the teacher a general idea about how many words are likely to be new or unknown in the subject-related context. The next two sections look at managing the groups commonly associated with subject learning: general academic and subject-specific words.

Learning general academic words: Notice and apply to other subject areas

General academic words are likely to be used in more than one subject area, so, although they are less frequent than everyday words, it is important to draw attention to them. Table 4.1 gives examples of the categories from the subject texts we looked at in Chapter 3.

Try making your own list with those in the table. What do you find in a subject text you are planning to teach?

Table 4.1 General Academic Words from Geography, Maths and History Texts

General academic purpose	Word class	Examples from subject texts
Abstract notions	nouns	*strategies, evidence, features*
Specific reference to 'things'	nouns	*examples, material, structure, layer*
Processes	nouns	*eruption, conquest, invasion, events*
Processes	verbs	*form, establish, occur, release, trigger, become establish, depict, organize*
Definitions	verbs	*is referred to, equals*
Instructions for tasks	verbs	*calculate, square, find*
Descriptions	adjectives	*powerful, cone shaped, bowl shaped, the kinds of, senior, supporting*
Concepts of frequency	adverbs	*usually, similarly, frequently*

Would this be a useful activity for learners? They could gather words through a lesson and group them as word bank tables like this on the classroom wall.

Learning subject-specific words: Use reformulations to make synonymous phrases

Subject-specific words are important to learn because of their centrality to carrying meaning in a particular subject. They are hard to learn because they have very particular meanings and contain a significant amount of information relevant to the subject. The word 'reformulate' is used here to mean 'saying or writing something in a different way'.

As mentioned above, we do not really come to know a word until we have encountered it several times in different modes and different contexts and when we have used it successfully in the appropriate context (Sökmen 1997). Reformulating provides a learning opportunity by exploiting the fact that in many subjects there are several ways of expressing the same idea – they are synonymous phrases. Our example here is a written task to practise *noun phrases from Chemistry* where the learners have been studying *Solvent Concentration of Water Molecules*. The teacher asks the learners to refer to their diagrams illustrating the ratio of solute to solvent in a solution, then look at the phrases that are scattered below the table. (In the case of Table 4.2, *the answers here are filled in for you.*)

Learner task: Put each phrase in a column in Table 4.2 to match the meaning of the phrase in the top line.

Table 4.2 Match Synonymous Phrases About Solvent Concentration of Water Molecules

High concentration of water molecules	Low concentration of water molecules
more water molecules	less concentrated solution
more solute particles	fewer water particles
stronger solution	lower concentration of solute molecules
more concentrated solution	fewer water molecules
higher concentration of solute molecules	lower concentration of free water molecules

Adapted from teaching discussions.

Collecting synonymous phrases such as shown above is a normal event in a *language aware* pedagogy. It underlines the flexible nature of wording in subject literacy. Learners can get used to using these new subject-specific words, trying out their meanings orally, visually or by writing in a task. Perhaps set up as a competition?

⭐ The aim is to make the meaning clearer to the learner and move towards *knowing* a word or phrase. This is to be distinguished from being able to make a general guess at the meaning or recognize a word because you have seen it before.

⭐ The task of matching synonymous phrases can be adapted to a topic in any subject area and also helps with work on building definitions. Reformulations can be supported by word banks on the wall with sentences to refer to.

Learning everyday words for specialist purposes: Note them down and compare with other subject areas

As we saw in Chapter 2 (page 50), everyday words will often occur with particular meanings in a subject text, and perhaps shift word class, e.g. 'mean' = noun or verb. In Chapter 3 (page 72), we found everyday words such as 'earth' and 'crust' are put together to form a 'compound noun' in 'earth's crust'. In this case they take on a particular meaning in the context of a subject text. This tendency of English speakers to extrapolate the core meaning of a word to use it figuratively for an abstract concept occurs in other European languages. For example, the word for 'earth's crust' in German is '*Erdkruste*' and in French is '*la croute terrestre*'. Draw attention to them. Use lists in word banks on the wall.

When planning a lesson with a text, estimate how many words will be unknown, and how many will be both new and *essential to the learner for the initial stage of predicting the content*. Avoid more than 10% unknown.

If there are more than 10% *essential new words*, prepare more scaffolding work before presenting the target text.

- Use exploratory talk with visuals and realia as triggers to encourage the learners to bring to mind mental images of the topic and what they already know.
- Make strategic use of hyperlinks to dictionaries, and encyclopaedias, plus key words and images on the wall in the classroom grouped according to communication purpose, and integrated into tasks.
- Encourage learners to use their own language with a dictionary, with a peer or with a teaching assistant who has the language (see policy advice Chapter 2, page 59).

Any lesson has a shared purpose and more than one language can be used to achieve it.

Having looked at finding a hook to trigger mental images related to the topic, and managing support for new words, we turn to the third factor involved with text difficulty: the complexity of language.

Dealing with the challenges of complex language

We need to recognize the components of language complexity when considering the level of challenge in a text because it reflects the complexity of thinking skills and the cognitive load involved.

Sometimes the challenge lies in the fact that some information is left out, as we saw in the examples of shared background knowledge above, but in other cases the challenge is the information density: the amount of information in the few words selected to give precise meaning. The teacher needs to be aware of both types of challenge.

To work out the meaning, it helps to deconstruct the sentences into word groups. In the same way that building up a supply of synonymous phrases can help with word meanings, so deconstruction and reformulation of complex sentences can help with complex language.

Have a look at this example of a Maths task. How challenging do you think the instructions are?

'How much change would a boy receive if he bought a book for £3.20 and he gave the shopkeeper a £5 note? Calculate the change received'.

Our EAL learner, Wu, working at PiE level B (Early Acquisition/Becoming Familiar with English) is puzzled by the last sentence. Fortunately, the teacher has integrated into her practice regular checks to confirm that the learners have followed the lesson. She invites requests for clarification. When she went through this task to check that everyone knew what to do, Wu put up his hand and asked,

'What mean "Calculate the change received"?'

The problem with the instruction is that the expert user of the language often leaves out some of the words that make the grammar explicit and the meaning unambiguous, because they assume another expert user will automatically be able to supply the missing grammar. The instruction is a command, with a missing subject, missing question words and a missing object. If we fill in the missing language the instruction would say,

'(You must) calculate (how much) change (the boy) received.'

This type of language complexity may challenge EAL learners and lead them to underperform in formal assessments or written tasks. How does the teacher support this challenge?

She decides to use the support of the class to *reformulate the instruction, to find other words with the same meaning to make the meaning simpler and clearer.* If a learner has difficulties of this kind, it helps to broaden the range of thinking by inviting others to give their answers or add to answers of others.

Notice the strategies used in the following exchange to show *flexible ways of saying the same thing*:

Teacher: Jakub, can you help? What are you going to do when you "calculate the change received"?'
Jakub: I am going to work out how much change he received.
Teacher: Thanks. And what operation will you use?
Jakub: Subtraction.
Teacher: Good. Shaheen can you give me another way of saying what you do when you subtract?
Shaheen: Take away.
Teacher: Well done! And another way? What are we going to *find*?
Mehmed: Find … the difference between the cost and what he paid.
Teacher: Great, so Wu, what are you going to do?
Wu: Errrm … subtract!

So now, in the reformulations, Wu has heard *everyday* and *specialist* terms for what he is going to do. The teacher has asked the class to remind her of all the different ways of expressing, 'Calculate the change given.' She can then write them on a wall board for future reference.

She might need to go further with making changes to different parts of the troublesome instruction such as those in the text box below. We can see

- verbs to express the **required action** (**in bold**) and
- *noun phrases/clauses* identifying *the object of the action* (*in italics below*).

The clauses have got the subject and verb underlined to help you identify them.

> 'Calculate the change given' reformulations
> - **Work out** *how much change he was given by the bookseller*
> - **Work out** *how much change he received*
> - *How much change did he receive?*
> - **Find** *the difference between the cost and what he paid*
> - **Subtract** *the cost of the book from the money he gave the bookseller*
> - **Take away** *the cost of the book from the money tendered*

This approach helps to deal with challenges provided by complex language and further exemplifies how long noun phrases and clauses can be built up (as discussed in Chapter 2 page 51). The example makes another explicit contribution to understanding the flexibility of the language for all learners, and provides a supportive *language aware* way of dealing with the problem for Wu.

The teacher has modelled a useful strategy. Learners can try the habit of finding another word for themselves if they come across another puzzling instruction.

Be careful not to make assumptions about comprehension skills of any learner! A nodding head could be 'polite', or it could be a defence strategy.

As mentioned earlier, try not to confuse EAL learner language difficulties with learning difficulties.

Deconstruction, paraphrasing and glossing a meaning

Reformulation is one way of dealing with complex language. Another is deconstruction, paraphrasing and glossing meaning. In this section we demonstrate this by comparing language complexity in two texts of equal length about *the difference between climate and weather*. Deconstruction means we can analyse and label the groups of words to illustrate how to talk about them. We can then consider ways of paraphrasing or using more and simpler words to gloss meaning.

In the text box below, Text A is from Wikipedia and Text B is the teacher's rewrite. To avoid retracing steps, let us assume that the topic and key words (highlighted in grey) are known to the learners. So the focus here is on complexity of language.

What language features can you find that make Text A harder? Where are the similarities? Where are the differences?

Text A: Wikipedia
Weather is the condition of the atmosphere at a particular place over a short period of time, whereas climate refers to the weather pattern, using statistical data, of a place over a long enough period to yield meaningful averages.
1 sentence = 39 words
(for contributor references see https://en.wikipedia.org/wiki/Weather_and_climate)

Text B: Teacher's rewrite
*Weather means the daily conditions of the atmosphere.
In the UK, weather can change quickly.
One day it can be dry and sunny and the next day it may rain.
The climate of a place refers to average weather patterns that are recorded for longer periods, e.g. a year.*
4 sentences = 8 + 7 + 15 + 19 = 49 words

What did you notice?

Similarities in word choice and length. Both texts

- use abstract nouns, e.g. *weather, climate, condition of the atmosphere*;
- contrast the two concepts by referring to a short versus a longer period of time and
- have similar length: A = 39 words and B = 49 words.

Differences in complexity of language. Text A is harder than Text B due to

- a higher level of information density: more concepts in fewer words;
- sentence length: 1 long sentence of 39 words, with more than one concept, and 3 commas. The reader must process the meaning of 'whereas' to make sense of the logical relationship between two quite complex ideas;
- a complex noun phrase object consisting of a **noun phrase + preposition phrase + infinitive of purpose + noun phrase (in bold)** below is used to make the time period and purpose for data collection unambiguous.

This difference in complexity is set out in Tables 4.3 and 4.4, where the sentences are segmented with '/' inserted to show word class groups.

How Can I Support EAL Learners to Engage with New Knowledge? 117

Table 4.3 Deconstruction of Text A

Weather......./is.../the condition of the atmosphere at a particular place
Noun subject/verb/noun phrase object............... + adverb phrase (where)
over a short period of time,
+ adverb phrase (when),
whereas................../climate......../refers to   /the weather pattern,
Conjunction (contrast)/noun subject/verb + preposition/noun object,
/using...................................../**statistical data of a place,**
*/subordinate clause verb (participle)/**noun phrase object + prep phrase,**
/over a long enough period/to yield................./meaningful averages.
/adverb phrase (when)....../infinitive of purpose/noun phrase object.

The actual text is shaded and segmented (/). The grammatical analysis is in the row below the text line, *in italics*, where the labels identify the word class.

The language complexity of Text A is likely to present challenges to all learners unfamiliar with understanding this kind of language, but in particular there are challenges for the EAL learner. For this reason, when dealing with a complex sentence, finding the basic structure of subject and verb is a useful start, so that the other parts of additional information can be worked out separately.

Table 4.4 Deconstruction of Text B

Weather......./means /the daily conditions of the atmosphere.
Noun subject/verb..../noun phrase object.
In the UK.........../Weather......../can change quickly/ – one day
Adv phrase (place)/Noun subject/verb +adverb (how)/ – adverb (time)
/it..................../can be/dry and sunny....../and............ /the next day
/pronoun subject)/verb/adjective + adjective/conjunction/adverb (when)
/it................../may rain. /The Climate of a place/refers to............
/pronoun subject/verb......./Noun phrase subject/verb.....................
/average weather patterns/that are ..../for longer periods,
/noun phrase object........./relative clause verb/adverb phrase (when)
/e.g. a year.
/adverb phrase (when)

The grammatical deconstruction of Text B set out in Table 4.4 shows the comparative lack of complexity, compared with Text A. The text is shaded and segmented (/) and the *grammatical analysis* is given in the row below, *in italics*. There is

- lower-level information density supported by a paraphrase: the middle sentence helps the meaning of the first one;
- sentence length: it has 4 quite short sentences of 8, 7, 15 and 19 words.

Segmenting a sentence into grammatical parts like this is a useful habit to explore, particularly with complex sentences that need to be reformulated to make synonymous phrases. It helps to find the core of the sentence, and seeing how a sentence is built is beneficial knowledge for the learner's writing too.

So how do we apply our understandings of the components of challenging texts to classroom practice to support learners' engagement with new knowledge?

Apply these strategies systematically to engaging with challenging texts

In this section we draw together strategies for engaging with the topic, new words, and language complexity to deal with approaching challenging texts. Because we see reading as an interactive process, when we plan to use a text we take account of reader and textual variables (Meyer, Marsiske and Willis 1993):

(a) the textual variables of communication purpose, word length/frequency/familiarity, sentence length/complexity and logical linking;
(b) the reader variables of background knowledge, familiarity with the content, interest and reason for reading.

So it is not just the reader, but also the complexity of the text that will work together to make meaning during the reading process.

Making use of purposeful activities developed for a high challenge/high support classroom, the next sections offer practical steps for supporting the learner to engage with texts in subject English and Geography, along with suggestions for application to other subject areas.

Subject English: A poem

Approaches to texts in subject English are often structured in three ways:

(1) pre-reading activities: preparation to support prediction,
(2) while reading activities: questions to focus reading for information and
(3) post-reading activities: response and discussion to build and extend meaning and understanding.

Pre-reading activities: Prediction

To get to know the topic and link it with what the learners already know, support strategies for prediction of content will engage the learner with finding out what this text is about. The question for the learner is 'What can you learn or predict from the title?'

To reflect the potential challenges facing learners, we have chosen a text that might appear to be both linguistically and conceptually difficult. It is a poem called 'Was Worm' by May Swenson, a 20th-century American poet. We know that the concerns of subject English are the skills with which language can be used for a purpose or effect, informational or affecting, so the challenge in the poem lies in the fact that the language alone is used to convey the images. The poem is from a collection called *The Complete Poems to Solve*, so there is *a riddle to solve*: *What is the poem about?*

The answer, 'Butterfly', is for the teacher to know and the learners to find out because the word 'butterfly' is not used anywhere in the text. It is a good illustration of how metaphorical/figurative language can be used in a poem. The question to the learners is this:

'What information does the poet give us to solve the riddle?'

To trigger mental images for the 'pre-reading activities' we use two visual clues to find the answer to the riddle, along with questions to initiate exploratory talk to build meaning. One step at a time. If there are misunderstandings they can be clarified: perhaps a fellow learner will draw a picture to demonstrate a point. The aim is to trigger schematic knowledge and prepare questions for active reading. Here we want to find out how the poet uses specially chosen words to give clues to the reader.

Visual clue 1 – Ask: *What does this make you think of? Who can tell me what this is?* (Use a brightly coloured image of a butterfly if you can; Figure 4.4.)

Build on the suggestions from learners until you get to 'butterfly'. The butterfly exists in most countries, so the question for the EAL learners is

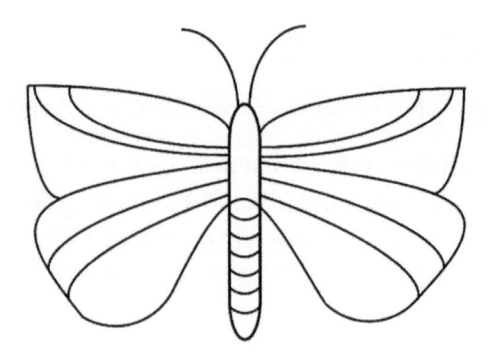

Figure 4.4 Visual clue 1.

'What is this called in your language?'

This will raise the profile of language investigation for all learners, and give you some interesting words to write on the board, or the learners could draw pictures if they are more comfortable with that. Having used this visual to hook into existing knowledge of butterflies, here is the second clue. (It might be wise to check with the Science teacher that the learners are likely to have this biological knowledge.)

Visual clue 2 – Ask: *What is the link between the butterfly and this diagram from Biology? What story does it show you?* (Figure 4.5).

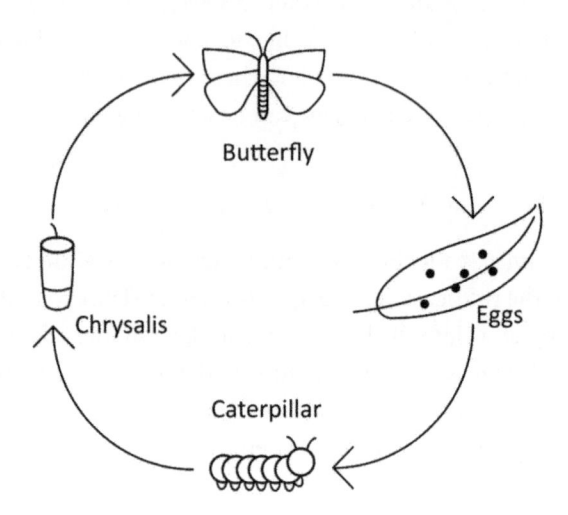

Figure 4.5 Visual clue 2.

You might get suggestions using everyday or more technical terminology: no matter. Once the learners have reached the idea that Visual clue 2 tells *the story of a life cycle*, here is the Visual clue 3.

Oral/Visual clue 3 – The riddle: use an introduction along these lines:

> 'This is the riddle – here are the first and last lines of the poem. What do think the connection is between these two lines? What happens?'
>
> 'Was worm' ➡ 'is queen'
>
> (Remember that in a poem, not all words have exactly the same meaning as if we were using everyday language. The poet likes to suggest rather than give whole meaning explicitly.)
>
> 'What is "the worm"? What is "the queen"? Which stages in the life cycle do they represent?'

If the exploratory talk is going well, working in plenary should elicit the ideas of 'change of state', 'growth', 'transformation', etc. Then the questions can become more specific to predict the kind of language they might find in the poem:

- 'Which stage is the one where the creature is a bit like a worm?' (answer = caterpillar)
- 'How do we describe a worm?'
- 'What words and pictures do we like to use to describe a butterfly?'
- 'What sorts of words do we use to describe a queen in a fantasy story or film?'
- 'How can a butterfly be like a queen?'

Perhaps this kind of inferential discussion based on the visual image will help to justify the labels 'queen' and 'worm'. Perhaps the class will come up with words used in the poem. You might get some words referring to *riches, bright colour* and *sparkling beauty*. Accept everything. This will generate confidence in the learners and more responses. You can follow up by getting the learners to justify their offerings and then by indicating what is relevant to this topic.

Having established any knowledge gaps at this level, the teacher can judge whether the 'new' or 'unfamiliar' words need to be presented visually, with a dictionary translation or general paraphrase.

Glossaries of word meanings are helpful to build up. Some books have glossaries at the back or use boxes in the margin (see Coates, Fitzpatrick, Hughes, Keay, Liddell, Robertson, 2008). Other subjects offer online resources, e.g. BECTA for Science. Having glossaries and labelled visuals on the wall is a much used strategy.

Another way of doing this is for the class to start with the riddle in Clue 3 and then move on to Visual clues 1 and 2.

Whichever choice you make, the next step is for the learners to hear and see the poem, on a slide or paper handout to check their predictions. They can work individually or in groups to match their ideas with what they find and try to create meaning with reference to other words and their peers.

While reading activities: Skimming, scanning and close reading

Use questions prepared at the pre-reading stage to answer from the text (possibly supplemented by the teacher). The aim is to find main points of the story.

Popular approaches include skimming (getting the gist) and scanning (hunting for specific words or information). In each case the teacher might set a limited time period to find answers from the text.

In the early stages of using these approaches, the teacher may need to model the strategies, being explicit in describing what she is doing in each of the processes. In the long run using a timed approach to finding the general idea of the message, or 'gist reading', is step one in training the reader to read efficiently.

Here are some scanning questions to use with the copy of the poem below.

- Can you find any of the words you predicted to describe a queen, in the poem?
- What other words you predicted can you find?
- Can you find any words to tell you what the worm looks like?
- What stage of the life cycle do you think it refers to, when it is most like a worm?

Tell the learners: 'A few meanings are given to you in the text to get you started. You can use a dictionary or guess if you like.'

Was worm — wrapped like a baby
swaddled in white.

Now, tiny queen — sparkling
in sequin coat
peacock bright,
drinks the wind and feeds
on sweat of the leaves.

Is little chinks
of mosaic floating,
a scatter of coloured beads.

Alighting, pokes,
with her new black wire,
the saffron yokes.

On silent hinges
openfolds her wings
applauding hands. — *getting used to another kind of food/stage in life*

Weaned
from coddling white
to lake-deep air, — *gently protective*
to blue and green,
is queen.

May Swenson (1993)

Learners might come up with 'tiny queen', 'sequin coat', 'peacock bright', 'little chinks of mosaic', 'a scatter of coloured beads'. And for the worm, 'swaddled in white', 'weaned from coddling white' (referring to the chrysalis wrapping the caterpillar).

These examples illustrate how the poet uses language to present an idea in such a way as to create mental images that are moving or entertaining.

The language is difficult because

(a) there is a mix of words used with every day and slightly extended figurative meanings, e.g. 'tiny queen'. The figurative meanings are ones that we can recognize by associations with our knowledge of the world.
(b) the word order and sentence grammar belong to literary style, which means that word order may be jumbled and some parts of the grammar such as the subject of the sentence is missing, e.g. 'was worm'.

The process of making meaning of this poem is to link the literal and figurative kinds of meaning in the six sentences. The challenge is to match the predictions with what you find.

Optional 'While reading' activities: Skim reading for gist
There is a lot of potential here for directed activities during reading to give purpose and questions to answer. The learners could identify the communication purpose of the poem. Which of these two patterns would they prefer?

   i) a series of events with causes and results or
   ii) a process of change with a description of the outcome.

While reading activities: Close reading
While reading activities can include close reading for particular language features such as incomplete sentences, word order, made up words. Or the learners could look for figurative language to describe the behaviour of the butterfly, examples below. Clue – look at the verb phrases,

- 'drinks the wind',
- 'feeds on sweat of leaves',
- 'is (little chinks of mosaic floating'),
- 'pokes with her new black wire the saffron yokes' and
- 'openfolds her wings' applauding hands'.

Interestingly, all the verbs used here deal with *actions* and *being/having*, as we saw in the Geography text describing the features of the volcano. There is no *thinking, feeling* or *saying*, as in a story.

The teacher can exploit the fact that this poem is a model of poetic language rather than a grammatically 'correct' scientific prose description of the appearance and habits of a butterfly. The writer suggests rather than states. And the information density is high. This poem uses 65 words. When I tried to write it out as a story, I had to use 190! The challenge might interest the learners. Perhaps the meaning could be rendered in other formats: visually or acoustically?

Post-reading activities: Extending understandings

Post-reading activities will build on and extend these understandings. In subject English, activities will depend on the learners' responses and creativity with the words and meanings. It might lead to colouring in a black-and-white image, or using similar language patterns to produce something in a different format for another text purpose. Groups might be given the task of using the indirect language of metaphor to create their own riddle for classmates to solve.

We will deal in more detail with lesson planning based on target learning outcomes in Chapter 5. In the meantime, how might this approach be applied to other subjects?

Apply pre-, while and post-reading activities to other subjects

Subjects	Trigger for previous knowledge	Examination of input and analysis	Response: plenary and group construction
Art: Picasso painting *The music lesson*	Multimodal resources associated with subject material – the music lesson/style/image created/the artist	Reasons why Picasso painted this way. Learner responses brainstormed as words, images, sounds. Justified	Collect data, report in groups and plenary. Guidance for group construction of response/appreciation
Music: Rap	Key words associated with rap/topics/creation/language resources and rhythm/performance	Watch a performance and note features of one selected aspect, or note how combination of features has a particular effect	Share response to content/performance. Work on group construction of rap on similar or other topic
RE: Natural burial grounds: Humanistic beliefs and value systems	Key words associated with end of life rituals, questions for investigation	A video story illustrating natural burial or discussion of end of life decisions with talking heads. Task to take notes on 5 aspects (given in a listening frame)	Group or individual presentation of an argument presenting a position of on the views encountered in the input material and group thoughts

Subject Geography: A discussion report

In the Geography class the topic for discussion is 'Your diet: is it traditional, Western or international? How is it produced and prepared for your table?' Along with language, food is part of cultural identity. So the communication purpose is an enquiry with a community focus that offers the opportunity for the learners to share knowledge about the food that makes up their diet, how it is prepared and where it comes from. They will produce a report at the end of the unit.

To gather material they can find out and make notes on

- what their diet is made up of,
- how the food they eat is produced,
- how it is prepared,

and then

- consider the evidence and come to a conclusion as to whether the range of foodstuffs they eat constitutes a traditional, a Western or an international diet.

The label 'traditional' is negotiable. They might prefer 'national' depending on where they are from. The discussion can touch upon globalization, where the food is sourced, how it travelled to their home, its contribution to a healthy lifestyle and so on. If the project takes off, it could be broadened to cover a survey of the whole school.

The teacher has written a model discussion text of the kind learners are aiming to produce when they have gathered evidence for their report (see Section 'How can I support learners to take notes?' on page 127). It covers the last question in the project brief: *whether their diet should be labelled 'traditional, Western or international'.* The teacher can decide where such a text is placed in the unit of study: the beginning, the middle or the end.

The text itself has high processing demands, so similar support tasks to those used above are used. But as the goal in this case is report writing, the support activities pay attention to

- text title, key words and main points to facilitate note making;
- producing a summary from notes;
- selecting main findings to put in a sequence that can be linked to build an argument;
- making use of language patterns to be precise with clear logical links.

How to kick off the topic?

You can adapt the kind of visual and textual clues used in the example from subject English, bearing in mind that the aim in Geography is to describe and classify. Here, the general 'hook' is *food that makes up your diet*. To support the enquiry purpose, the teacher can use pictures, realia, and get learners to google pictures of their favourite food, to give descriptions of their favourite meal.

The more specific hook is the question of whether the label should be 'traditional', 'Western' or 'international' diet. The focus is the culture of food: *What is its role in their lives? What are the methods of production and preparation – in various regions in the UK, in various regions in the world, etc?*

How should the learners prepare for information gathering? Perhaps brainstorm activities to create more precise questions based on their own ideas about food and its place in their culture?

They may then consult books, internet sources, interview peers, family and community members as appropriate. The title 'your diet' can refer to more than the individual; it might be a community.

How can I support learners to take notes?

This is a different kind of reading purpose from the *riddle poem*. Learners are not identifying meaning from literary language or other mode of expression where one could say that 'the medium is the message'. This time they are looking for specific information to reuse in another context: *their report*. So this text, or a similar one, can be used for note-taking practice. The following activities are based on breaking down the big task into three manageable stages, as above, but here the target skill set is to practise finding and recording key words and main points in the source text they are working on for use elsewhere.

(i) *Pre-reading*: refer to the brainstorming questions to see if any of these might help with predicting what the text is about. Use the title. These two activities should bring up key words. Pool language resources to check meanings and associated images of words.
(ii) *While Reading*: check the text (scan) for key words – the ones that occur more than once, the words and phrases that share synonymous meanings.

Skim read to get main points. How? The learners focus on the first sentence of each paragraph to identify the main points. The assumption here is that a paragraph is constructed with a topic sentence followed by supporting material.

In the following text, marked up for teacher's use, the key words and those associated with them are in **bold** (e.g. *diet, ways of producing and preparing food, traditional, Western, international*). The topic sentences are underlined.

Title: 'Your diet: Is it traditional, Western or international? Are traditional ways of producing and preparing food disappearing? '

Many people claim that **traditional ways of producing and preparing food** are disappearing because the **diet** of people around the world is becoming more **westernized**. This claim is true to some extent. However, it is not clear that it is due to **everyone's diet** becoming more **westernized**.

My impression is that the disappearance of **traditional ways of producing and preparing food** is more likely to be due to the huge increase in world population. For example, one hundred years ago it was nearly 2 billion, 50 years ago it was 3.5 billion, and today (2018) it is 7 billion. So more **mechanized ways of food production** are required to meet these needs. Nowadays fish are **farmed** in many places instead of being **caught in the wild**. **Hydroponic methods** are used to grow fresh vegetables **instead of soil**. **More powerful seeds, fertilizers and tractors** are used for cultivating staple crops such as maize, rice and wheat, with irrigation in many places.

Secondly, it may be true that more people around the world eat beef burgers and drink coca cola than 50 years ago. But it is also true that many people like to try **new dishes** from different cultures such as Lebanon, India, and China. This appears to be due to more people moving to live and work in other countries.

<u>So in my opinion increased population and demographic movement are the main factors affecting</u> **our ways of producing and preparing food**. And as a result, **the diet** of people around the world is becoming **more international**, rather than **more westernized**.

Adapted from an idea in Morgan (2012)

  (iii) *Post reading for notes*:

    (a) The learners make notes, taking careful account of the noun phrases (in *italics*) that are used to carry a lot of information in a few words.
    (b) They deconstruct the noun phrases to help them make a summary or paraphrase of the text – with a word limit of 100 words.
    (c) They compare the points they selected for the summary with what others did, and then hand in for feedback.

At this stage, learners might prepare group presentations as interim reports on their project. This would give practice to see how successful they are at picking out main points, planning a sequence of points for the outline and coming to a conclusion. They might need more support before writing up. More importantly it offers a chance to share ideas with classmates, and get feedback on their findings.

Identifying language features for organizing the text

Before they start to plan the outline for a presentation or for writing, the learners might consult the model above (or similar) to identify language features that are used to signal or signpost (make clear) to the reader how the text is organized. This time the focus is on words used (a) to signal opinions and (b) to provide logical links between the ideas. Here they are identified (for the teacher): <u>markers of opinion (underlined)</u>, logical linkers (shaded).

 (Long noun phrases are in *italics* as we will refer back to this text in part (c) of the next section.)

Hunting for <u>markers of opinion</u>, logical linkers and long noun phrases as models of writing style

'Hunting' for words, as suggested in Chapter 3 (pages 74, 79, 86) is a language awareness activity that can be extended to hunting for other aspects of language here, in order to support both the reading and the writing processes. Use these steps.

Step 1: How can text signposts help the reader?

(1) Cut up the text into paragraphs and get the learners to sequence them.
(2) When they have finished, they should explain what clues they used to help them.
  - If they are unsure of how to do this, the teacher can model the task by using the start of the first and last paragraph. (*It is true to some extent; so in my opinion.*)
  - Ask the learners to identify which is from the first and which is from the closing paragraph and what word signals the difference. (They are both sentence/paragraph starters to introduce the writer's opinion, but the last one starts with 'So'.)
(3) They discuss the shaded phrases that signal the *logical structure* of the text, think of alternatives and decide which ones could be useful to include in their text.

Title: Traditional ways of producing and preparing food are disappearing because the diet of people around the world is becoming more Westernized. Discuss

It is true to some extent that *traditional ways of producing and preparing food* are disappearing. However, it is not clear that *this is due to everyone's diet becoming more westernized.*

My impression is that *the disappearance of traditional ways of producing and preparing food* is more likely to be due to *the huge increase in world population.* For example, one hundred years ago it was nearly 2 billion, 50 years ago it was 3.5 billion, and today (2018) it is 7 billion. So more *mechanized ways of food production* are required to meet these needs. Nowadays fish are farmed in many places instead of being caught in the wild. Hydroponic methods are used to grow fresh vegetables instead of soil, and more powerful seeds, fertilizers and tractors are used *for cultivating staple crops such as maize, rice and wheat, with irrigation in many places.*

Secondly, it may be true that *more* people around the world eat beef burgers and drink coca cola than 50 years ago. But it is also true that many people like to try *new dishes from different cultures such as* Lebanon, India, and China. This appears to be due to *more people moving to live and work in other countries.*

So in my opinion *increased population and demographic movement* are *the main factors affecting our ways of producing and preparing food.* As a result *the diet of people around the world* is becoming more international, rather than more westernized.

Step 2: Collecting markers of opinion

The markers of opinion are just samples of a huge range of styles. The teacher has used 'My impression is that', but avoided 'I think' because the learners will gradually start to write in a more impersonal style. In the style they will tend to use in Humanities and Sciences, the writer does not write 'I'. But it is implied through a statement such as "It is true to some extent", which means '(I think that) it is true to some extent'.

What is helpful in the language samples in the teacher's text is that most of them are *introducing* statements ending with 'that', so the writer can then give us the viewpoint. For example, 'It is not clear that ....'

Step 3: Collecting logical linkers

The samples here give the learner quite a range for different text purposes. They are important as they act as *signposts for the reader*. The use of these kinds of words is seen in research as a sign of maturity in writing skill, as it indicates awareness of communication purpose and *writing for the reader* (Cameron 2003). The ones from this text are set out in Table 4.5 to show their communication purpose.

Table 4.5 Signposts for the Reader from the Geography Text

Communication purpose	Examples
Contrast	*however, but*
Comparison	*more than*
Exemplifying	*for example*
Alternative	*instead of*
Number sequencing	*secondly (firstly is implied)*
Time sequencing	*nowadays*
Result	*as a result, so*
Addition	*also*
Reason	*due to*

The ones missing are 'indication of purpose', such as 'in order to'. For a more detailed set of logical linkers see Teaching Resources of this chapter (page 134).

Step 4: Collecting models of writing style: Long noun phrases

Long noun phrases are useful in such texts as they are

(a) a source of general academic and subject-specific words and
(b) models for how to write in a precise style (more information fewer words).

The clue to give to learners for general academic words is that they are likely to have come across them in other subjects, and they are more frequent than subject-specific words. For example: *disappearance, huge increase, main factors,* and *different cultures*.

The subject-specific words for Geography are possibly 'Hydroponic methods', 'staple crops', 'mechanical ways', 'ways of producing and preparing food', 'food production'. But since the concerns of Geography can overlap with other subject areas, it is better not to make definite assertions on how language is used.

The general advice remains: break the task into stages, and if the text is hard like this one, make the tasks easy. If the text is easy, ask detailed questions.

Decide what learning outcomes you are looking for with texts based on how hard or straightforward it is. Is it ideas? Is it language patterns? Both?

Sample outline from another subject

As a *pre-presenting* or *pre-writing guide*, EAL learners might find this sample framework produced at the end of a PE project useful (Table 4.6). The goal was to find out 'Reasons why people use leisure centres' (see Department for Education and Skills 2002). It has a sentence starter for the introduction, the sections and the conclusion, along with sample linking words.

Alternatively, this might be used as a sample framework before the data gathering stage on a different project topic. This means learners can make their own boxes to complete with any notes they might make.

All these strategies for meeting the challenge of unfamiliar topic, new words and complex language may appear to be time consuming, but as pointed out in the Introduction, teachers who spend time on focusing on the language of subject literacies find that this is a valuable way of supporting deeper levels of learning and the ability to communicate ideas effectively. Teaching Resources to support you are offered at the end of this chapter.

This approach to subject literacy in the Lower Secondary phase of Secondary Education will lay a good foundation for study at Upper Secondary level. In Chapter 5 we build on these understandings as we explore the principles of producing a task that meets the needs of the EAL learner.

Table 4.6 Reasons Why People Use Leisure Centres

Type of reason	Sample introductory and topic sentences
	People use leisure centres for a number of reasons
Personal	Firstly there are personal reasons. These include ….
Health	Next there are health reasons. These are ….
Fitness	Then there are reasons linked to fitness. These are ….
Social	Lastly there are social reasons. These are ….
	In my opinion, the most important of these reasons is … because ….

Adapted from Department for Education and Skills (2002:18)

Teaching resources

High challenge/high support framework for EAL learners' engagement with new knowledge

(1) *Use meaningful tasks* that

- require active engagement;
- are purposeful – to answer general, detailed or inferential questions;
- are set up for success.

How?

- Use scaffolding, monitoring and feedback from peers and/or the teacher.
- Break down the new information and support into stages related to text and learner variables. The learner's comprehension might not be immediate. Let each stage build on another.
- Use talk at each stage in plenary and in groups, accepting all contributions.
- Encourage reflection on types of talk to notice the relative values of *exploratory*, *disputational* and *cumulative* (summarized in Mercer 2008). Set ground rules for groups to encourage learners to recognize when they are stuck with non-productive disagreement or purely additive talk. Remind the group of the goal – to reach a joint decision on the task they have been working on.
- Encourage comprehension checks to give a chance to repair problems of understanding, particularly at an early stage to avoid failure.

(2) Be clear on *the concept and communication purpose* of the topic so you can find triggers to activate previous knowledge and support engagement.

- What resources can I use to trigger previous knowledge of this word, or concept? Title? Visual? Tactile? Audio? Textual (spelling and syllable segmentation), Translation of previous knowledge in school?
- How can I identify communication purpose to support questioning the text? The teacher needs flexible thinking processes.

(3) Be clear on *how to read logical linkers and signposts* to find organization pattern.

(4) Be clear on *characteristics of words*:

- What kinds of words are involved: *everyday, subject specific, general academic*.
- How much attention do I need to pay to a particular word: *exact meaning, general meaning, ability to use it accurately*? (Teaching Resources, page 135).
- How to work out word meanings of selected words – using images and labels, a monolingual dictionary, exploratory talk with the teacher or in a group.
- What to learn about them: spelling, pronunciation, word stress (Teaching Resources, pages 134, 135–6).

(5) Be clear on *how to identify language complexity* so that your *text selection* takes account of both reader (what they already know) and text variables (challenges presented). E.g.

- sentence length (how many ideas? How many words?),
- sentence complexity (subordinate clauses and information density),
- signalling words (linkers) to ensure clarity of structure.

These aspects support

- deconstruction of multiple ideas in a sentence to unpick meaning,
- clarification of the logical links between them,
- reformulating phrases using similar general and specialist words to try out meaning,
- glossing meaning using more words with everyday meaning.

(6) *Avoid giving your learners long noun phrases without support.* Reformulate them until you have worked with the learners and they understand how to deconstruct them.

(7) *Be clear what macro and micro features to note in texts* as models for writing.

(8) *Adapt these strategies to other modes* to use as triggers, e.g. break down tasks for listening to music, looking at a video in French, critiquing a picture or a play.

(9) *Refer to the kinds of language patterns identified in Chapter 3* Teaching Resources (pages 93–6) to support finding

- a communication purpose,
- a suitable organization pattern and
- language features for particular purposes.

Answer to the title puzzle page 104: *Lesson planning*

Word stress rules in English

(A stressed syllable is marked by accents over syllables in a dictionary, by CAPITALS in this text):

(1) *Stress the first syllable of*
   - most two-syllable nouns (e.g. CLImate, KNOWledge) and
   - most two-syllable adjectives (e.g. FLIPpant, SPAcious).

(2) *Stress the last syllable of*
   - most two-syllable verbs (e.g. reQUIRE, deCIDE).

(3) *Stress the second-to-last syllable of*
   - words that end in *-ic* (e.g. ecSTATic, geoGRAPHic) and
   - words ending in *-sion* and *-tion* (e.g. exTENsion, retriBUtion).

(4) *Stress the third from last syllable of*
   - words that end in *-cy, -ty, -phy* and *-gy* (e.g. deMOCracy, unCERtainty, geOGraphy, radiOLogy) and
   - words that end in *-al* (e.g. exCEPtional, CRItical).

https://www.toeflgoanywhere.org/learn-these-4-word-stress-rules-improve-your-pronunciation
https://www.really-learn-english.com/word-stress.html

Communication purpose and sample linking words in text

Adding something	Showing a result, effect, consequence
In addition, additionally	So, therefore
Also, moreover	As a result, the result is, this leads to
Apart from this	The implication, this implies
A further point	Consequently, as a consequence
Another aspect, besides this	This is caused by, the cause of this is

Offering an alternative	Showing aim or purpose
- Alternatively	- So that
- In other words, to paraphrase	- In order to, with the aim of
- That is to say	- To allow
- To clarify	- To enable/to facilitate

Showing contrast	Showing reason
• However, although, whereas • In spite of this, despite this, except • Even though • Nonetheless	• So, because • For this reason, the reason for this • Since, due to • Caused by
Exemplifying	**Showing sequence**
• For instance, for example, such as • Including • Show, demonstrate	• First, second, to start with, initially • Subsequently, then, followed by • Finally

Questions to ask yourself FREQUENTLY about words

- Am I using this language figuratively or literally? Does it need glossing?
- Which register does it belong to? Informal, formal, dialect, standard? Is it an *everyday word* used with *a subject-specific meaning*?
- Can the language origin of this word help with meaning and spelling? e.g. Greek, Latin, French (*beef, mutton*), Anglo-Saxon (*cow, sheep*). In English, half of the high-frequency words and two-thirds of all academic and technical words are derived from Latin, French and Greek. Identify these in your subject area, e.g. the names of your subjects (History, Geography, Mathematics, Biology, Chemistry), parts of the body, plants, techniques.
- Can *the root/stem* of the word take *prefixes* and/or *suffixes*? For EAL learners, some of the most useful *suffixes* are -*ful*, -*est*, -*ing*, -*less*, -*ly*, -*er* and *prefixes* are *re-*, *un-*, *dis-*, *mis-*, *pre-*.

Examples:

Root/stem	Prefix	Suffix
determine	indeterminate	determination
enter	re-enter	entrance

- Is this an Anglo-Saxon phrasal verb? Can I use an alternative *general academic word*?

come in vs. *enter*	*get off* vs. *leave*;
get on vs. *embark*	*go out* vs. *leave, depart*

- Should learners memorize the spelling of this word? How frequently used is it?
- Is the pronunciation different, despite similar spelling patterns (*read/read, though, through, enough*)?
- Does the *prefix* need to be emphasized when I say this word? E.g. prefixes like '*en*' in 'encouraging' are easy to miss if you are not expecting them: 'necessary' and 'unnecessary' are common confusions. It is sometimes helpful for the teacher to put *stress on the negative prefix* of the word to distinguish it from the *positive version without prefix.*
- Are the meanings of these words confusing because they look similar? For example, 'affect' and 'effect' can be confusing:
  - 'Affect' is normally used as a verb to show a change, 'Many schools are affected by this local decision'.
  - 'Effect' is normally used as a noun, 'The effect of this decision is significant'.

5
What Are the Key Principles for Adapting Pedagogical Tasks and Tests to Suit the EAL Learner?

Chapter Outline

Starting points: Opportunities for participation	137
Setting up a Science topic for small group discussion	139
Planning, setting up and supporting a group task in subject English	151
Planning, setting up and supporting an individual test in Climate Science	157
Drawing together principles for *language aware* task design	164
Teaching resources	168

- *How can I best represent the ideas and concepts of the task in a way that my EAL learners will recognize?*
- *How can we adapt pedagogical tasks to make the most of EAL learner funds of knowledge and to meet their needs?*
- *How do we write a good class test that is sensitive to EAL learners' needs?*

Starting points: Opportunities for participation

This chapter invites you to plan your activities in the classroom from the point of view of the EAL learner, taking account of the language and knowledge they bring with them. We have identified in previous chapters some of the subject literacy challenges facing EAL learners, along with strategies of good practice for inclusivity and supporting engagement with new knowledge for EAL learners.

As part of every lesson, subject teachers set up and carry out a range of pedagogical tasks with their learners through which prior knowledge is shared and new knowledge is created. Such tasks might include

- listening to a teacher's explanation,
- watching and responding to a demonstration,
- responding to a creative stimulus,
- carrying out some practical work,
- predicting an outcome of an experiment with a partner,
- reading and analysing some primary source materials to make notes for an essay,
- preparing an outline for a presentation and
- writing a response to a class test question.

Within your lesson plans you include opportunities for participation. However, as we have seen, the language demands can be very challenging for our EAL learners. If these activities are not set so that learners can recognize ideas to start from, they may struggle to engage with the task and be denied the opportunity to demonstrate their subject knowledge.

The communication purpose of a task needs to be clear in the teacher's head so you can deconstruct language components and identify what support the learner needs to engage with the concept. What language will they need to talk about it? In this process you are an interpreter of your own subject literacy, an intermediary in the process of showing how to represent the knowledge of your topic.

As we mentioned in the Introduction, student teachers find the challenge of being taught in another language a useful way of reflecting on an EAL learner's classroom experience.

In the process they rely on existing knowledge of visuals or similarities in subject specialist words, e.g. *photosynthesis (English) versus Photosynthese (German)*. What other resources could you draw on?

Bearing in mind the *high challenge and high support* goals mentioned in Chapter 4 (page 98), in this chapter we look in detail at how we can set up tasks in a *language aware way*. Our template for task design consists of a series of questions, set out in Table 5.1.

Using the questions in this template, this chapter looks at language demands more closely to show how we as teachers can adapt our standard pedagogic tasks to support our EAL learners' emerging subject literacy.

Table 5.1 Template for *Language Aware* Task Design

Step 1	How can I best represent the ideas and concepts of the task in a way that my EAL learners will recognize?	• Do my learners know enough spoken or written English to recognize what I want to say in verbal form? • Would a diagram be easier to understand? • How abstract are the terms? • Would a direct translation of the term from the learner's own language help them to understand the task?
Step 2	How can I provide opportunities for my EAL learners to participate in the task using a language that is understandable to them?	In which language and/or mode of language could my learners participate – spoken, written English, diagram/illustration, gesture or home language?
Step 3	What language is new to my EAL learners and would be useful for them to know for future tasks?	How can I isolate this language and draw their attention to its form (pronunciation and spelling), meaning and use (the grammar)?

In the next three sections we set out how we can go about planning, setting up and supporting the following tasks in the classroom with our language learners.
- A small group discussion
- A class task
- A class test

Setting up a Science topic for small group discussion

This section presents five aspects of planning, setting up and supporting a Science topic for small group discussion that allow us to focus on what happens in the process: where are the opportunities for participation and the challenges that need support.

Planning: Identifying the communication goal

In this section we look at a class discussion between the teacher and learners at the start of a topic to establish what the learners already know, followed by a small group discussion. When planning such a session, it is helpful to think of tasks in terms of 'Backward design', a planning framework discussed with reference to Secondary

Maths in Roddick and Sliva Spitzer (2010). This means the teacher starts with the learning goal and asks: What kind of outcome is the learner being offered to experience?

With the end goal in place, the teacher can plan how to find triggers in the *knowledge* our EAL learners already *bring* to the activity to help them engage. Taking a positive view of the situation helps us focus on the opportunities each task gives to build new knowledge, even though, as teachers, we work against set standards prescribed to us by syllabi and curricula.

That said, teachers' assumptions as to how to build on the learners' current knowledge might vary widely. For example, our work on lesson planning with some Design and Technology students in the second year of their four-year BEd was interesting. Their topics were 'Desk Top Publishing (DTP)' or '2D-3D modelling'. Where would you start?

Most of them wanted to start with new terminology to assess what learners already knew. To their credit they showed awareness of a gap between their specialist knowledge and that of the learners, but *their Step 1 amounted to a test*.

One or two students suggested letting the learners have a go at designing a poster using DTP Software. True, this is another way of finding out what learners know, but the teacher needs to offer a scenario for the poster. What is the reason for using this technique?

Both topics involve *procedures for a particular purpose.* One student suggested discussing what DTP is *for (communication)* and *what it consists of (a combination of text and graphics)*. And for 2D-3D, the purpose is *to communicate a visual representation of a designed shape by extending 2D to 3D.*

> Notice it is not just the terminology the student teachers need in their plan but also *the purpose behind the procedure* in order to build the concept behind the terminology.

> Our learners will use whatever resources they have at their disposal to interpret what we do in the classroom. Much of this will be filtered through our EAL learners' home language until their English skills reach a certain level.

To engage them, they could be shown images of a poster advertising their country or a product from their country. Inevitably they will use their everyday knowledge of the world and their own home language to make sense of what is going on in front of them. They could compare a 2D image of a house with a 3D one using their own language, or they could be encouraged to use Google Translate for key words like 'poster', 'communicate' or '3D modelling'.

If our EAL learners are encouraged to see that the knowledge they bring to the task is not only interesting but *essential* if they are to make progress, they are far more likely to remain engaged. And we might learn from them!

Setting up: Preparing for the small group discussion

Using research data from Zacharias (2018) we look at an example of setting up a topic for a small group discussion to meet the needs of an EAL learner in a Year 8 (S1) Science class. In this class 65% are EAL learners, including Zhou, our Chinese learner who is a recent arrival. Although he has learned English in China, he is working at the start of PiE level B (Early Acquisition/Becoming Familiar English: page 42). He needs time to become familiar with classroom processes. He is generally silent, but listening and noticing. What can we learn about integrating *language aware* strategies into the task to make it inclusive and support the needs of an EAL learner?

The topic in the classroom exchange is to 'examine or look at living material', or 'living things'. You will see below that Mr Dalel is skilled at using general academic words like 'examine', closely followed by a gloss for the meaning, i.e. 'look at'.

An important concern for Science is *to establish categories that frame the way we think about the physical and living world*. The questions for the class are: '*How do we describe or define something that is living to separate it from something that is non-living? What does it do?*'

You can probably anticipate the key words associated with this topic. They are shaded in the class transcript below.

As preparation, you could ask the learners to find Google images before class for the words 'living material' 'describe', 'define', 'classify' and to choose ones they predict will be used in the Science topic they are about to start on. When they share the images in plenary, try not to be judgemental about their predications. Accept everything and let them simply say what they think. If they give you several meanings for the word, draw these associations as a mind map on the board. You could add your own example to extend the vocabulary range, then go back to it to check their predictions. It's a helpful way to raise awareness of how we can use the same words in different ways according to context in English.

Note how the teacher, Mr Dalel, talks about the concept of 'living material' and uses questions to develop the thinking of the class.

> Mr Dalel: What we're going to do today … guys … We are now going to start to examine or look at living material. Right. Things that can be thought of as living. You're living. Animals are living. But biology isn't just the study of animals. Other things are living as well. Adam, what things do you know about things that are living … apart from animals?

Adam: Humans?
Mr Dalel: Humans? Okay, well, they can be classified as living. Humans can be classified as a group belonging to animals, yeah.
Ammar: Insects?
Mr Dale: Insects. Yeah, okay, they are animals. Amy?
Amy: Plants?
Mr Dalel: Plants. Yeah. The trees outside. Plants are also living things. How would you define … how would you describe or define or say what it means to be living? Name one thing that a living thing does.
Zarif: Does it live for a long time?
Mr Dalel: It might. Some don't. Some live for a few hours, a few days maybe, just for a few weeks. They don't necessarily live for a long time. What does a living thing do? For example, if I say to you 'scissors'. Are they living?
Class: No
Mr Dalel: Right. If I say 'pen'. Is it living?
Class: No

As you probably noticed, to establish a shared understanding of what is meant by 'living', Mr Dalel presents to the class the idea of 'living' as a category: *either something is living or it is not.*

Support for comprehension of the topic

To consolidate this shared meaning, Mr Dalel uses a visual to demonstrate the language and provide an opportunity for Zhou to participate in the task. To represent the concepts of *living* and *non-living* he shows them as two circles on the board (Figure 5.1), with 'living things' written over the left hand one and 'non-living things' over the right hand one.

Living things   Non-living things

        Animals
       (Humans   Pen
        Insects)   Scissors
      Plants (Trees)

    Animals are living   'A pen is non-living'

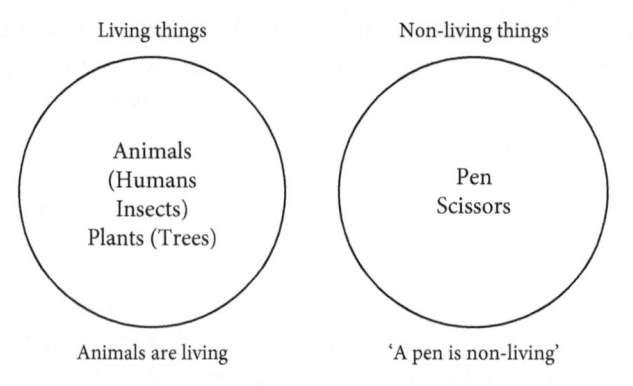

Figure 5.1 A visualization of two conceptualized categories, with written language to help EAL learners engage with lesson.

Then he asks the class to tell him where to write the things they already mentioned as 'living'. To get them started he writes the statement 'Animals are living' underneath the 'living things' circle. He puts the *non-living* items they agreed on into the second circle, with the statement 'A pen is non-living' underneath, as shown above.

These visuals are likely to help Zhou engage with the task by activating his schema of 'living' and 'non-living' things. Mr Dalel then says,

'What about the bird?'

'Is it living or non-living?'

He asks Zhou to point to the appropriate circle. Taking this approach ensures Zhou has an *opportunity for participation*, right at the start of the lesson.

Having looked at how Mr Dalel introduces the categories to learners, let's consider the language he uses for *categorizing, i.e. description and definition*. We want to make sure Zhou is not left without knowing how to express these ideas when speaking, which is key if Zhou is to participate in the other activities of the lesson.

Mr Dalel uses the verb **to be** (**in bold**), along with the passive form '*can* ***be*** *thought of*'.

- things *can **be** thought of* as living
- biology **isn't** just the study of animals other things ***are*** living as well
- if I say 'pen', ***is*** it living?

What we have to appreciate is that Zhou may not recognize the individual words used for the definition in the stream of the teacher's talk. However, having seen the visualization of the living/non-living concepts in the circles, he might match the English he hears with what he would use in his own language.

Interestingly, Mandarin Chinese, like English, uses the verb 是 (shi) – 'to be' to describe and categorize the world in a similar way to English:

things *can be thought of* as living
Direct Chinese translation: 些东西能 (can) 被认为 (be thought of) 是活的。

But in Chinese, the passive construct 'can be thought of' is generally avoided when speaking, so the teacher would probably express the idea in a different way:

我们 (we) 来 (are going to) 分辨一下 (examine) 什么东西 (what kinds of things) 是 (are) 活的 (living) (and) 什么东西 (what kinds of things) 是 (are)死的 (dead)。

(An anonymous Chinese informant)

These examples show that it is not necessarily the idea that we can categorize things as being either *living* or *dead* that could make it difficult for our EAL learner to understand, but *the language Mr Dalel is using to express the idea*. Many learners of

English have problems with the passive form in English because conceptually it is not a form they use in their own language. Also, the passive voice relies on using the common verb *to be* as a *helping verb* or *auxiliary*, e.g. Geography **is** *formed*, Maths we **are** *said to* ....

This information about how learners express ideas in their own language can help us rethink our strategies and devise an approach that is inclusive. Perhaps, you have already thought of one?

For further hints on potential difficulties learners with different language backgrounds might have, see Swan and Smith (2001) for grammar, and O'Connor and Fletcher (1989) for pronunciation.

To support Zhou's English development, he needs explicit examples of how concepts of living and non-living can be represented verbally. And to accelerate Zhou's learning of this language the examples need to be made explicit at the time they are used in class, with attention given to the meaning and grammar of the language.

A straightforward way to do this would be to insert the key statements 'A plant is living /A pen is non-living' next to the visual, as shown in Figure 5.1. It is also important to ensure Zhou has heard the language too. This way, Zhou is able to *hear* and *see* the relatively simple language he needs to talk about the phenomenon.

Before we move on, can you think of other applications of the visuals for categories with key labels and statements beneath? Would this work in your subject area?

Whatever your answer, working through this example demonstrates the importance of tapping into what the learner already knows, providing opportunities to participate and offering the new language needed to do the task. This is especially the case for a learner like Zhou, working at PiE level B. This is a step that teachers need to pay attention to if they are to carry out tasks in a *language aware* manner.

Setting up the group discussion task

The next step in the lesson is setting up the group task. Teachers know the benefits of getting pupils to work in small groups. As Littleton and Mercer (2013) remind us, everyday problem-solving often relies on us working together with other people, sharing ideas and working towards a shared goal. We offered this strategy in Chapter 4 for working on the riddle poem. Working together with peers provides our learners with an opportunity to interact with others that a teacher-led discussion does not afford. For our EAL learners, group tasks can provide the opportunity to practise the language in a more private arena than in front of the whole class.

At the same time, small group activities can present their own set of challenges for our EAL learners. As mentioned in Chapter 2, if they come from classroom cultures where learning from the teacher is the normal channel, learners might help each other outside the class, but learning from each other in class is often not regarded as useful. So there have to be ground rules. Look at Mr Dalel's instructions:

> Mr Dalel: Okay. So what sort of things do living things do? What I want you to do, guys, is to think about that a bit. Discuss amongst yourselves and write down your answers. Come on, get busy.

He has already alluded to the question for discussion, when he said 'Name one thing that a living thing does' above: the focus shifts from the verb 'to be' to the verb 'to do'. At that point Zarif asked, 'Does it live for a long time?'

In response, Mr Dalel commented that not all things did; i.e. the statement could not be used as a generalization.

Without knowing these words Zhou will be lost. Zhou will probably know about living organisms but will not have the language in English to represent these ideas to the group. So how can we help Zhou to engage with the ideas and concepts in the discussion?

(a) Write, mime and say the task: 'To **think** (with gesture) about What sort of things do living things do?'
(b) Write sample language that answers the question, e.g. 'it lives for a long time' (on the board or word banks).
(c) Mime 'groups **discuss**' with gesture. Allocate groups carefully to ensure support.
(d) Mime '**write down** answers' to make clear the goal.

These gestures may appear simple, but they are very effective. As suggested in the Introduction, perhaps teachers across the school could come up with an agreed *gesture code* for instructions such as *think, discuss, write down* and so on?

The target outcome is that these descriptions will be distilled into a definition, so that the learners can make statements starting, 'It's living because …', 'It can't be living because ….' So if Zhou has relatively little classroom experience in English, this level of support will help him understand the classroom processes and have an idea of the topic. He will also have a model for what a simple definition looks like in English: not just the key words but the grammar.

Opportunities and challenges in the group discussion

The group consists of two learners, Sara and Zarif, who both have English as their first language and Zhou, who is listening and noticing what happens. The success of the exchange relies on the learners being able to construct mental images of the living organisms each one adds to the ongoing dialogue.

As you read the three sections of the discussion, think about these questions:

Where do you think Sara and Zarif's knowledge of living organisms comes from? What mental images do they have? Is it likely that Zhou will share these?

What pedagogic purpose does this exchange serve for the learners?

Section 1

> Sara: All living things need oxygen.
> Zarif: What about fish? They don't need oxygen?
> Sara: They do.
> Zarif: Turtles don't. They can stay under the water more than ….
> Sara: They grow.
> Zarif: Not all plants.
> Sara: They breathe.
> Zarif: Not all ….
> Sara: Not everything that is living does the same thing.

This first section of the exchange starts straight in with a series of *assertions and rebuttals* covering fish, turtles and plants. Sara's statement sounds more like a definition of something she has heard or read. On the other hand Zarif has a mental image of a fish where 'oxygen' probably refers to the air that is above the water that surrounds the fish. Zarif associates fish with turtles, suggesting his mental image at this time is of water, possibly the sea.

The success of the exchange relies on the learners being able to construct mental images of the living organisms each one adds to the ongoing dialogue. The exchange flows quickly, with incomplete sentences. Sara's style is *cumulative*, adding more and more information uncritically. By contrast, Zarif is more *disputational*, tending to disagreement. In the 9 contributions there are 5 with negatives.

Both the *cumulative* and *disputational* discussion styles, along with the more constructive *exploratory talk* are described and exemplified by Mercer and Dawes (2008).

The transcript shows how memory and imagination play key roles. The contributions demonstrate ideas that the learners have either directly experienced or have created by drawing on the schematic knowledge that they have accumulated from reading books or watching films.

They appear to assume that Zhou knows these words. They do not seem to have written anything down. It would help Zhou if they had written the words shaded above: 'need oxygen', 'grow', 'breathe'.

Section 2

> Zarif: I tell you something. That nothing that is living can survive without water, like oxygen is really important and everything … but fish ….
> Sara: Trees breathe.
> Zarif: They breathe water. They don't come out of the water.
> Sara: Yeah, they do, they stick their mouths out the water to get oxygen.
> Zarif: Not all fish ….

In this section Zarif seems to be trying to regain the upper hand by making claims. He grabs attention with a long start to his sentence – 'I tell you something. That nothing that is living can …' with the result that Sara is slightly wrong footed. Perhaps Zhou would be confused as to who 'they' refers to: fish or trees? This part of the conversation is not productive, but the tone shifts in Section 3.

Section 3

> Sara: What about the ones that live at the very bottom?
> Zarif: I think oxygen is like water to the fish.
> Sara: I think water is the most important because to have life you need water.
> Zarif: I could be down at the bottom and then I needed up to get oxygen.
> Sara: Maybe it's … that millions and millions of fish ….
> Zarif: Do you know, for fish, do you think that water is like oxygen for them?
> Sara: Yeah, I think so, but there is nothing that can live without water …, Name me something that lives without water?
> Zarif: Errr fish? [*laughs*]

In this section, Zarif and Sara both start to show some evidence of criticality: Zarif with 'I could be' and Sara starting a contribution with 'maybe'. They both *give an opinion* rather than *take opposing positions*. But although Sara finally agrees with

Zarif's assertion that nothing can live without water, the link with oxygen remains unresolved.

This is verging on *exploratory talk*, which is seen as the ideal for both plenary and group work. In the group context, it means people ask questions, ideas and opinions are shared. The flow may well be disjointed and hesitant as the participants try out ideas. Opinions are listened to with respect. They might be offered in a tentative way: 'It might be …', 'it could be …', 'Perhaps', 'I suggest …', 'What do you think of this idea …?'

In this kind of productive talk, there is an atmosphere of trust, there are clear roles and there is a sense of a shared purpose to investigate the issue. Opinions are backed up by reasons and so are challenges. A learner might offer evidence from a book, a visual or from their own experience. The group seeks agreement on joint decisions for the group to report, or, in the case of the teacher managing a plenary discussing, the teacher draws together points to make a final pedagogic decision.

If the purpose of the discussion is to construct shared knowledge, who is most confused after this? Sara? Zarif? Zhou? What did they report to the teacher? They have explored their knowledge, started to consider alternative views and finally agreed on one point: 'There is nothing that can live without water.'

How will they resolve the link between water and oxygen? Will Mr Dalel invite them to ask any question that arose during the discussions? Perhaps Mr Dalel has been monitoring the groups and heard this quandary. Perhaps another group knows the answer to this question. It might encourage the emerging knowledge that the learners have constructed here to find a resolution.

You will have noticed that in the process of discussing the abstract concept 'what is living', the learners are anchored in concrete nouns: *fish, turtle, trees, water, oxygen*, and the action *'breathe'*.

But what about the links between the nouns and verbs? The success of the discussion relies on the learner being able to use the grammatical constructions required to represent this knowledge. So they have moved on from using the verb 'to be' with the adjective 'living', to verbs that represent *what living things do*, shown in Table 5.2.

Table 5.2 Language Options Modelled for Zhou

Living things	What they do
trees	breathe
fish	swim
turtles	need oxygen
plants	grow
	need water

The important point for Zhou's language development is having a point of reference to model language options so that he can become familiar with the patterns of the verb 'to be' and practise adding the basic subordinator *because* in a statement.

Tables to model language options can be used for any subject to support practice in similar basic language patterns.

At the end of this discussion the learners will have evidence to contribute to a class discussion to combine the ideas and distil them to come up with a definition:

- *X are living because they* …………….
- *All living things* …………….

These examples show how the various textual features in a spoken, written, or visual text such as of vocabulary and grammar constructions can trigger elements of the schemas that are needed to understand the text, picture or diagram and contribute to building knowledge.

When you consider the explanation example for 'categorizing' presented, notice the sequence Mr Dalel chose.

Mr Dalel started with *the purpose* (*to examine how to build a description*) and then moved on *to build that definition*, i.e. he took a bottom-up approach.

Text books, by contrast, take *the definition as the starting point of a procedural explanation, followed by an outline of how to carry out the procedure.* As we saw in the Maths text example in Chapter 3 (page 76) the pattern is a *definition, followed by steps in the procedure.* Similarly the Geography text (page 68) starts with *a definition, followed by steps in the formation event and a description of the outcome.* Perhaps this feature of text books is behind the instinct of the second-year Design and Technology student teachers mentioned above to start with the definition.

But when applying pedagogic knowledge, it is preferable to approach the topic from the '*bottom up*', with an *exploratory discussion of concepts with the class*, and then in groups to gather shared knowledge for *the definition* (the end goal in this case).

This view of setting up a group discussion in a *language aware* way shows both challenges and opportunities for participation that can apply across all subject areas for EAL learners engaged in this kind of task. Have a look at how they are set out in Table 5.3. Are there any points that strike you?

Table 5.3 Challenges and Opportunities of Small Group Discussion

Challenges of a small group discussion	Opportunities for participation

1. Success of activities relies on pupils having
   i. some background knowledge about the subject and
   ii. the language to represent this knowledge to each other.
2. The background knowledge can come from recall of prior reading, film or a real-life event. If that is not available, learners need external resources, e.g. visuals, gesture and translation, to help establish or reinforce a common ground.
3. The language to represent this knowledge means that memories need to be transformed into verbal language. For an EAL learner this may require effort and a certain level of knowledge about language.
4. For an EAL learner, as we saw in Chapter 4, spoken English has the challenge of rapid shifts from one topic to another, sentences started and not finished, and words joined together in a stream.
	1. Group work provides opportunities for sharing creating and challenging new knowledge.
	2. Pre-teach language required for task (see Table 5.2).
	3. Supply Zhou with a picture dictionary.
	4. Encourage pupils to draw illustrations to communicate ideas with each other.
	5. Model the strategies that are productive in reaching a consensus. They should
	   i) all speak in turn,
	   ii) make a note of main points they agree on and
	   iii) note down points where they had problems reaching agreement.
	This will give the opportunity for further exploration and clarification in the group or in plenary. Activating of schematic knowledge to build the shared knowledge of the classroom provides an opportunity for personal engagement with material.

★▲★ You will notice the focus in the template on using multimodal resources to convey meaning, giving explicit focus to subject-specific words and also the grammar to support them in sentences. You could check against the template when planning. You will probably find you can add to it.

Let's look at applying the strategies outlined above for planning, setting up and supporting an activity to other kinds of explanation. Much of what is taught at Secondary level is based on abstract concepts that are not directly experienced through our senses. It is much harder to represent them pictorially. These next two sections explore two representative examples of working with abstract concepts.

Our two explanations focus on

(a) an enquiry task that records a response to the expression of feeling in a novel (that could be transferred to a painting, a piece of music, a price of drama);
(b) a test to display knowledge of how to explain cause and effect (or consequences) in an aspect of Climate Science (that could be transferred to other tests requiring an explanation).

Our learning purpose is to develop and rearrange existing schemas in the minds of our learners so that we can extend existing knowledge to create new shared classroom knowledge and language. Ideally, the subject literacy skills that start to emerge will resemble the language (and thinking) of your subject. Learners are aiming to learn. Several Science student teachers we worked with commented on the high motivation levels of many EAL learners in the classes they saw. Some asked more questions than their Scottish classmates.

Planning, setting up and supporting a group task in subject English

The group task and language to be planned, set up and supported in this section involves data gathering for an enquiry activity in a Year 9 class that includes the EAL learner, Yusra, who is working at PiE level C (Developing competence/Becoming a confident user: page 42). When planning the lesson, we need to bear in mind the language Yusra might already know and what might be new.

The nature of this enquiry differs from the group discussion in Section 2 that required thinking about creatures in the natural world. It relies on triggering story templates for adventures to engage with the text we have chosen. It is from the novel *Wolf Brother: Chronicles of Ancient Darkness* (Paver, 2004), the first in a series where the hero is set a challenge that draws on existing 'world knowledge' of human interactions and leads the reader to want to find out more.

Unsurprisingly, basic story plots follow a pattern similar to the one we identified in the History text in Chapter 3 (page 84): *situation or setting, problem, solution*. This sequence repeats through the book until a final resolution takes place at the end of the tale. We may *read* a story at home, but as we saw in Chapter 4 (pages 119–24), Subject English is interested in the skill of how the writer uses language and structure. So we *study* a novel in school to learn to recognize these features. In this novel, the writer generally chooses *frequently used* everyday words and most sentence structures are relatively simple.

Step 1 is to predict content from the title, *Wolf Brother*. Start with the title. Ask the learners, *What do you think the novel is about?* Taking the concept of 'adventure' as the starting point, what might be key words for the learners to google? *Problem, challenges, bravery, companion, brother, feelings, safety, danger, wolf, dangerous animals.*

To generate specific ideas and images, it is good practice to ask learners to google the key words associated with the topic and bring the meanings and images to class.

This can be done in English, or EAL learners could check the meaning of the word in their own language. Different web browsers in different languages can trigger different results, e.g. google.ro versus google.fr or google.com. As policy guidance recommends, as teachers we should not discourage our EAL learners from using their home languages or to refer to their home experiences and past memories as this is an active part of the learning process. Indeed, we view what they bring to the classroom as *resources to be used productively*.

The class can share the images and meanings they find. Are they similar or different? Ask learners to point to images that are familiar to them. When have they come across the idea before? What is the word in English? Or in another language?

This is the first of four steps to encourage engagement and prediction. Try to support *hearing comprehension* by repeating words and phrases and writing them on the board. Be prepared to offer some of your own key words to complement what the learners bring as they try out the language. As with Zhou, it is important to anticipate language resources needed to reach the next step and to fill in any gaps from the task.

Step 2 is to establish the setting. Show a slide of the front cover of the book because the adventure is set in prehistoric times, the Bronze Age. One of the strengths of this text lies in the visual images on the cover, in chapter headings and a map that lays out the terrain in which the adventure takes place. Perhaps there is a learner in the class who has a historic or archaeological interest in fossils that might offer a link?

Helpfully the front cover (Figure 5.2) looks like a Bronze Age cave painting. It shows a figure with a bow and arrow accompanied by a creature running alongside him. This is the wolf cub that grows into the 'Wolf brother' companion in the story. The questions for the setting might be

> 'What sort of places do people find pictures like this?'
> 'What does it show?'
> 'What time in history do you think this story belongs to?'
> 'What do you think this novel is about?'

Language might emerge for you to write on the board. If not, be ready to supply the kind of language that is needed. There are may be predictions for you to note that are not relevant or likely, but can be acknowledged, justified and then checked against what the class finds as they go through the novel extract. You might exploit the clue about the *companionship* in the image on the front cover. Perhaps you have a learner who is interested in wolves and their characteristics?

Figure 5.2 Front cover of Wolf Brother (2004 Edition), design John Fordham.

Step 3 is to find out the mission for the main character. Present the background information in the text box below on a slide, or in a handout, or use graphics with stick men if needed for comprehension. Questions could be

(1) What task does Torak have to do?
(2) What is dangerous about a bear? (A picture of a bear in threatening pose might be helpful.)

Background

This novel tells the tale of a thirteen-year-old boy, Torak, who is travelling in the forest with his father when the father is killed by a demon bear. Before he dies, Torak's father tells him that he must find and kill the bear to save all the people in that area. His advice is: 'Look behind you Torak'. There are numerous hard tasks and challenges to overcome on the way. What can they be? How does Torak feel?

★ As with many works of fiction, meaning is expressed indirectly. In this case there is no language in this extract reporting how he feels. There are only actions that reflect his feelings.

At this point a light hearted demonstration of *indirect communication* might be useful. The word 'indirect' needs to go on the board for reference. Think about the indirect ways of making a request mentioned in Chapter 1 (page 14). Learners might rise to the challenge of demonstrating to their peers how they might ask their parents for something indirectly, in order to be sure to get it. The listener has to *read between the lines* and put in the information that is left out.

With this expectation of indirect communication in mind, the learners could look at the extract to find out what is happening to Torak and *read between the lines* to work out how he feels. We are looking for clues, as we were in the riddle poem (pages 119–24), but this time the clues are about feelings. There will be universals here. As set out as a Starting Point for this book, humans share many common physical and social experiences including associating friendship with warmth and happiness: resources we can draw on to trigger a familiar mental image for the topic.

Step 4 is to prepare for reading. Set the scene in the forest before reading the text extract from the book. Show a picture or draw a graphic on the board to show and label the setting, with 'trees', 'stream', 'bracken' and 'dock leaf'. 'Trees' is probably a known word, but paraphrases for 'stream', 'bracken' and 'dock leaf' would be helpful as well as general images of water flowing, green undergrowth and a plant leaf big enough to serve as a drinking vessel.

Ask the learners to take one minute to 'skim read' the text in the text box below to get the general picture, where the verbs are shaded, and then discuss with a partner to choose a headline from the three options that follow.

> Torak reached the stream, where a mist floated above the bracken, and willows trailed their fingers in the cold water. Glancing quickly around, he snatched a dock leaf and moved forwards, his boots sinking into the soft red mud.
> He froze.
> Beside his right boot was the track of a bear. A front paw twice the size of his head, and so fresh that he could see the points where the long, vicious claws had bitten deep into the mud.
> *Look behind you Torak.*
> He spun round.
> Willows. Alder. Fir.
> No bear.
>
> (Paver, 2004:8)

Group task: choose a headline

(a) Torak finds evidence of the vicious bear
(b) Torak gets a dock leaf so that he can have a drink at the stream but forgets to look behind him
(c) Torak goes to look for willow, alder and fir trees

The answer is (a).

These steps will afford a general overview of the text meaning. So the next questions are the ones for the task.

Step 5 is to prepare the task. Work on the wording. As we saw from Wu's difficulty in Chapter 4 (pages 113–15) and revisited in our template for task design, wording is key to representing the ideas and concepts in a way that the learners will recognize. The final goal in this task is a piece of text that answers the questions below.

Wording of the group task:

(1) Read the text and answer this question: How did Torak feel when he saw the paw track?
(2) How do you know from the language in the story? Which words does the writer use to tell you? Check out the *nouns, verbs, adjectives*. Try to find three or four which give you clues. Be careful. They may be words that tell you *indirectly* how he feels.
(3) Share your words and phrases with your group.
(4) Nominate a scribe to write up your group answer, using the words you have found as evidence to explain and justify how the writer tells us Torak's feelings.

This task can be co-constructed with a group, but the teacher needs to offer initial modelling before the group starts co-construction.

To generate data from the text, lead a plenary discussion to guide the search.

The discussion of language in plenary with the class might *focus on a word hunt* for

- *nouns* that name what he saw (a front paw), e.g. *Who can find me a word that shows the bear was there?*
- *adjectives* that add colour to those things (*twice the size of his head*),
- *verbs* that name what was around him in the environment (*mist floated*) and what he did (*reached, snatched*).

Mime might be a useful way to create the events and the atmosphere for the extract. The teacher or a learner could enact Torak's role, with someone speaking the words of the dead father that Torak hears in his head.

Step 6 is setting off the group. Once the task has been modelled with a general focus on language, it would help to limit the scale of the group task, e.g. focus on the verbs to scaffold how to use inference and deduction from detailed reading. To help the teacher, the verbs in the text above are shaded. The learners could be advised to underline them and then match up to a crib sheet, with the verbs shaded, in the same way.

The questions could also be about the kinds of meaning in the verbs.

- Do the verb meanings give us descriptions of what is there? being/having? actions? sights? words spoken?
- Can you find any sentences where the writer has left out a verb?

To help you identify the verb meanings, they are listed in Table 5.4, set out according to type of meaning, with *a missing verb indicated by '…'*.

Table 5.4 Verbs from the Extract Expressing *Doing, Being/Having, Seeing* and *Saying*

Doing	*Being/having*	*Seeing*	*Saying*
reached	was	glancing round	'look behind you'
floated	… Willows. Alder. Fir.	could see	
trailed	… no bear		
snatched			
moved			
sinking			
froze			
had bitten			
spun round			

The verb examples represent a combination of *moving, seeing and hearing*. Some of them are *everyday words* ('reached, moved') and others have an *indirect meaning* that implies how Torak did something: 'glancing', 'froze' and, the kind of mark the paw made, 'had bitten into the mud'.

As the group shares their data and decides what feelings are represented, the scribe can set them out in a list, followed by examples, as in the text box below.

haste: he came to the stream *glancing quickly round* and *snatched* a dock leaf;
fear: when he stopped, he *froze*;
panic: he *spun round* when he heard the ghostly voice of his father.

Now the group has 'evidence', a straightforward way to model presentation of that data in an 'appreciation' or 'report' is to work out a Writing Frame with Sentence Starters in plenary and write it on the board. For example,

> We looked at .... to examine how the writer ....
> We found three examples of ....
> The first ....
> The second .....
> The third ......
> These examples show how the writer creates an atmosphere of ....

This kind of model can be enabling, but risks becoming restricting. It should be a scaffold, not a set procedure.

Try to use such a model alongside your planned opportunities for interaction in plenary and small groups or pairs to facilitate oral rehearsal of the language. The best approach is to develop the writing frame for the task with the learners. This sharing will support the emerging construction of knowledge. Perhaps this kind of group task might create interest in drawing a response, or further reading of the text, e.g. working out the plot, or investigating the language used to create an atmosphere of suspense in a further extract.

It is a key feature in the plan of the activity that group work occurs before individual activity. We now turn to the last example of an explanation task in this chapter: preparing for a test.

Planning, setting up and supporting an individual test in Climate Science

Our third example is from Climate Science, where the class has been studying 'The Greenhouse Effect'. We want to prepare an End of Unit test task in *a language aware way*: *Explain the causes of the Greenhouse Effect.*
With 'Backward design' in mind, the learners need to know

- the purpose of a test: to display their individual knowledge of the subject;
- the success criteria:
  ○ fulfil the requirements of the question,
  ○ show a level of content knowledge,
  ○ demonstrate a level of subject literacy to express it appropriately.

In this case the *subject literacy* includes

- understanding what 'explain' means in the test task;
- choosing a logical structure to present the key facts involved in the causes and effect, making use of key words and clear sentences;
- demonstrating the ability to work out the relationship between the facts.

The teacher should cover these key points so learners know what is expected from the test. To help with this kind of explanation, science often uses an analogy to represent a phenomenon. However, an analogy may have pedagogic limitations because the learners often take the metaphor literally and, in this case, consider what they know about *greenhouses*, rather than take hold of the *concept of cause and effect* that is behind the original use of the analogy.

The label *Greenhouse Effect* caught the public imagination when it was first introduced. But it is important to make clear to learners the characteristics of a greenhouse that are similar to the scientific phenomenon so that learners can see why it is used as an analogy. It's also a culturally coded analogy: perhaps your EAL learners are not familiar either with what a greenhouse looks like or its purpose. Again, it might be helpful to google images, as suggested for the novel task above, or to offer another metaphor for the phenomenon that might be nearer to the learners' context, e.g. 'canopy' (of trees) or 'blanket'.

The topic occurs in the classroom as part of a curriculum requirement in Chemistry to study *the production of CO_2 by human activity and its effect on climate*. The data below comes from research investigating how learners interpret the meaning of words and metaphor in Climate Science (Deignan and Semino 2018). A group of 14-year-old learners were interviewed as they were finishing the unit on *The Greenhouse Effect*.

Interviewer: So what is the greenhouse effect? Who can tell me about that? All right? ⟶ Applies analogy

Student 1: Er like in greenhouses they trap err heat in for plants to erm stay warmer and all that, and that's happening to the earth. The earth is like the plant, and the CO_2 is making like a glass shelter around it, and it's trapping heat in. ⟶ Literal use of 'greenhouse'

Student 2: We have greenhouse things because then, the plants, when you put plants in there, it helps 'cos they don't, they get like everything so they don't get too much rain and too much sunshine, they have a variety of different things.

Interviewer: Anyone else know anything about the greenhouse effect?

Student 3: It's a mixture of different gases, it isn't just one.

Interviewer: What happens to the gases?
Student 1: They make a layer around the earth, like we've got atmosphere yeah, and they make a layer like the atmosphere, trapping all the heat in.
(Interview data Deignan and Semino, 2018)

It is clear from this exchange that the metaphor of the greenhouse has been applied in a rather literal sense. The learners use key terms they have been taught, but there is little sense of the link between *cause* and *effect* in the dialogue. They report the story as a sequence of events joined by 'and'. The learner data was compared with input in school materials which indicated that the model provided by the input materials also present a sequence of events. For example: 'Now carbon dioxide and methane are building up in the atmosphere. They are acting like a greenhouse around the earth' (Deignan and Semino 2018).

This is an area for caution because teachers often use this kind of figurative language to put across an abstract concept and the learners repeat the words or versions of the words in their work. But the fact that learners *use* technical terms does not mean that they have *accurate understandings* of the underlying cause effect links involved.

Supporting the synthesis of ideas for cause and effect

It's important to support the synthesis of ideas when we prepare the learners for a test. We want to set up opportunities for the EAL learner to demonstrate their knowledge. To activate the schemas the learners have for links between the concepts of cause and effect, we use images and sample language.

Here is an example to adapt. Find a picture on the internet of heavy snow falling around buildings and add the caption '24.02.2018 Beast from the East', labelled 'cause'. Follow this with a picture labelled 'effect' which shows a school buried in snow with the sign 'Closed' hanging on the school gates.

Apply this concept to learners' everyday lives. Have the learners work in pairs. Give each pair two sets of pictures with captions, one set labelled 'causes', the other set labelled 'effect'. Pictures can be of pairs such as

- Forgot money ➜ can't go on the bus
- Soaked in the rain ➜ bad cold
- Eating sweets ➜ tooth decay
- Car belching smoke from exhaust ➜ air pollution
- Tsunami ➜ devastated villages

The pairs match the two sets of picture so that each *cause* is matched with its *effect* or *consequence*. To support the language of this task, the final slide has a text box with three sections: on the left is a picture of factories belching smoke, labelled 'cause'. On the right is a picture showing a city covered by a cloud of pollution, labelled 'effect', and in the middle section a set of verbs that can link the two 'caused', 'led to', 'resulted in', as set out below. You might want to add the cautionary 'appear to have contributed to' to avoid potentially offending readers. It is important not to confuse Climate Science with Climate Change.

Picture of factories belching smoke **CAUSE**	**joining verbs** 'have caused' 'have led to' 'resulted in' 'appear to have contributed to'	Picture showing a city covered by a cloud of pollution **EFFECTS**

Adapted from teaching discussions.

This type of trigger can offer an engaging way of making it clear to the learners that they are working on an explanation that involves events and contributory factors: causes and effects. Combining pictures with captions gives a reasonable amount of support, and the joining verbs help with the language for linking the events in the cause/effect chain in a style appropriate to subject literacy, i.e. not just *saying* 'there's been a lot of smoke belching out of factories and now there is pollution'.

Google Translate could be used for *cause and effect*, and *greenhouse effect*. EAL learners can be invited to add examples in words or pictures that are culturally relevant to them, perhaps a farmer sowing seeds matched with a poor crop of maize caused by drought.

What key words relating to Climate Science is the teacher expecting the learners to come up with in a test? This is for the teacher to decide when designing the test and the strategies to support it. As in many subjects, we can offer numerous related terms that are possibly synonymous (illustrated in Chapter 4, page 112).

Planned opportunities for oral rehearsal of ideas

As mentioned above, synthesis implies drawing together ideas and understanding the relationship between them, how they fit together and how they affect each other. So in this section, following the practice of *language aware pedagogy*, we set out an oral task idea with two extension tasks for learners to find out and practise the language in order to take some kind of ownership of it. These routes into new language are likely involve both *everyday and specialist terms* being used as the new knowledge is created and the subject literacy emerges, as we saw in the Heat Transfer transcript in Chapter 2 (page 53).

Task idea

- Aim: learners produce a diagram to explain the causes of the *greenhouse effect* synthesized from information from three sources of professional knowledge.
- The teacher sets up the task using a schematic representation to explain the greenhouse effect that has previously used in class as a model.
- To make their explanatory diagram, tell the learners to find three different images representing *the production of CO_2 by human activity and its effect on climate* from internet or textbooks. They might use sites like these three and/or a textbook:

    https://en.wikipedia.org/wiki/Greenhouse_effect
    http://www.environment.gov.au/climate-change/climate-science-data/climate-science/greenhouse-effect
    https://www.bbc.com/bitesize/guides/zx234j6/revision/2

- Learners use this information to create their own diagram with arrows to reflect how they want to explain the causes. Use language from their own understanding to present the diagram to the class.

These text boxes give you some samples for language support if they get stuck. They can be on a handout or round the wall.

Nouns	Verbs	Linkers
human activity	release/is released	when, so
combustion	trap/are trapped	because of, due to
emissions	causes/is caused by	as a result, the result is
atmosphere/layer	escape	
thermal energy/radiation	are a result of/result from	
analogy	shelter	
heat		
CO_2 (Carbon dioxide)		
blanket		

Extension task 1

Ask the learners to make sentences using key words and language patterns such as those above, or from their presentation, or from the input materials of the unit. Example task questions:

- How many different sentences can you make with (a set of) key words?
- How many of these words are synonymous in meaning?

This is particularly good practice to help the learners distinguish between the *active* and *passive* voices for the verbs. For example, the Deignan and Semino (2018) research data also showed confusion between 'release' (active) and 'is released (passive)' as shown in this written example, using *active* voice.

> 'Like, increased human activity's affecting the amount of carbon emissions that *we're releasing* into the atmosphere'.

The agent of 'release' appears to be 'humans' rather than 'the human activity' that we might say causes carbon emissions 'to be released'. It would help to compare versions that learners come up with to check they are making explicit the logical relations of cause and the effect. For example,

> Emissions of carbon and methane (resulting from /caused by human activity) are building up in the atmosphere. These gases are not released from the atmosphere (which means/ with the result that) parts of the atmosphere are acting like a greenhouse around the earth. The effect is to make the earth warmer.

Extension task 2
Ask the learners to build up a definition of *greenhouse effect* by adding to this starter.

> The greenhouse effect is an analogy for ………………………………………………

You might expect something like 'the effect of too many greenhouse gases in the atmosphere'. Working in groups the learners can support each other's learning.

Support understanding of the purpose of a test

As set out at the start of this section, the purpose of a test is to display individual knowledge. The learner should show they

- understand the question – so the teacher can support work to deconstruct the topic and the instruction (*explain, discuss* etc.);
- know the key words for the key facts they need to include – so the teacher can support practice in using key words in different phrases and sentences as in the task ideas above;
- know how to present them in a logical way to explain the causes of the greenhouse effect. The teacher can offer a two-step model for the answer.

What Are the Key Principles for Adapting Tasks and Tests   163

Table 5.5 Setting Out Causes and Effects

Causes	Effects

Step 1

Offer a table to help the learners organize the statements into causes and effects (Table 5.5).

Step 2

Offer a template to structure the test question. This text box gives a Writing Frame for 'Explain the causes of the greenhouse effect'.

Plan – Introductory statement to say what is going to be explained i.e. causes of the greenhouse effect	Content – overview of what the causes are and comment on what this analogy means
Setting/situation	Atmosphere: what is it? What is it for?
Contributory factors/processes 1	? radiation
Contributory factors/processes 2	? thermal energy
Contributory factors/processes 3	? human activity
Contributory factors/processes 4	? trapped gases
Result	the greenhouse effect: rises in temperature

These steps offer learners a route through the tangle of relationships between specialist words and the concepts they are trying to capture. We all use figurative language, analogy and metaphors to put across ideas in our subject areas. But there is not always a one to one equivalence between a concept and the chosen metaphor or analogy, so a certain amount of inference or reading between the lines is required. Similarly, as pointed out earlier, learning involves more than memorizing terminology. It also involves thought and reasoning, so the logical relevance of a concept has to be established in the mind of the learner.

This kind of modelling can give a learner a strategy to deal with any test, however significant, whether worth 2 marks or 20. These *language aware* approaches to coping with metaphor can be applied to other subjects, as can this approach for planning, setting up and supporting a test.

Apply a check list for a planning, setting up and supporting a test to other subject areas

- Ask yourself 'What am I looking for?'
  Have a clear communication purpose in your mind. It helps to write a model answer or key points for an answer to identify the success criteria, *e.g. demonstrate knowledge of key words, key facts and ability to present the information in sentences in a structured way that shows the relationship between them.*

- Have these criteria been outlined to the learner?
  Yes, we discussed a how to deconstruct the assignment instructions, what key points to include and how to organize them.

- Have I used language to present the material with explicit focus on language features of this topic and the writing conventions?
  Yes, in class we looked at typical language patterns and practised variations in how to say the same thing, ranging within the appropriate register.

Drawing together principles for *language aware* task design

The principles for *language aware* task design set out in this chapter show key stages in planning, setting up and supporting opportunities for learning. At the same time, they show the teacher is making flexible use of resources available in the funds of knowledge brought by the EAL learners as much as in her own pedagogic and subject knowledge.

Planning makes use of the classic Kolb structure modified to suit the needs of the EAL learner identified in the Chapter 2 Teaching Resources (page 58). This includes presentation, deconstruction of topic elements and co-construction of outcome. The process involves participation in plenary, group and individual activities with oral rehearsal so that the teacher can monitor the learners' interpretation of the classroom processes. This is relevant to *all* learners who need to extend the range of their English vocabulary and understanding in order to build knowledge and express themselves clearly.

We have identified four principles, as follow.

Work on the communication purpose

As set out in Chapter 3, the teacher needs a clear communication purpose in mind. In the subjects of Science and Humanities, the communication purpose often involves describing features that are observable and then providing reasons for these observations by referring to an underlying mechanism, cause or theory.

In subjects such as subject English, Music, Art and RE, the focus is on identifying features of the text, considering the expression of thoughts and ideas through language, sound or visual, and commenting on an aspect, perhaps the effect, an emotional, intellectual response, or how the ideas contribute to a value system

Teachers' explanations will vary according to the subject, the level of understanding required and whether it is a description, a procedure, a process of events or an inquiry. As set out in Chapter 3, some may be more descriptive than others, but they all have one feature in common. They all provide a reason; they refer to contributing factors of cause, and show an outcome or effect.

Identifying this communication purpose will take you to the key words and sample language structures you need to model.

Model the structure and language features of a task or test

Using 'Backward design' models the structure of the task or test as part of the planning. This means the teacher identifies the target learning experience and the language to be used. The model structure offers two kinds of support for you to offer the learners: *the logical sequence of the communication purpose of explanation* and *the key words and sample language structures* that you want the learners to encounter and use in the classroom.

It may be a narrative of the enquiry process as in the example of the text analysis above. This type of exploration to find data and offer interpretation can be applied to subjects as shown in this text box.

English	Interpretation of 2 poems
Music	Appreciation of structure/performance
Art	Comparison of treatment of a theme by two different photographers
PE	Critique of performance (live or video)
RE/PVSH	Comparison of treatment of one theme in two belief systems
Spanish	Composition of a letter to a friend

It may be a task requiring synthesis, as in the account of *the greenhouse effect*. This assemblage of actors, actions and contributory factors where their relationship with one another needs to be untangled can be applied to other subjects as exemplified in this next text box.

History	The causes of the First World War
Design and Technology	The relationship of text and colour theory in DTP

Plan for engagement in a *language aware* way

It is important to offer maximum support for engagement in the topic by applying the questions from the three-step model of *language aware* task design introduced at the start of this chapter (page 139):

1. How can you tap into what the learner already knows?
2. How can you provide opportunities for the learner to participate?
3. What language will you make explicit for your learner to learn?

In the same way that the teacher found scenarios relevant to learners to activate schemas of language and background knowledge for *cause and effect*, the lesson activities can be resourced by images and sample language (both words and grammatical structures to carry meaning), such as

- other languages: translation, comparison of how concepts are expressed in different languages;
- visuals: from a range of sources, from simple to complex, to introduce ideas and concepts based on concrete entities, that is, objects of our immediate physical world. They can also be used as summaries representing the relationship of more abstract concepts such as the *greenhouse effect* (this chapter, pages 159–60), or *changes of state solid, liquid and gas* (Chapter 4, pages 101–2);
- gesture/mime to confirm the message and even indicate logical relationships. For example, a *thumbs up* can work as a kinetic code for learning logical relationships through gesture.

Consult the *Explanation model* in the Teaching Resources at the end of this chapter (page 168).

Be aware of the challenges and opportunities for participation in a task

Awareness of challenges and opportunities for participation inherent in a task as set out in Table 5.3 (page 150) can be applied to any task. Ask yourself: How can I frame the challenge to engage the learner? What opportunities for participation can I set up? Where does the learner need support?

Apart from identifying communication purpose, key words and language structures as mentioned above, to support engagement, we know the importance oral work, whether listening or speaking. In these activities there will be thoughtful composition of groups to challenge yet support the EAL learner. If there is a choice, is there a place for the EAL learner to work with others in her own language? Will it be more useful for her to work with other English speakers? (See Chapter 2 Teaching Resources, pages 56–8.)

- Do the groups have established ground rules for the procedure and a clear idea of the success criteria of the target outcome?
- Are they aware of how we talk to each other: in an *additive, confirmatory* way, in a *disputational* way, in an *exploratory* way to hypothesize, imagine and try out ideas?
- Are they aware of which kinds of talk are productive of learning?

Further examples of subject lesson plans designed to suit EAL learners can be found at https://www.naldic.org.uk/eal-teaching-and-learning/eal-resources/science-eal/ (an archived NALDIC page).

Using this *language aware* approach to task design will offer opportunities for EAL learners to demonstrate their knowledge. These steps are set out for your reference in the explanation model we have adapted for EAL learners in the Teaching Resources for this chapter (page 168).

And when we see their work, what kind of feedback will be useful for further guidance? This is the question for the next chapter.

Teaching resources

Table 5.6 Explanation Model Adapted for EAL Learners

The explanation model	Adaptation for EAL learners
Planning Establish the goal in terms of learning and the communication purpose of explanation: process, description, procedure, events with cause and effect. Break the topic down into manageable parts. Establish links between parts. 　Write a model of your goal • Definition • Appreciation • Explanation Take time to find out about the EAL learner backgrounds. Find a trigger to tap into that knowledge and build on what they know as a platform for new knowledge.	Label visuals, diagrams, equipment, with English words. Give abstract terms before lesson for learners to check on Google Translate. Plan differentiated activity/crib sheet, e.g. • *Before listening:* match key words with picture • *While listening:* Picture/word chart to tick when they hear the word during explanation • *After listening:* Gap fill missing words and phrases of written explanation.
During the explanation Aim for clarity and fluency • through defining new terms • through use of explicit language • through avoiding vagueness	1. Language of defining in spoken English *It's a ..., we call that a ..., it's a sort of ... it's like a ....* 2. Take care with analogies, metaphors, figurative language such as greenhouse effect. Although essential for abstract thought, pupils often understand it literally.
Emphasis and interest • with gestures • by use of media/materials • by use of voice and pauses • by use of repetition, paraphrasing, starting sentences and getting learners to finish them • by encouraging interaction	1. Support your meaning with non-verbal modes of communication (a systematic code of gestures, visuals). 2. Articulate clearly, and sometimes more slowly. 3. Repeat and recycle language. 4. Write new language to emphasize pronunciation, word stress and spelling. 5. Nominate EAL learners to encourage interaction. Non-verbal responses such as pointing, frowning, nodding are better than nothing!

The explanation model	Adaptation for EAL learners
Organization • Logical and clear sequencing. • Use of link words and phrases.	1. Language of logical sequencing: because, so, therefore … etc. 2. Signposting language: First, second, after that, then ….
Providing examples • Clear appropriate and concrete • In sufficient quantity • Positive and negative where applicable	1. Based on your knowledge of your EAL learners' cultural background, ask yourself, 'Will they have seen the examples you use before?'
Feedback • Opportunities for questions provided • Understanding of main idea assessed • Expressions of attitudes and values sought	1. EAL learners could use question prompts on wall: What is/does? How/Why? etc. 2. Use own L1 with buddy to talk through? 3. Use non-verbal cues to demonstrate understanding (put pictures in right order etc.)

Adapted from Brown and Armstrong (1984:123)

6

What Constitutes 'Useful Feedback' to Support EAL Learner Subject Literacy Development?

Chapter Outline	
Starting points: The supportive role of feedback	171
What does emerging subject literacy look like?	175
How do learners manage the complexities of language to support the vocabulary of subject literacies in a test?	177
How do learners use subject-specific and general academic words to explain abstract concepts in an essay?	187
Drawing together features of *useful feedback* to support EAL learners	195
Teaching resources	197

- *How can I recognize the patterns in subject literacy that I need to support?*
- *What should I respond to?*
- *What does language aware feedback look like?*

Starting points: The supportive role of feedback

Giving feedback means responding to learners, offering support of an important kind for the challenges inherent in learning. In this chapter we meet our EAL learners again, but viewed through the lens of learner data. As we saw in Chapter 2 (pages 47–9), the pragmatic EAL learner generally finds that working out how to use everyday language is relatively straightforward, but school knowledge is more challenging because it is expressed in more complex ways. As anyone who has struggled with preparing a graphic, a presentation or an assignment knows, in this more formal mode there are expectations: What does the teacher/examiner/class need to know? How should I say it?

Our EAL learner data will show us what emerging subject literacies can look like. This will draw together threads from previous chapters where we have highlighted aspects of subject literacy that the teacher can integrate into practice to support subject literacy development. In the learner data we are looking for patterns of language choices that indicate areas of conceptual understanding and areas for useful formative feedback, along with advice for ways forward.

Our reciprocal view of learning implies participation in meaningful interaction that is a three way process. This is between the teacher, the multimodal resources available in the classroom (including classmates) and the EAL learners, who play an equally significant role in terms of the knowledge they bring to the lesson themselves.

In this dynamic process, teachers have to make on the spot pedagogic decisions as they monitor, evaluate and decide on next steps at every stage of the lesson. And to support subject literacy in culturally diverse classrooms, the feedback teachers give is the same as to any other learners, except that it is *language aware* feedback.

What does that look like? You are familiar with the ways knowledge is represented in your subject and, as you have read through this book, you will have noted how to make explicit the language patterns involved in that literacy. We extend this to how you make decisions on feedback. Learner responses show teachers what the learners have made of the lesson material, so learner data shows teachers what to do next. This will guide you on how to integrate the subject literacy focus into your feedback practice.

The view of feedback we take in this chapter is based on the well-established concept of 'formative assessment for learning' (Black and Wiliam 1998). In their work *Inside the Black Box* they focus on creating opportunities for learning and feedback throughout the lesson.

We touched on this idea in our chapters about engaging with difficult language (4) and difficult concepts (5). Feedback is therefore iterative, much repeated and always there. It can be anything from a smile to a crib sheet. It has a significant place in the teaching cycle because it leads to the next event, whatever that may be. And because we all like to give supportive feedback, it

- involves a judgement or an evaluation of some kind;
- offers active guidance on how to continue building knowledge and
- requires an active response that encourages learners to reflect on how they learn.

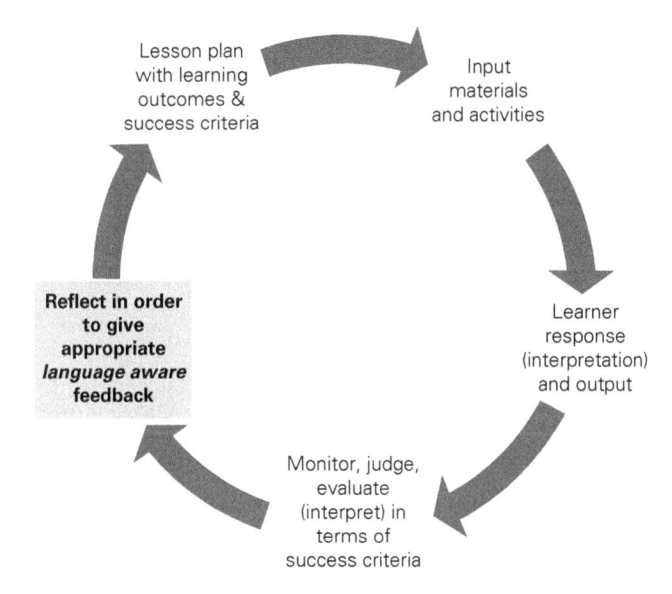

Figure 6.1 The place of *language aware* feedback in the teaching cycle.

This conceptualization of the place of *language aware* feedback in the teaching cycle summarizes our perspective.

From these starting points, this chapter links the language patterns of subject literacies identified in previous chapters, with the interpretations EAL learners make. We take evidence from oral transcripts and written output.

This will build up a portfolio of different kinds of *language aware* feedback to apply to subject literacy in your own subject area.

What are your preferred modes of feedback? Your answer is probably 'it depends' because the wise teacher will match the type of response to needs, either *of the moment* or for *more long-term learning*.

The key principle is to match the type of feedback you give to available resources, learning outcomes and success criteria. Feedback on an individual basis is what every learner wants, but this is only feasible on occasions when time and resources permit. Some advisers (Jones and Wiliam 2008) suggest giving detailed feedback on 25% of work handed in. The remaining material will receive other types of interactive feedback.

According to this advice, it should be 'coherent', 'structured', 'progressive', and 'differentiated'. In other words, to be supportive, it should match the needs of a learner and be consistent with *the goal of personalized learning*.

Feedback activities offer another opportunity for learners to engage with the knowledge they are developing (Schleppergrell 2012). So, included in the *high challenge/high support* environment planned for learning, well-designed feedback can set up learning opportunities in collaborative work with the teacher and with peers. We offer examples of various kinds of feedback activities so that they can be adapted to all subject areas.
They may be

- from the teacher:
    - when? immediate or delayed,
    - context? in plenary or individual,
    - mode? visual, spoken or written;
- collaborative from peers in a group;
- self-assessment guidance for monitoring and editing.

Where do we start? The challenges for EAL learners identified in previous chapters were in the areas of

- familiarity of topic/information,
- interpretation of conceptual meaning in key words,
- how the words are supported by sentence grammar and
- mastering logical links to make a coherent text.

Based on this knowledge and the *assessment for learning* approach, we look at evidence of what an EAL learner can make of those challenges.

Subject teachers will find the following broad criteria of assessment useful as a basis for feedback:

- Concept knowledge (any problems with the topic?)
- Control of subject literacy (any problems with language choices?)
- Next steps advised

We use data from general classroom interaction and from more focused End of Unit events. After each example we discuss options for feedback: *teacher, collaborative, self-assessment guidance*. At each stage we refer briefly to the PiE scales (see Chapter 2, pages 42–3) to benchmark the subject literacy skills a learner working at that level is likely to demonstrate. The following sections answer these questions:

- What does emerging subject literacy look like?
- How do learners manage the complexities of language to support the vocabulary of subject literacies in a test?
- How do learners use subject-specific and general academic words in grammatical sentences to explain abstract concepts in an essay?

What does emerging subject literacy look like?

To get us started, here are two samples of oral classroom language to illustrate two kinds of emerging subject literacies. As you will see in the comments following each sample, both teachers use a similar kind of 'in the moment' feedback i.e. *exploratory talk to shape learner responses*.

Sample A: A problem with register.
Setting: Year 9/S3, Geography class. General information gathering session about dangers to human life from earthquakes and tsunamis prior to making an outline and writing.

>T: What can you tell me about the Indonesian Tsunami in 2014? Yes, (………)?
>L: Miss, there was this massive wave, Miss!
>T: A massive wave! Yes, that's right, we saw it on the news. But let's think about it as *Geographers*. How do we explain what caused it?

(adapted from teaching discussions)

Comment
We can see that the teacher decides to interpret the informal register problem in Sample A as a joke. The exchange could occur during a co-construction with the rest of the class to remind them what a *Geographer* would say by referring to *the specialist register* to explain causes. This problem *could occur at any level of PiE*. The teacher uses *in the moment* feedback which she can then actively extend by referring to the *everyday/specialist word* register continuum for consolidation (as set out in Chapter 1 Teaching Resources, page 27).

Sample B: A problem with range of expression (finding the language)
Setting: Year 10/S4 Topic: History of medicine: 'The work of Ambroise Paré in the treatment of gunshot wounds in the 16th century. What effect did his ideas have?' This transcript is from the follow up with the EAL teacher after the subject teacher's presentation.

>T: (*Reading from the board*) 'Why was Paré important?'
>L: He knew the … (*gesture, moves hands apart, searching for word*) of wounds and gunshot.
>T: Yes, (*dictating*) he knew about gunshot wounds. What did he do?
>L: Some of them … (*gesture*) gunshot was poisoning, but it was not. Bacteria was poisoning … like Miss said.
>T: Yes, (*dictating*) other people thought that gunshot was poisonous, but the wounds were poisoned by bacteria. What did he do?
>L: He used … (*hesitates, gestures, find word*) egg … yolk of egg … something like oil of egg … boiling oil? No, oil of roses and paint … painting … turpentine.

T: Yes, well done, he used yolk of egg, oil of roses and turpentine. And did it work?

L: No it didn't. … Yes it did … *(confusion, searching for the language to connect the two statement because the teacher has stressed that the new treatments were not adopted in Paré's own lifetime).*

(Qualifications and Curriculum Authority, 2000: 39)

Comment

The limited range of language available to the learner in Sample B illustrates the kind of challenge facing an EAL learner regarding how long it might take to acquire the language for subject literacies (5 to 8 years, see Chapter 2, page 52). This transcript involves Alena, who has been in the UK system for a year. She is struggling to find the specialist words and the logical links for the grammar to carry the meaning. With reference to the EAL proficiency scales (pages 42–3), we would place this sample at PiE level C (Developing competence/Becoming a confident user) because a lot of listener interpretation is needed.

What kind of feedback do we see in the transcript here? The EAL support teacher avoids direct error correction. She repairs communication breakdowns in order to keep the interaction going. Her feedback focuses on content, as she recognizes Alena's subject knowledge and shapes her words into sentences to express it. She dictates, to confirm how the words that Alena has in her mind should be supported by the grammar.

When it comes to logical links, Alena's answer to the question 'Did it work?' is accurate in terms of concept, but her expression of it as 'No, it didn't …. Yes, it did …' shows the language problem. How should she connect the two statements to reflect the fact that Paré's treatments were not adopted until after his death?

> In classroom discourse, the need to express *opposing positive and negative meanings* is common. The teacher often uses a 'thumbs up' and 'thumbs down' as a universal gesture to reflect this.

In this case how do we help the learner to link the two? It is the time reference (*when*) that is missing. So to offer supportive feedback the next question is 'Tell me about *when* it didn't work and *when* it did work'. Perhaps a sentence starter like 'It didn't work when … but it did work after …' will help to make the logical link clear. If the sentence starter can be written down for future reference, all the better.

> You could add sentence starters like this to the language you include in your classroom 'word banks' on the wall.

We saw similar examples of *in the moment* feedback in Chapter 4 where the teacher used exploratory talk to shape Jamila's response with the meaning and use of 'calculating' (page 108) and to clarify for Wu the meaning of 'calculate the change received' (page 114).

So *language aware* pedagogy can offer explicit feedback to shape learner responses, not only to support the registers of subject literacy (Sample A) but also to support the logical connection of phrases and concepts (Sample B).

The summary of 'in the moment' feedback in the text box below matches our comments on Sample A and B with our three criteria.

> *in the moment* feedback
>
> - Recognizes adequate *concept knowledge* of the topic.
> - Identifies difficulties in *control of subject literacy* in the areas of register and sentence structure to carry the language and the logical relations.
> - Provides next steps guidance to reformulate, to recast and to note for future reference.

Can you apply this model for *in the moment* feedback to your own subject area? The teacher may choose this kind of feedback for a number of pedagogic purposes. Perhaps it is to clarify understanding? Or a language choice?

This approach offers an active way of drawing learners' attention to an area for development.

How do learners manage the complexities of language to support the vocabulary of subject literacies in a test?

In this section we look at examples of how learners manage the complexities of language in data from the End of Unit test on Heat energy transfer given to the Science class that we met in Chapter 2 (page 53).

We look at the language and cognitive challenges of the test, how the challenges are supported by the task design and how they are met by the students.

As with any test data, we have questions in our heads as we read:

- What was the input for the test?
- What were the learning outcomes and success criteria?

Input for the End of Unit test

We draw attention to two types of input the learners have had.

i) In Chapter 2 (page 53) the classroom transcript for the Science lesson showed how the teacher mixes *every day and specialized language*. The aim is to clarify the meaning of the specialized terms for talking about *Heat energy transfer*. *Key words* in that part of the lesson were *heat will travel along the rod, we call that transfer of heat, the fancy name is 'conduction', heat travels along solids in a straight line*.

ii) Another part of the input involved role play, where the learners stood up and took on the role of particles, vibrating in response to heat, and colliding with one another to transfer heat energy.
Key words in this activity were *vibrating, colliding to transfer heat energy*.

In the End of Unit test, as we emphasized for the enquiry activity in Chapter 4 (page 155), *the wording of the task* is crucial to the learners' interpretation of what they should do. This test question has two sentences, (i) giving the scenario and (ii) the instruction, as set out in the text box below:

Scenario	During an experiment Matthew finds that when the end of a copper rod is heated, the Vaseline melts and the paperclips fall off.
Instruction with key words and marks value	Describe how particles of the solid copper rod carry the heat energy (2 marks).

Points for the learner to note in the wording of the test are that

- the first sentence *describes the physical event* and
- the second sentence *asks for a scientific explanation*.

It is *supported by a visual* with which the learners will be familiar (Figure 6.2).

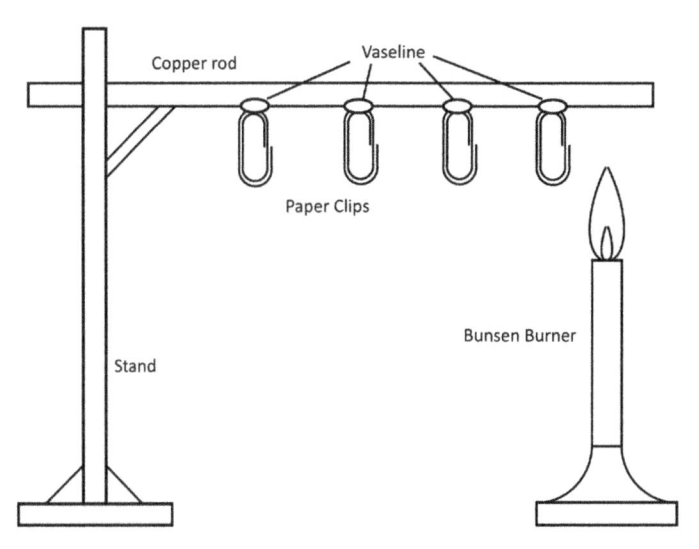

Figure 6.2 End of Unit test question on Heat energy transfer.

Learning outcomes and success criteria: What does the teacher expect in the answer?

When asked what he was looking for from this task, the teacher gave the following response. We've set the sentences out in separate lines to make the organization of the points clear (Figure 6.3).

> 'What I would say is that the copper rod carries heat energy.
> The copper rod is made of particles, packed quite closely together.
> When one end is heated, the particles in the solid vibrate more quickly.
> These particles collide with the other ones, which then vibrate more quickly, and that's the way heat energy is transferred.
> That is what I would have written.'

Figure 6.3 Teacher's model answer (Interview data, Zacharias 2018).

We can see that the teacher's answer is organized as a *classic scientific explanation*. He is explaining a process with *an introductory statement*, *stages* and *a conclusion*. So in the marking, the teacher is looking for a structure like the one we represent schematically in Table 6.1 to make the language features explicit.

The left hand column sets out *the structure of the explanation* and the right hand column sets out *the language features*. The shaded phrases show how the teacher has made clear the logical relations, the underlined words show his key nouns and the words **in bold** are his **verbs**.

Table 6.1 Text of Teacher's Scientific Explanation Showing the Organization and Language Features

Organization	Language features
Introductory statement	The copper rod **carries** heat energy.
How? Description of the copper rod composition (*noun phrase to give precise description with added detail*).	The copper rod is made of particles, packed quite closely together.
How? Event 1 + Result 1	When one end **is heated**, the particles in the solid **vibrate** more quickly.
How? Event 2 + Result 2 + Result 3	These particles **collide** with the other ones which then **vibrate** more quickly.
Concluding statement from evidence	(and) that's the way heat energy **is transferred**.

Based on these expectations, the teacher will look at the answers to identify the level of subject knowledge and the extent to which it is represented in appropriate language.

To give you a general idea of the range of answers, Table 6.2 gives the marks from the class of twenty learners. The class is not streamed.

Table 6.2 Class Test Results

2 marks	1 mark	.5 marks	0 marks	No answer
4	5	1	6	4

Let's look at three of these answers and associated difficulties under our three headings to try to understand the scores. And then use our three criteria to guide what feedback we offer.

- Concept knowledge: scientific explanation of heat energy transfer
- Control of subject literacy: the terminology, grammar, and linkers?
- Next steps advised

In these examples, as in the model answer, the main focus is on the **verbs** in bold and the nouns underlined. The key points for comment are shaded.

Example 1: 2 marks: communicates the general idea

The particles in the copper rod **vibrate** and they **touch** the next set of particles and that **keeps on happening** until they all **vibrate**.

Concept knowledge: Scientific explanation. General concept knowledge is conveyed, but the learner assumes a significant amount of shared knowledge with the reader. There is no mention of 'how the rod carries heat energy', i.e. the reader expects a first sentence introducing the topic and a closing sentence completing the explanation.

Control of subject literacy: The learner uses '**vibrate**' and is able to use noun phrases successfully adds detail to make explicit which particles he is talking about (shaded). The use of '*until*' as linker shows *understanding of cause/effect*.

Next steps advised

i) work on a more complete scientific explanation to meet the needs of the reader;
ii) select more precise words;
iii) work on how to link ideas in a sequence with words apart from 'and'.

Example 2: 1 mark: partial communication of the general idea

When heat **gives** energy to particles Particles **vibrate** *then* this process **happens** all the way through the copper (**happens** best in solid *because* particles are close).

Scientific explanation: Conceptual knowledge good: many key words and a general idea of the link between solid rod and closely packed particles and vibrating 'all the way along'. But explanation incomplete: the writer assumes shared reader knowledge. As in first example, there is no first and last sentence.

Control of subject literacy: The learner has heard the two words 'heat' and 'energy', but not conceptualized them as the terminology for 'heat energy', the topic of the unit. He separates the two words in the sentence 'heat gives energy'. This connection needs reworking so that he can refer to what heat 'causes', i.e. 'heat causes the particles to vibrate'. The linkers 'When', 'then', 'because' show awareness of logical connections, but are not used effectively due to poor *sentence punctuation*.

> *Next steps advised*
> (i) work on the complete structure of the explanation to meet the needs of the reader;
> (ii) rework key terminology to build practice phrases and sentences;
> (iii) work on sentence punctuation;
> (iv) write for the reader: *avoid writing as you think/speak*.
>
> ### Example 3: 0 marks: no communication of the general idea
>
> <u>The particles</u> **vibrate** *and* **travel** <u>through the rod</u>.
>
> *Scientific explanation*: little evidence of conceptual understanding. The first three words are probably memorized from the input. The rest of the sentence is inaccurate.
> *Control of subject literacy*: the word 'travel' has been misapplied to 'particles'.
>
> *Next steps advised*
> i) Look at the complete structure of the explanation to notice what is included;
> ii) Rework key terminology to build practice phrases and sentences.

The misapplication of the verb 'travel' might well occur in any subject area. Do you recognize patterns of variable success with learners using new words in your own subject? What practice do you offer to support this?

What feedback on this test can we offer that is relevant to other subject areas?

The areas for next steps we have identified in the test scripts are relevant to other subject areas. Many answers are likely to show

- lack of familiarity with *writing for the reader* and *using the structure of a scientific explanation*;
- use of *everyday* instead of *general academic* words;
- some *formulaic knowledge of the key specialist words demonstrated*, but these words are frequently *misapplied in poor grammatical choices and linking* (a similar problem to the use of 'release' in Chapter 5, pages 161–2).

What feedback can we offer the learners to develop their subject literacy into fuller responses, showing awareness of the difference between *writing as if speaking to a listener* and *writing to communicate with a reader*?

In the next three sections we offer practice tasks for these difficulties for you to adapt for your own subject area. They focus on the

- structure of the explanation,
- use of specialist versus everyday words to make meaning more precise and
- sentence formation to show logical relations.

They are suitable for the *whole class to work on collaboratively in groups*.

The structure of the explanation

Here are three possibilities to adapt to your own subject.

- Focus on *writing for the reader*: Choose a model explanation type from your subject area. Emphasize that the learner must write for the reader. She cannot assume shared knowledge with the reader as if she is a listener and knows what she is talking about.

  Tip for learner: Make sure you start off with an introductory statement to show the reader you know what the question is asking you to do. Use words from the question to restate what you are required to explain.

- Focus on *sequence and logical links*: Deconstruct information elements in a model explanation from your subject area to illustrate what is expected. Emphasize sequence and logical linkers.

  Learner task: Put individual sentences cut up from an explanation into logical order, with suitable linkers based on the list in Chapter 4 Teaching Resources (page 134).

- Focus on producing a process *explanation of a process*: adapt the template in Table 6.3 to use with an example from your subject area. Model with learners. Apart from structure, include the relevant advice on language patterns: *words, complex language and logical relations* (see Chapter 3 Teaching Resources, pages 94–6).

  Learner task: Complete this template to give an *Explanation of process* answer to an End of Unit test question.

  Tip for learner: Use words from the question to start (and finish?) your answer. Use key words and link them clearly.

Table 6.3 Template for the Process Explanation

Explanation of the process	
Introduce the process or activity – *use language to define or present claim*	
The key terms – *choose language for classification of general class and specific types*	
The stages in the process, including the contributory factors – *choose language to represent specific features selected for description in words and visuals, plus logical links to show causes & effects*	
The result, with examples to make it relevant – *choose language to make clear cause and effect*	
Conclusion – *choose language to present opinion clearly*	

Increase awareness of differences between specialist and everyday vocabulary

Three possibilities based on the *Heat energy transfer* example for you to adapt. The first two are for *groups* and the third is for *individuals*:

- Refer to the register continuum for *everyday/specialist* words (Chapter 1 Teaching Resources, page 27). Model where the words 'bump into' and 'collide with' should be placed on that continuum.

    Learner task: Look at the words in the text box below and put them on the continuum on the wall to show which words are *everyday* and which are used as *specialist* words in *Heat energy transfer*.

> Words: *vibrate more quickly, keeps on happening, collide, bump into, touch, knock into, heat transfer, pass heat.*

In your subject, you can ask groups to look at a sample text of learner work. This could either be anonymously selected by the teacher from the class work, or selected by a group in consultation with each other.

- Refer to the way a Scientist talks about *Heat energy transfer* in *everyday* and *specialist* words.

    Learner task A: Model two sample phrases and ask if they are *true/false*? Groups receive some phrases of specialist terminology and should decide which are true and which false, e.g.

> Heat energy transfer means? T/F
>
> - Conduction
> - The transfer of heat energy along a conductor
> - A copper rod is a good conductor of heat
> - Particles vibrate …. *Teacher to add some more incorrect phrases.*

Learner task B: Which words mean the same in this topic? Model two words and ask if they have the same or different meanings. Groups receive a selection of words and should decide which ones have the same or similar meaning and which ones are different, e.g.

> *Collide, bump into, touch, knock into, transfer heat, pass heat, carry heat, heat travels, heat energy is transferred.*

- *Individuals*: Discuss in plenary what 'Editing before handing in' means. Brainstorm what kinds of checks the learner can make on their own work. Set out the checks as a set of criteria for each learner to use to check their work before handing in. They could be questions such as

> - Is the meaning of the key words precise enough?
> - Do I need to add additional detail?

These questions can be adjusted and added to as the class goes through other subject areas. As learners become familiar with the kinds of difficulties they are insecure about, they can be guided to add their own questions to the list of what to check.

Learner task: Check through your work using these questions before you hand in.

Some teachers ask learners to estimate a mark for their own work when handing in. They check against the feedback they receive. Would this work in your subject?

Sentence rewrite *for a reader*

This model can be applied to various contexts where feedback on sentence formation needs to be given. It is modelled *collaboratively in plenary* and *worked on individually*. This will offer a forum for individual learners to look at their own language work more critically.

- Discuss *writing for a reader* and *writing as you speak* with the class. Focus on the idea that *the writer is not present to clarify for the reader, but the speaker is there for the listener to clarify any problems.* Deconstruct a learner text with *writing as you speak* problems such as the one in the text box below. Then model how to sort it out into single ideas so that they can be combined appropriately into *sentences for readers*. Follow the model layout in Table 6.4, with groups of words with one idea (sentences/clauses) in the left hand column. The possible learner rewrite is in the right hand column. Problem verbs learners need to change are shaded for your benefit. Working with the language in this way will also give opportunities to learners for trying out the language and making the ideas their own. Memorizing the words of scientific principles, instead of trying to understand and use them is a false short cut. As we saw in Chapter 4 (pages 111–12), reformulating new concepts in similar words can be a useful way of becoming familiar with them and practising how to express them.

Learner task: The test answer in the text box below lost marks because the meaning is not clear. *The writer was writing for a listener (as if speaking) rather than a reader (with clear punctuation).* Can you make it clear by sorting the words into groups with complete ideas, so that they can be organized for a reader to read? To help you, the **verbs** are in bold and the nouns are underlined.

> When heat **gives** energy to particles Particles **vibrate** then this process **happens** all the way through the copper (**happens** best in solid because particles **are** close).

You should use the format in Table 6.4 to set out the groups of words, and then rewrite them *for a reader to read*.

Table 6.4 Sentence Re-write.

Deconstructed phrases with word problems shaded	Possible learner rewriting
Heat gives energy	Heat causes particles to vibrate
Particles vibrate	-
Then this process happens all the way through the copper	Then this process *(heat energy)* continues *(to travel)* through the copper rod
Happens best in solid	A solid *copper rod is a good conductor*
because particles are close	*because* particles are close*ly packed*

Is this exam training? Or preparation for study at Upper Secondary level? We suggest this type of directed writing practice lays a foundation in subject literacy for the development of confident independent writing at Upper Secondary level study.

How do learners use subject-specific and general academic words to explain abstract concepts in an essay?

In this section we look at emerging subject literacy in a History essay. This presents more writing challenges than an End of Unit test as it involves preparation of an argument and extended writing, such as we saw in Chapter 4 (pages 125–30), where the report on diet required gathering evidence, planning an outline and then writing. What are the practical *language aware* approaches to giving useful feedback on an essay assignment?

We start with the input for a Year 9 (S2) History essay on what led to the Second World War and then look at the essay text to identify problem areas and suggest feedback approaches. The learner data comes from a Qualifications and Curriculum Authority document on assessing EAL learners (2000: 35–6). The problem areas we identify are likely to occur across subject areas, so the feedback approaches suggested here can be adapted.

Input for History essay

Setting: The class has been studying the rise of Hitler and the Nazi Party in Germany for which the assignment is an essay with the title 'The five steps leading to World War 2'. In the lesson, to prepare for the writing, the teacher's input was recapping previous lessons and asking learners to read extracts from the textbook and respond to oral questions. The teacher then summarized responses on the board, setting out the five steps to war, along with key words and brief notes: in other words, her expectations.

Yurek is from Poland, where he has had continuous schooling before arriving in the UK, five months prior to writing this essay. His English is at PiE level C (Developing competence, Becoming a confident user). The teacher prepared differentiated tasks for the EAL learners in the class that consisted of a key word list (some to be looked up in class, some at home), a photocopy of two pages of text to read and highlight key words associated with each step in a different colour. Some words were broken down into parts to show the prefix and help the pronunciation of syllables e.g. *re-mil-i-tar-i-za-tion*.

The essay 'The five steps leading to World War 2'

After class, the essay was hand written unaided. This is a typewritten version of the original, where some words were crossed out. As you read the first paragraph in the text box below, think about your immediate response to the work.

> *Five steps to war is the one of Adolf Hitler's plan to win with all the world and he want be a king of all the world. The first step is about army. Adolf Hitler when he want fight with another countries he must be has a very good army. Adolf Hitler tell for people German people very good things, he give a German people lot of money also he tell he give for Germany power and he broke the Treaty of Versailles.*

Now apply our three criteria for feedback: conceptual knowledge, control of subject literacy and advice for next steps. We set out comments in the next sections

Concept knowledge: History essay explaining causes

Ask yourself, *is he showing signs of having grasped the main points of the topic?* YES?/ NO?

We suggest that the text shows signs of a good grasp of the historical content and the expected organization pattern, though the explanation of the reason behind each step could be clearer.

Control of subject literacy

Ask yourself, *Is he writing as he speaks? Is he writing as a Historian?* GOOD? AVERAGE? POOR?

To support your answer to this question, we offer a marked up version of the text in the next text box to draw your attention to language features you might have noticed above when looking at content:

- his control of <u>general academic vocabulary: some puzzles underlined</u>,
- his control of appropriate **verb tense (all in bold)**: 19 are in the present tense, 4 are in the past,
- his control of the use of the article 'the', 'a', or 'Θ' (zero article) (problems are shaded).

Five steps to war

Five steps to war **is** the one of Adolf Hitler's plan to win with all the world and he **want** be a king of all the world. The first step **is** about army. Adolf Hitler when he **want fight** with another countries he **must be has** a very good army. Adolf Hitler **tell** for people German people very good things, he **give** a German people lot of money also he **tell he give** for Germany power and he **broke** the Treaty of Versailles.

Another step **is joined** Austrio-Hungary to Germany for strongest country and army and when he **joined** with Austrio-Hungary he **broken** the Treaty of Versailles, also another step **is** remitlerization Rhineland. Adolf Hitler **put** the soldiers in Rhineland.

The step 4 **is** about Czechoslovakia and Sudetenland. Adolf Hitler **want** Sudetenland because this place **is** very good for defense and an attack, and Germany **need** this because **he has** everyone the side North, West, East, but not side with Sudetenland. The last step **is** about Poland. The Treaty of Versailles **give** for Poland and German free city Danzig but Germany **want** only this city, and Poland **don't want give** this city for Germany.

Qualifications and Curriculum Authority (2000:36)

What is your impression? He has learned the key specialist words (almost). His work has structural organization and a basic logical progression of ideas, suggesting that he has made good use of the scaffolding provided by the History teacher. He is not writing as he speaks. This essay is a good example of *an emerging ability to write at length*.

For learners needing more support, a writing frame adapted from Chapter 3 Teaching Resources (page 94) or Chapter 4 (page 131) could be used.

In some places Yurek appears to have memorized key topic phrases. But overall his representation of Hitler's aims and opinions is simplistic, lacking evidence of different views on the events and his own interpretations.

The emerging subject literacy we see here is patchy, by which we mean that if the reader tries hard enough, most of the reasons for the five steps can be identified despite *limited general academic vocabulary* and *inaccurate use of verb tense and the article*. Yurek's control of *the specialized register* is restricted by his use of *everyday words*. He manages well with these in everyday life, but they limit his ability to demonstrate his knowledge in this written essay. The *emerging general academic language resources* need support to develop.

From these comments, the next steps advised are

- expansion of general academic vocabulary,
- support for use of the appropriate tenses and
- focus on the use of the article.

What feedback on the essay can we offer that is relevant to other subject areas?

Here is a mix of six *collaborative and individual feedback* activities for adaptation that focus on the areas identified above, i.e. the development of general academic vocabulary, awareness of tense and guidance on the use of the article.

For this set of examples, let's suppose that the teacher has prepared the ground for a choice of feedback by diagnostic marking all of the scripts to identify some common areas where improvement is needed in learners' work.

(1) Two stars and a wish

This model of feedback, adapted from Jones and Wiliam (2008), encourages learners to undertake shared reading of an anonymous learner's writing. The aim is to identify *two strengths (stars)* and *one area for improvement (a wish)* when matching the script against a template or an agreed set of criteria e.g. the structure of the explanation, or feedback on presentations.

This activity can be set up in different configurations

- *as teacher to individual or groups;*
- *as groups to groups in plenary;*
- *as groups working with another group or with individuals within a group.*

Start by discussing the concept of *two stars and a wish* and model the task by working in plenary on one sample. Enlist the help of the class to find *two stars and a wish* to complete Table 6.5.

Table 6.5 Criteria for Two Stars (Strengths) and a Wish (An Area for Improvement)

Use of general academic vocabulary	2 stars………… The wish…….
Awareness of tense	2 stars………… The wish…….
Use of the article	2 stars………… The wish……….

Learner group task: Using a similar text of their own, the groups then each work on one of the criteria and explain reasons for their feedback in plenary, using the whiteboard or slides.

For a good example of this feedback activity look at the guidelines for developing group evaluations of performance in PE lessons (Department of Education and Skills, 2002: 14). Examples of this kind of feedback in PE obviously focus more on style of movement, but language is still required.

Check out the 'Access and Engagement' document for your own subject area (see Teaching Resources Chapter 2, page 59). This feedback will identify target areas for learners to work on.

(2) Find and Fix feedback

The scripts/calculations are marked using a *Feedback codes* sheet to identify the language problem for the learner to fix (see Teaching Resources this chapter, page 198). For example, the teacher might use codes such as follow to sort out problems with *tense (T)*, *article (Art)*, *wrong word (WW)* or *register (Reg)*. The learner then fixes the problem following one of the routes set out below:

Learner tasks: (Some use different modes of delivery depending on pedagogic aim).

- Individual (calculations/scripts/presentations): learner invited to sort out problems with reference to own knowledge/guidance sheets/register continuums or word banks on the wall.
- Groups: teacher marks a few scripts and gives them to groups to improve. They share ideas of what is right with each other and return to teacher for checking.
- Each group reads one script/calculation and uses the *Feedback codes sheet*. They should underline and code problems with two or three specified language items in the learner text, e.g. *WW*, *T* and *Art*. Give to another group to fix. Hand in to teacher to check.
- Teacher gives specific words from test answers that do not fit the register (Reg). Get the learners to find them and place in the appropriate position on a *register continuum* on the wall.

(3) Group shaping to make the best text

- Teachers or groups negotiate three criteria to create *a feedback form* for peers to use in groups.

    Learner task: In groups, learners 'share read' each other's texts (no longer than 50 words) and choose one to fix up to create the best version.

⭐ These various forms of feedback that require an active response provide a safe forum for the individual learner to develop a sense that language plays a worthwhile role in demonstrating learning.

(4) Brainstorm to expand vocabulary

Brainstorming is a useful way of sharing resources to expand vocabulary range. It is particularly appropriate to support the development of *general academic vocabulary* that makes up around 10% of a school text (see Chapter 4, page 110).

This activity also offers learners more opportunities to practise using the new language. These are reformulations that are similar to the ones for learning how to use subject-specific words that we saw in Chapter 4 (pages 111–12). But this time the focus is *on their own work to check their choice words to express their meaning*: a goal similar to the grammar focus of the *Sentence Rewrite task* presented in this chapter (pages 185–6).

It works best modelled in plenary for groups. Adapt the examples below for your own subject areas.

Two possibilities

(a) *Focus on verbs*: the example in Table 6.6 aims to encourage learners such as Yurek to replace the *general purpose verbs* of the kind EAL learners use for survival (*put, do, have, make, go*) with verbs with more explicit meanings to express *concepts such as plans, intentions, aims, claims* and *control*.

Table 6.6 Expand the Range of Yurek's *Everyday Verbs* to *Verbs with More Explicit Meaning*

General purpose verb	Verb with more explicit meaning
is (is the one, is about)	means, refers to, relates to, involves, concerns
want	aimed, intended, planned, Wanted to gain control of
must has	needed ..., planned to expand ..., aimed to increase and improve .... It was necessary to have
tell	promised
put	sent, set up, stationed,
has everyone the side	controlled the North, West and East
give	gave access to Danzig
don't want give	did not want to give up/lose their right of access

⭐ These new possibilities can be recorded by an individual learner or added to a word bank on the wall.

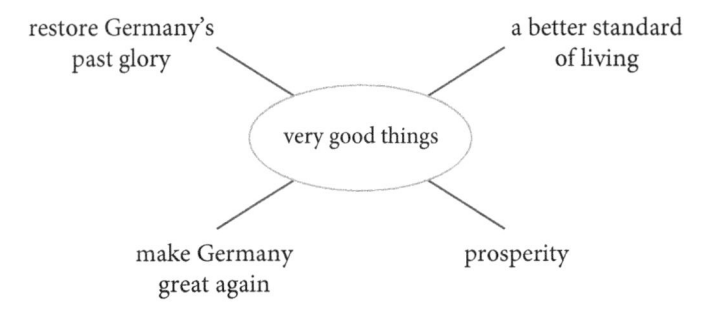

```
        restore Germany's                      a better standard
           past glory                              of living
                           ╲                  ╱
                            ( very good things )
                           ╱                  ╲
         make Germany                           prosperity
          great again
```

Figure 6.4 Brainstorming spidergram to expand vocabulary of noun phrases.

(b) *Focus on noun phrases*: the groups can brainstorm more precise phrases and words in a Spidergram. The example we have below is to replace the vague language Yurek uses, such as 'very good things' (Figure 6.4).

Another example would be to sort out Yurek's phrase 'plan to win with all the world', which the reader takes to mean 'plan to rule the world' or 'plan for world power'.

(5) Choose a tense

Learners find tenses in English difficult to get right, even if they are high-level learners. The choice depends on the perspective of the speaker or writer. Many textbooks use the present tense to set out generally accepted truths. Perhaps that is why Yurek is comfortable with the present tense. When he came to the UK, he was able to answer questions in the present tense about himself, where he lives, where he is from, his family, his likes and dislikes (Qualifications and Curriculum Authority 2000: 34).

In his History essay Yurek relies mainly on the present tense (*19 cases*). But there are signs of other verb forms emerging (*4 in the past tense*), which is what would be expected as History generally discusses events and ways of life that took place in the past.

What is the most common tense you use in your own subject area? Check a few websites and texts to confirm your hunch.

The most helpful way to approach choice of tense is to offer a *Tenses timeline chart*, setting out time reference and verb form. We have included one in the Teaching

Resources for this chapter (page 199). Or you could look at other representations such as these:

- http://tonyeosenglish.weebly.com/verb-tense-timelines.html
- Learn verb tenses with diagrams https://www.youtube.com/watch?v=A9xVaDaOUg8
- British Council/BBC https://www.teachingenglish.org.uk/article/timelines

Feedback for the learner on tenses fits neatly into the *Find and fix task (for individuals or groups)* to check.

- Model by asking the learners to notice the tense at the start and the end of a text to see if they match up. This is good *noticing practice*. You want to avoid starting in the present and ending in the past, unless you are referring to a specific event in the past. Refer to the *Tenses timeline chart* for verification.
- Set up the *Find and Fix* task by marking yourself or having groups mark, as appropriate.

   Learner task: Sort out the problems indicated, with reference to the *Tenses Timeline Chart*.

(6) Guidance for the use of articles

This is another area of challenge for learners of English. The EAL learner will have had instruction in this area, but still be hesitant with whether to use 'a', 'the' or 'nothing'. If you go back to Yurek's essay you will see that there are problems with his choice throughout, but he writes 'broke the Treaty of Versailles' with no problem. *This is probably a learned phrase, heard and read many times in the classroom.*

We will follow the most common approach to dealing with this problem: present some rules and then give a gap-fill task with a blank in front of each noun phrase for the learners to complete. The general gist of the rules is represented visually in Figure 6.5 using the word 'HOUSE' to demonstrate how we use the article differently according to which or what house or houses we are referring to.

The graphic shows that the *same word 'house' can belong to one of three groups, A, B or C, according to what it refers to.*

- *Group A* – Use 'zero article/nothing' when you are referring to *a general group or plural* – 'HOUSES' – all the x's in the circle.
- *Group B* – Use 'a' when the identity of the noun makes *general reference to a single 'house' in the whole group of houses.*
- *Group C* – Use 'the' when *the identity of the 'house' is known or has been specified*: 'The house I live in.'

Teacher: Find a subject text to use for gap-fill, and set up gaps in front of every noun phrase.

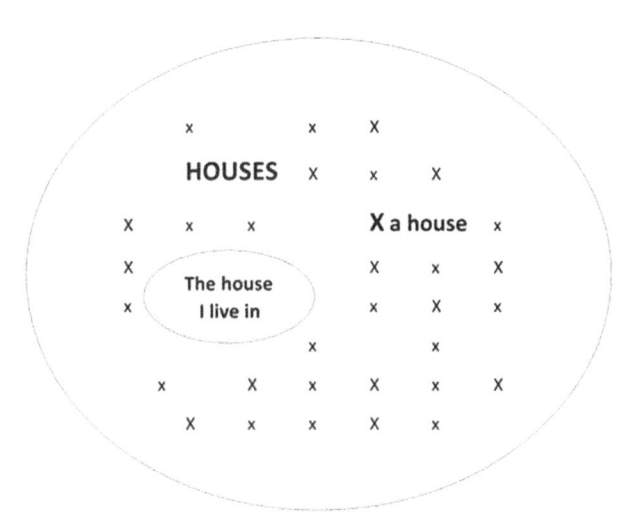

Figure 6.5 Graphic representation of the rules for the use of the article (see Williams, 2006).

Learner task: Complete gaps in front of nouns. Justify your choice by referring to one of the rules above. Check with the original text.

This feedback task can be done *individually or in groups*. In groups, the learners have to convince each other that *they are right*.

Be prepared for disagreement where both choices are *grammatically correct*. A person might make different choices depending on point of view or style choice.

Drawing together features of *useful feedback* to support EAL learners

Feedback as a response to learner activity is a kind of assessment for learning that occurs *at each stage of the lesson. The more opportunities for active participation the learners have, the more evidence of the emerging subject literacy we see.* In this chapter we have seen that the kinds of feedback teachers give in response will have their own pedagogic purpose. Some feedback starts and ends with *the teacher*; other feedback starts with the teacher who models for learners so that they can work in *collaborative groups* to give feedback to peers, and/or as *individuals to monitor their own work*. Learner learning is an important aim: to encourage learners to reflect on how they learn.

The teacher's priority is to focus on both the *content* and the *language features*, so the *language aware* approach to feedback uses the three criteria presented in this chapter:

- Concept knowledge
- Control of subject literacy
- Steps for improvement

What we have seen in the data discussed in this chapter is that the learner may well know the information, but the emerging subject literacy skills might mean it is organized or presented in ways that do not match the subject literacy expectations. The teacher may have the impression that the learners' mastery of topic knowledge is variable because, although they appear to have mastered some phrases, they have not managed to build them into appropriate sentences.

Evidence of this problem occurs in

- content that is unexpected – an interpretation that suggests misunderstanding;
- register/style choice;
- the word choice or grammatical construction.

With this evidence the teacher is in an informed position to respond with a variety of *language aware* strategies to maintain learner engagement and meet her pedagogic aims. As we saw in Chapters 4 and 5, support for learners' conceptual understanding can be provided by images and creative interpretation, with reformulations, paraphrasing to gloss meaning and so on.

The more active feedback the learners can receive, the more opportunities for practice there are to expand these aspects of subject literacies. A *high challenge high support* classroom will have *self-aware learners* who are not shy about making requests for clarification. Learners will be accustomed to making use of available support to find something familiar as *a hook* to *the new*. They will have the habit of reformulating what the teacher or text has said to check their understanding. More practice also means the learners are encouraged to reflect on their own skills as learners, and gradually embark on the road to becoming independent learners.

These *language aware strategies* are summarized in a portfolio of feedback in the Teaching Resources at the end of this chapter (page 197).

Using the kind of EAL learner data examined in this chapter allows us to monitor progress and code the type of difficulty to some extent. This is significant to planning progression systematically, which is the focus of the last chapter.

Teaching resources

The *language aware* feedback portfolio

This portfolio is best supported by resource bank of relevant images and simple sentences to gloss meaning. The class can construct their own for future learners.

- Immediate *in the moment*: teacher to individual or plenary to shape learner responses
  - drawing attention to *Register Continuums* on the wall for register/style (Sample A, page 175),
  - *reformulating grammar* to support meaning (Sample B, page 175),
  - clarifying understanding with *exploratory talk or drawing/googling an image* (this chapter, page 175 or Chapter 4, pages 102, 103, 108, 113–14, 119–21),
  - monitoring how group discussion operates to **encourage productive talk for task completion** (Chapter 4, page 132 and Chapter 5, pages 146–9).
- Delayed: teacher to individual or groups, groups to groups in plenary, or groups working with another group, or with individuals within a group:
  - **Sentence rewrite task:** rewrite deconstructed phrases with word problem highlighted (this chapter, pages 185, or rewrite multi-clause sentences Chapter 3, pages 72, 86),
  - **Model the structure of the explanation:** make own template or deconstruct from subject text (this chapter, page 184),
  - **Deconstruct** teacher's explanation (or other model) (this chapter, page 180),
  - **Two stars and a wish**: template (this chapter, page 190),
  - **Find and Fix:** use **Feedback codes sheet** (this chapter, page 198, illustrated page 182); refer to the **Tenses timeline chart** (this chapter, page 199), and **Guidance for use of articles**, illustrated in this chapter, page 194.
  - **Group shaping to make the best text:** manageable with six groups in the class.
  - **Expand vocabulary**
    - *Everyday versus Specialist* (this chapter, page 192)
    - *True/ false match definitions* (this chapter, page 184)
    - *Which words mean the same?* (this chapter, page 185)
    - *Brainstorm*: verb table and Spidergram for noun phrases (this chapter page 192 and illustrated Chapter 2, page 51)
- Self-assessment guidance for monitoring and editing.
- Set up a set of **criteria for the learner to check their own work before handing in** (this chapter, page 185).

Feedback codes for writing guidance (Make a parallel one for calculations?)

Overall clarity of text purpose and organization

Symbols	Meaning
⇐	These ideas/ paragraphs need a clearer link.
//	New paragraph needed.
?_____	Not clear: choose another word or way of expressing this idea.

Words and grammar

Symbol	Meaning	Example
Reg	Register/style	The imagery all adds up to being frightening.
V	Vague	In this choice are a lot of good things.
WW	Wrong word – check meaning:	Subordinators indicate casual relations between ideas.
WC	Word class	USA can defense Berlin.
S/P	Singular/plural agreement	The use of pesticides are controversial.
Art	Article problem: 'the'/'a'/'Ø'	A sun radiates energy.
∧	Something is missing	The teams consists ∧ 11 players.
T	Tense	Supermarkets charged the new prices tomorrow.
Vb	Verb form	The heat carry on through.
WO	Word order	Picasso painted in his life many pictures.
X	Not needed	Although the arm is extended, but it is not straight.
P	Punctuation	The UN could only work if the Security Council members agreed, also the Security Council could ….
Sp	Spelling	misslies on Cuba
Rep	Repetition	When heat gives energy to particles, particles vibrate.
NS	Not a sentence	Vibrating and bumping into each other.

Adapted from Hedge (1988/2005)

The English tenses timeline chart

This timeline sets out the English tenses to show how they locate the verb meaning in the past, present and future. Verbs are highlighted in **bold**. There are some empty boxes in the chart because some verb forms are not used.

Simple active	Simple passive	TIMELINE	Progressive/ continuous active	Progressive/ continuous passive
		PAST TIME		
They **had** already **decided** when I arrived	It **had** already **been decided** when I arrived	PAST PERFECT	They **had been discussing** for 3 hours when the result was announced	
The team **trained** hard last week	The team **was trained** by a new coach	PAST	The team **was training** when I saw them	The team **was being trained** when I saw them
He **has designed** computers for many years	The computers **have been manufactured** in China for the last 10 years	PRESENT PERFECT	The company **has been marketing** computers for 6 months	The users **have been supported** for the last 3 years
Five times five **equals** twenty-five	Volcanoes **are formed** by earth movements	PRESENT	The particles **are vibrating**	The result **is being recorded**
		FUTURE INTENTION	They **are going to launch** the new iPhone tomorrow	The new iPhone **is going to be launched** tomorrow
The new term **will start** next week	The timetable **will be published** tomorrow	FUTURE SIMPLE	I **will be working** tomorrow	
He **will have completed** 30 laps by the end of the race		FUTURE PERFECT	He **will have been studying** for 3,000,000 hours by the age of 16	
		FUTURE TIME		

7

How Can I Monitor Emerging Subject Literacy and Plan Progression?

Chapter Outline

Starting points: Situating the EAL learner in the trajectory towards Upper Secondary-level study	202
Monitoring a newcomer to your class (PiE levels A–E)	203
Monitoring learners working at low level (PiE B): Wu, Sophia and Jamila	205
What are the areas to work on to reach level C?	206
Monitoring learners working at mid-level (PiE C) Alena and Yusra	208
What are the areas to work on to reach level D?	209
Monitoring learners working at upper level (PiE D) Yurek	210
What are the areas to work on to reach level E?	211
Monitoring and supporting learners working at high level (PiE E) Sabih	213
Four steps in planning progression	218
Teaching resources for further study of language	222

- *How can I monitor the aspects of subject literacy that the EAL learner is working with?*
- *What trajectory is the bilingual learner in my class likely to take in developing literacy in my subject?*
- *How does that trajectory guide my practice in monitoring progress and planning ahead?*

Starting points: Situating the EAL learner in the trajectory towards Upper Secondary-level study

You can probably write this chapter yourself! Through the chapters we have set out a metalanguage for talking about key aspects of subject literacies and offered strategies to engage and support the EAL learner to use their available communication resources to construct knowledge. The EAL learner data analysed in previous chapters has set out examples of those emerging subject literacies. To close the book we move from monitoring these literacies in single tasks (Chapter 6) to monitoring emerging skills in subject literacy for planning progression.

To do this we place the EAL learner at the centre of the subject literacy trajectory that links Primary with Upper Secondary study. As we emphasized in Chapters 1 and 2, at Lower Secondary level it is important to acknowledge and build on what has been covered at Primary school in order to make progress towards what learners need to be able to do at exam level. Whether the EAL learner in your class is already familiar with the UK system or is new to it, significant adaptation is involved as new skills for learning emerge.

We build on the approach set out in Chapter 5 to establish a *language aware* classroom environment that can support short-term targets such as a group discussion, a task or a test. Here, we use similar parameters to set up long-term goals to plan progression.

The principles of syllabus design tell us to select and sequence content (Breen 2001). Based on the discussion of key aspects of subject literacy in previous chapters, this is what we select for *content* in our subject literacy progression plan.

- Be aware of differences in language register choices for everyday and classroom purposes
- Identify a communication purpose in an explanation, along with key ideas
- Deconstruct and construct the organization/format/notation used
- Be aware of how to gather information in order to organize, link and express ideas in complex ways in an extended piece of work
- Manage everyday, general academic and subject-specific vocabulary flexibly
- Deconstruct and construct *complex sentences* to carry the meanings

To sequence the level of challenge in the subject literacy skills we use a combination of the PiE descriptors set out in EAL proficiency tables (Chapter 2, pages 42–3) and *cognitive principles for sequencing language tasks* adapted from Skehan (1996: 23). They are similar to the ones we identified in Chapter 4 in discussion of text difficulty, i.e.

- Familiarity of material: abstract versus concrete
- Reasoning operations required

- Degree of structuring required
- Range of vocabulary
- Grammatical complexity

From these starting points, we exemplify the skill trajectory for managing control of subject literacy to express conceptual understanding by drawing together the data of emerging subject literacy skills we have seen through the book. We start with a newcomer to your class who might be working at any PiE level, then set out subject literacy skill profiles for EAL learners working at low (B), mid (C) and upper (D) levels of PiE. We complete this overview of progression by adding an EAL learner working at high level. Sabih, working at PiE level E (Fluent), has a language competence that is equivalent to a learner with English as a first language. He can manage without EAL specialist support. Nonetheless, he will benefit from subject literacy guidelines such as you might offer home learners.

Let's look at the emerging subject literacy of our EAL learners working at these different stages to illustrate the trajectory they are on.

Monitoring a newcomer to your class (PiE levels A–E)

This newcomer represents any EAL learner who is new to your class, irrespective of what level of PiE he or she is working at. As we saw in Chapter 2 (pages 32–3), initial interviews and assessments on arrival in the school will provide a profile of the language resources and funds of knowledge the learner brings. Familiarizing yourself with this profile of language, culture and education gives you a starting point for planning inclusive lessons in terms of

a) using your intercultural curiosity to find a trigger to make the content relevant and
b) preparing differential support to match the PiE level the learner is working at, using resources in all modes.

Even at early stages of developing English, learners have a considerable amount of passive vocabulary and may understand words without necessarily being able to say, read or write them. They may show signs of literacy awareness such as *an interest in visual representations, drawing, print, awareness of the English alphabet* and *emergent reading and writing* (MacGahern and Boaten 2000: 116).

> Unsurprisingly, the learner will get tired. It is hard work operating in a new language. Patience is required.

Another EAL learner might act as a translator and write down the vocabulary in other languages. If the learner is literate in her mother tongue, she can use a bilingual dictionary. Learners not literate in their mother tongue can copy from a grid. In all cases drawing and annotation are emphasized as important aspects of language development (ibid: 118).

As mentioned in Chapter 2, a newcomer working at lower PiE levels might be in your classroom as an observer for perhaps one lesson per week for a while. But at higher levels, a learner such as Zhou, who we met in Chapter 5 in a Biology class, should become familiar with the routines and discourses of the class to start active participation relatively quickly.

Assessed as able to work at PiE level B, Zhou is becoming familiar with classroom processes as he is listening in plenary to the teacher's question: 'How do we classify something as living?' To support his participation, Zhou has visuals (*circles, a bird*) and language labels available, plus gesture and supplementary language on the board to help conceptualize the categories.

There are two steps to the outcome for Zhou: (1) identify what a living thing does and (2) express this in a sentence with basic causality: because + evidence, e.g. 'It is living because ….' Again, the support comes from language options modelled for Zhou in a table. As MacGahern and Boaten (2000: 119) point out, 'Such tables not only offer language but also the pattern of how the parts of the sentence fit together.' This is also important for the skills of reading, noticing word order, and sound and letter patterns in spelling (2000).

> Tables modelling language options can be simple or complex and made for any subject. Chapter 3 Teaching Resources (pages 94–6) show options for describing, presenting procedures, etc.

This Biology lesson illustrates how the reasoning operations become more complex through the lesson as the task of *description* shifts to naming *defining characteristics* in a classification. Nonetheless, the focus is still on *What do they do? (verbs)* rather than *concepts (nouns)*. If you think back to the Magnets lesson in Chapter 1, we saw that the teacher starts with verbs ('*Magnets stick/attract*') before moving on to a noun phrase, '*Magnetic Attraction*'.

We also noted that it is important to support Zhou listening to ideas about 'what all living things do' in the small group discussion by guiding emerging perceptions about procedures and expectations. A focus on productive talk and outcomes is part of an inclusive ethos in the class for group work. And collaborative work on presentations will help to answer the newcomer's question, 'How can I learn from my peers?'

Until the learner is familiar with the patterns of language at different stages of the lesson, it is important for the teacher to be aware of how to signal them. The learner might be distracted if the thread of the lesson is broken when the teacher turns away to deal with something else in a different register. Remember to signal your return to the initial role.

Do you have the habit of using emphasis at the start of a sentence to signal an important point is coming? Or when you want to focus attention on something? You might use *Why/where/what* at the front of a sentence, e.g.

- 'What I want to tell you about this is ….'
- 'Why we are looking at this is ….'
- 'Where you can easily go wrong with this calculation/task is ….'

Do you recognize this pattern in your own classroom discourse? Make sure the EAL learners are with you when you use this special focus – perhaps gesture or mime – to signal your meaning until they are used to it.

And finally, be aware that the newcomer may consider that what counts as *achievement or success* is to score 100%.

The learner may be determined to get everything right in Science – even if this means imitating what others are doing rather than working out a problem (Edmunds 2000: 135). It may be confusing for the learner to be asked to show workings in Maths, or to describe mistakes and rethinking in Design and Technology. Adjustment of the view of success criteria can be supported by consistent valuing of what the EAL learner brings, and giving constructive feedback on any contribution they make.

Try to find an appropriate level of intercultural awareness and avoid making assumptions. There is more than one way of doing things. It helps to take the view that the other way is not *wrong*. It is *different*.

In the following sections, we set out profiles of EAL learners working at specific PiE levels, and then suggest what aspects of subject literacy they might focus on to progress towards the next stage.

Monitoring learners working at low level (PiE B): Wu, Sophia and Jamila

We met Wu in Chapter 4, working at PiE level B. This means he is at the stage of Early Acquisition/Becoming familiar with English (Chapter 2, page 42), where everyday communication is emerging. His level of understanding means that he can follow instructions and manage some key subject words and phrases. He will have basic knowledge of the language, but we saw his uncertainty in how to apply it in Chapter 4 (pages 113–15), where, even though his question came out as 'What mean "Calculate the change received"?' he had the confidence to ask it. He has completed six years of education in China, so will be familiar with mathematical processes. He has a communication purpose: to ask a question. At the end of the interaction he finds an answer when he recognizes the verb 'subtract'.

Despite working at a low PiE level, Wu may well enjoy the Maths, and other practical subjects like Design &Technology, P.E. and Science, where the practical nature of the activity supports meaning of language from context. The tricky subject might be History because of the text base, unless it is taught in an active way with plenty of investigation, diagrams with timelines, a trip and exploratory talk. Some teachers use a visual tool like Voki (see Chapter 2 Teaching Resources, page 60).

Sophia and Jamila also appeared in Chapter 4, expanding their vocabulary in a confident way by matching general academic words with everyday words to describe a character in the context of a story. They are seen to be working at PiE level B because Sophia's reading of a new word is hesitant, confusing the consonant clusters, saying 'inspringing' instead of 'inspiring' (Chapter 4, page 106). On the next word, when Jamila answers the teacher's question, 'If you were a calculating person, what would you do?' she makes several attempts to find the right words to start:

> You'll be like, you'll be, you'll do, you'll be like able to do anything and sharp. You'll be sharp like clever.
>
> (NALDIC 2009: Transcript 300509)

This opportunity for oral rehearsal allows her to find the right start for her answer. She is using the resources she has available, so she uses a mix of everyday language and informal register ('like') to suit her communication purpose.

What are the areas to work on to reach level C?

To help learners working at PiE level B to build their level to C, 'Becoming a confident user of English', they need as much practice as they can get. Since he has learned English as a Foreign Language in China, Wu might well know more metalanguage for word meanings and sentence structures in English than you do! Some of you may have come across this phenomenon in the course of learning other languages. Perhaps you are multilingual yourself, or you teach classics or modern languages, or have encountered the metalanguage at school when learning a classical or modern language. As you know, it's still a different matter putting language knowledge into practice.

It is important to offer as many opportunities as possible to practise the basic vocabulary and sentence structure so that a learner can build on that knowledge to extend the everyday vocabulary and can start to cope with complex language. The reader might find it helpful to refer back to Chapter 1 (pages 29–30), where we set out the formal language knowledge of basic sentence structure expected to develop at Primary level. As the language that learners encounter gradually becomes more complex, they can start to notice and use what are described as 'basic subordinators' in writing development (Perera 1984). For example,

- *'that'*, *'who'* – to clarify a noun phrase
- *'because'*, *'as'*, *'so'* – to show reason or consequence/result
- *'as … as'* – to make a simple comparison
- *'if'*, *'when'*– to show condition and time

(See examples with full sentences in Chapter 3 Teaching Resources, pages 94–6.)

To master these patterns, learners will all benefit from as much planned oral practice as possible, along with contextualized tasks to link existing word meanings with new ones. These could be in areas such as

- Word lists before class, to tick off as they are heard in class and gap-fill sentences on activity sheets for consolidation. This will provide a record of the main points and language of the lesson.
- Word banks on the wall (Deconstructing words in word families).
- Some tasks can focus on spelling to help with pronunciation, and focus on punctuation to help with sentence formation.
- Reading tasks can ask the learner to identify key words in the text, then match their meanings with everyday ones to check their meanings. Finally they can be used in a sentence.

In this way, learners can become comfortable in your subject as they name images, read words and practise writing sentences with subject-related language.

Your support in the classroom will ideally be complemented by work with an EAL specialist (up to five hours a week per learner working at this level).

Monitoring learners working at mid-level (PiE C) Alena and Yusra

These learners are 'Developing competence/Becoming confident users of English'. When we met Yusra in Chapter 5 her needs were included in our design of an enquiry task in subject English (pages 119–22). When we met Alena in Chapter 6, we were eavesdropping on her trying out her new language meanings that gave us a lot of information about her subject literacy skills (page 175). Her growing confidence in English is shown in the way she is actively expanding her language knowledge and participating with increasing independence (Qualifications and Curriculum Authority 2000: 38). She can manage oral expression, but there are significant inaccuracies in her use of grammar and word choice. She is coping, but literacy support is still required to engage with a text and to write. Useful strategies are focusing on titles, headings and topic sentences, as suggested in Chapter 4 to support learners reading the text for the project on diet (pages 127–31).

The cognitive challenge for Alena in Year 10 is the level of reasoning operations required: the two questions are 'Why was Paré important? What effect did Paré's ideas have?' Both questions focus on *facts (nouns), not deeds (verbs)*.

The transcript shows that she is starting to follow abstract concepts as she remembers most of the content words to report the facts about what Paré did (pages 175–6). But she is struggling to find the language structure to support her words. Alena is sometimes hesitant because she wants to be accurate. At the end of the extract she is searching for how to express the complex relationship between the facts she knows.

In the same source document there is evidence of her ability to produce, with the support of a writing frame and a fair amount of discussion, a very creditable piece on a story by H. G. Wells (Qualifications and Curriculum Authority 2000: 40). Although she has understood the abstract ideas set out in the writing frame, her response is expressed mostly in informal concrete language, e.g. 'the mystery is sort of solved'. At the same time there is evidence that she has retained some of the academic and literary register she will have heard in class; e.g. she uses the word 'figure' that the teacher will have used to refer to a character, and the phrase 'awoke in daylight' for 'woke in the morning'.

The combination of evidence from oral and written language suggests her emerging subject literacy is characterized by a conceptual understanding, expressed in everyday words, rather than the general academic or subject-specific ones, and at the same time lacks the grammar to support them.

What are the areas to work on to reach level D?

Alena is ready to receive abstract ideas, so now she needs to start expressing them. For example, talk about phenomenon such as the formation of volcanoes, calculation of squares and cubes (Chapter 3, pages 73, 78). To this end, Alena would benefit from work on her control of grammar to support her vocabulary. Work on logical links between pieces of information would also help her to progress. Her oral confidence could be boosted by participating in group work, to listen, as much as to contribute. She would hear models of how other learners talk fluently about their knowledge.

To meet this general aim, we refer the reader to tasks from previous chapters, as follows:

- *Expanding range of content words* could be supported by developing awareness of register, to notice how words are used by the teacher in class, by the learners in groups, and by writers in texts. Set up continuums on the wall for *informal/formal* and *concrete/abstract* registers to use during the lesson to model where words might go. Alternatively, the teacher and/or learners can adapt for specific topics the ones set out in Chapter 1 Teaching Resources (pages 27–8). Equally, encourage learners to have their own register continuums in the back of notebooks.
- *Developing control of the language to support her meaning* could be supported by giving group tasks with *synonymous phrases* (Chapter 4, pages 111–12). When they have sorted them to match the meanings, they can build them into sentences, following the models in Chapter 2 (pages 51–3) or in Chapter 3 Teaching Resources (pages 94–6).
- Alternatively the teacher can offer *model sentence starters to frame the communication purpose*, as follows in Table 7.1.

Table 7.1 Model Sentence Starters for Communication Purpose

Communication purpose	Frame for communication purpose	Learner completion
Reason	*Paré was important because ....*	
Result/effect	*Paré's ideas had an effect on ....*	

- *Awareness of how to link pieces of information logically* to match the communication purpose can be supported at text level by using the paragraph ordering task offered to model text organization in Chapter 3 (page 87). Or at sentence level she can work on using multi-clause sentences to express connections in her conceptual knowledge (Perera 1984). For example, she might use initial subordinate clauses showing *reason, time, concession*, etc., starting with *advanced subordinators*, such as *which, where, although, after, until, unless* (Cameron 2003: 31). Examples are modelled in Table 7.2, with initial subordinator shaded.

Table 7.2 Models for Advanced Subordinators

Initial subordinate clause	Main clause
When Paré was alive his ideas were not accepted,	but after his death, they became influential.
Although Paré's ideas were not accepted during his lifetime,	they became important after his death.

The teacher can prepare a learner task with a table like this where the subordinators are deleted. The learner task is to complete (see further models in Chapter 3 Teaching Resources, pages 94–6, and this chapter, page 207).

⭐ This kind of support helps all learners to consolidate their awareness of the communication purpose inherent in a lesson presentation, in activities during a lesson, in language used and in presentations or writing to be done.

⭐ Your support in the subject classroom will ideally be complemented by an EAL specialist offering one-off time-limited work on a specific subject literacy goal.

Monitoring learners working at upper level (PiE D) Yurek

Working at this level, Yurek, who we met in Chapter 6 (pages 187–90), understands the communication purpose of most social and learning contexts, engaging successfully in learning activities.

Yurek's extended writing on *5 Steps to War* showed he had clearly grasped the main ideas. The recognizable shape of the text as a chronological Historical account reflects a sense of a communication purpose. This can be compared with the test answers we looked at in Chapter 6 (pages 180–2), where there was little sense that the learners were writing a scientific explanation for a reader.

However, Yurek's text includes little *causality* or *interpretation as to the reason for the actions*. As we would expect from a learner working at PiE level D, his written English may lack complexity, contain grammatical errors and show varied success in word choice. He has most of the specialist words and phrases required, including a few memorized set phrases used by the teacher. But the range of general academic vocabulary shows limits. As noted in the assessment report of the Qualifications and Curriculum Authority (2000: 34), this partially explains why, although Yurek can read and understand a variety of texts, complex texts such as History still present challenges. His confidence is reflected in the fact that his oral English is fluent, though it may lack complexity and contain occasional errors.

What are the areas to work on to reach level E?

Yurek is already on the way to working at level E as we can see from an example of his work later in the year, discussed in this section below. As he is a relative newcomer to the school, he benefits from some one-off diagnostic support sessions to deconstruct meaning in complex texts, understand the tense system and expand his general academic vocabulary to include abstract concepts. Having received specific support to work on how to use 'signpost' words to indicate to the reader how the text is organized, how to link ideas and how to include detail, his work shows greater mastery of how to present different views on events with his own interpretations.

At this stage of the year, the History teacher has set a more complex topic that deals with *abstract ideas, i.e. choices, rather than a series of actions*. In this text of Yurek's the topic sentence, signposting phrases and links showing reasons are shaded to identify them.

Kennedy's choices

I think the best choice for President Kennedy will be Blockade.

In this choice are a lot of good things. USA can show for USSR it is serious, but it is not big reason for start war.

(Topic sentence)

(Signposting organisation)

> [Reference and evaluation] [Signpost opposing view]
> *That choice is good because* Khrushchev have to decide what do in future. *This decision will be very hard because* USSR doesn't have that big army ~~haus~~ like USA and if Khrushchev don't think anything USA can start another options. Blockade has one reason against which is missiles on Cuba. There were still on, and USRR can use it. *Another small problem is* Soviet Union might ~~retaltre~~ retaliate by blockading by Berlin, but USA can defense Berlin because we have bigger army.
>
> [Reference and evaluation] [Signpost 2nd opposing view]
>
> (Qualifications and Curriculum Authority 2000: 36)

Starting with *a signpost statement* such as 'in this choice there are a lot of good things' has a similar effect to 'there are three types of volcano' (Chapter 3, page 69). It immediately tells the reader how the text is organized.

★▲★ The shift of focus from 'actions' to 'abstract ideas' requires a clear framework of signposts for the abstract ideas and helps us appreciate the need to *extend support focus from vocabulary and grammar to text structure.*

If Yurek is able to continue to develop his sense of communication purpose, his work will be presented as something more than just a collection of information, like a shopping list. Writing frames often set up a series of *signpost* words and phrases to support the learner on what to include. Using linkers for signposting shows that the learner is starting to write for the reader with the communication purpose in mind. This feature is included in Cameron's 2003 study of writing development in home and EAL learners. Taking 'level' to signify expected GCSE results, she found EAL learners working at 'high level' were more likely to use signposting than home learners working at 'low level'. She concludes that 'signposting' is not a natural skill. It is instructed.

To meet this general aim, we recommend Yurek to focus on tasks from previous chapters, as follows.

- *Developing the ability to present clearly organized texts* with signposts and linkers can be practised using tasks focusing on paragraphing. For example, set out a text as a series of topic sentences indicating one point per paragraph.

  Learner task: work out what linker to use. Make a choice from the linkers in the Chapter 4 Teaching Resources (pages 134–5). Ask questions like, *What is the communication purpose? What is the logical link? Is it time? Cause? Comparison?* etc.

- *Adding more detail to the nouns and verbs in the text* could be practised using models for preposition and adverb phrases (Chapter 3 Teaching Resources, pages 94–6). Particular focus needs to be given to prepositions in 'set phrases' (words that are always used together, like a formula).
- *Developing skills to work out meaning* in sentences from complex texts. We have two suggestions here:

    (i) Deconstruction as illustrated in Chapter 2 (page 51) and Chapter 3 (page 72). We take a sample from Yurek's reading text;
    'The Depression of 1929–32/**increased**/*the support for extremist parties in Germany*.'
    Learner task: find <u>the subject</u>, **the verb** and *the object*.

    (ii) Devise a 'word hunt' to identify key content words that convey main ideas (Chapter 3, pages 74, 79, 86). Check meanings in a monolingual dictionary to help with recognizing the difference between *everyday* and *specialist* meaning. The examples in the sentence above are 'increase' = grow in size/number, 'extremist' = not moderate. This will help *all* learners to develop their register awareness.

- Expanding vocabulary can be supported using tasks similar to the suggestions from Chapter 6 (pages 192–3). For example, *Brainstorm to expand vocabulary*. Particularly focus on finding *verbs with more specific meaning*. These could include modal verbs to express opinion. Yurek's ability to do this in the 'Choices' text above appears limited. He uses the modal verbs, 'will' and 'can' to *express future intention and ability* respectively, rather than anything related to *possibility* (*could, might*) or *obligation* (*ought, should*).
- Improving accuracy at sentence level will benefit from *Find and Fix* tasks from Chapter 6 (page 191), and the *Correction Codes* in Chapter 6 Teaching Resources (page 198). Focus on appropriate use of active and passive voice would be useful (Chapter 3, page 73 and Chapter 5, page 162).

Your subject support in the classroom will ideally be complemented by one-off time-limited specialist EAL support for a specific subject literacy goal.

Monitoring and supporting learners working at high level (PiE E) Sabih

Sabih, working at PiE level E, is a fluent user of English. He is a second generation resident from Pakistan, so he participates in Pakistani cultural practices and uses his heritage language, Urdu, or a mix of Urdu and English, with friends and family. At school, his oral English, reading and writing skills are competent in a variety of *every day* and *subject-specific* areas, so he can manage without specialist EAL support. His growing familiarity with academic uses of English is at the same level as fellow learners who are born and brought up monolingual in the UK. So for this learner, the support you include in your lesson is similar to what you would use for any home learner who is developing subject literacy skills on the trajectory to the Exam stage. We suggest that this primarily involves a focus on continued development of the sense of communication purpose. You might include *managing instruction words for tests and exam questions*, such as *discuss, explain* and so on.

As Cameron (2003) suggests, EAL learners working at high level appear to respond well to language guidance. So it would be useful to offer support for a more complex task such as interpretation of graphs and data commentary. This involves *expressing a degree of certainty, being able to interpret data critically* and *make judgements from evidence*.

Supporting areas of challenge for the high-level learner: Comparison and interpretation

In English the many different ways of expressing comparison and interpretation can be confusing for the EAL learner. Addressing this challenge is important because these structures may be relevant to the reasoning operations involved in appreciations of works of art, music or literature, or in explanations of processes, procedures and evaluating results.

To model these reasoning operations, in this section we will discuss language for talking about charts and graphs. Charts and graphs are key visuals that carry significant information, as we saw in Chapters 3 and 4, where the *cross section of the volcano*, the *butterfly life cycle* and *changes of state* describe a process.

Going back to the comments of the Physics teacher, we note that his learners have to understand the relationship of one thing to another and present the results. In order to frame their meanings when they describe or interpret their work, they need similar support to the language tables offered for Zhou (Chapter 5, pages 142–9) and reformulations for Alena (Chapter 6, pages 175–6). The teacher can model the language and write it on the board, or perhaps have banks of *sentence starters* on the wall.

When it comes to data from simple surveys, the learners can generally cope with talking *descriptively* about results. They might use *simple comparison structures* to express *relative size of populations*, as shown in the following examples:

Simple comparison structures

- *more, most;*
- *large, larger, largest;*
- *more than, less than, the same as, as big as ...* and so on.

These phrases are similar to concepts in PE like *higher than, longer than, faster than, the fastest runner, the longest jump* (Department for Education and Skills 2002: 87).

Common comparatives relevant to a particular topic indicating relative size or quantity could be included in word banks on the wall.

More complex comparison operations
For a more complex task, the next stage would be to talk about the relative size of the variation and the relative certainty we have about the cause of it.

Let's look at a few examples from the possible interview data about diet generated in the Geography investigation task (Chapter 4, page 125). The task we modelled for supported reading, note-making and writing was to investigate whether the participants' diet is Western, Traditional or International. We have now imagined here the outcome of turning the investigation into a school wide survey. This allows us to look at the aspects of subject literacy that are involved in reporting data.

For the hypothetical survey, 300 participants from Years 7, 8 and 9 in our school were asked a number of questions about what was included in and excluded from their diet. The last question invited an overall view as to whether their diet was Western, Traditional or International. A bar chart has been used to record the responses to that question (Figure 7.1).

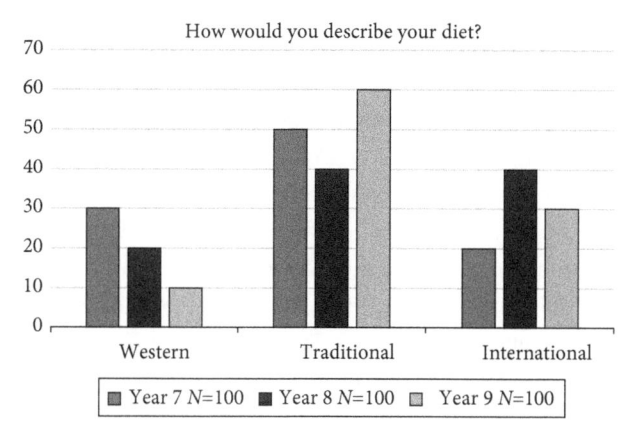

Figure 7.1 Bar chart giving results of survey question labelling diet.

A useful place to start when interpreting statistics is by making detailed descriptive notes and then working out the patterns of trends before planning how to organize it as a commentary. Here are some sample structures for notes, with expressions for quantity shaded.

Presentation of responses

1) Focus on totals:
   The totals for all 300 participants are Western = 60, Traditional = 150, International = 90
   Most of them/the majority say their diet is Traditional (150), fewer say it is International (90), then the fewest/smallest number say it is Western (60).

2) Focus on single groups:
   Year 7
   Half the group (50%) claim their diet is Traditional, while 30% claim it is Western. The smallest group chose International (20%)

   Year 8
   The respondents are equally divided between Traditional (40) and International (40), but only about a fifth (20) say their diet is Western.

   Year 9
   According to the results, just under two-thirds of the Year 9 participants have a Traditional diet (60), just under a third have an International diet (30) and only one tenth (10) have a Western diet.

3) What is most striking overall?
   The largest number = A high percentage of Year 9s have a Traditional diet,
   The lowest number = Few /not many Year 9s have a Western diet.

Interpretation

Giving an interpretation involves an opinion expressed with levels of certainty. Here we imagine that the question is based on a graph comparing the preferences of the three year groups: 'What trends does the graph show in participants' changes in preference between the ages of twelve and fourteen?'

To support this task, we could offer a table of language structures to express the view that preferences change between the ages of twelve and fourteen, giving options of certainty rated as *high, medium* and *low*. We often use modal verbs for this purpose. Here we have included *will, could, may* and *might* (Table 7.3).

Using the examples in Table 7.3, the same pattern choices can be applied to complete other comments on the trends. Learners fill in the gaps below.

Between the ages of twelve and fourteen

- Year 8s .... change to labelling their diet as a mix of traditional and international.
- Year 9s .... return to labelling their diet as traditional.

Table 7.3 Table of Language Structures for Expressing Degrees of Certainty from Trends Graph

The graph shows that Year 7s	*will,* *(or omit modal and just use 'label')*	high certainty	*label their diet as traditional.*
	could *are likely to* *will probably*	medium certainty	
	may *might* *will maybe*	low certainty	

As with other suggestions about language features, similar patterns can be adapted for commentaries and appreciations in other subjects. Learners can be offered sentence completion tasks, making use of a sample table as a model.

How learners use modal verbs as they learn to write was also included in Cameron's study of home learners and EAL learners (2003: 36). Her research showed

- EAL learners working at low level tend to use *should* and *must*;
- Home learners working at low level use *can*;
- EAL learners working at high level like to use *would*.

It is useful to look at how other modal verbs like *can, should, must and ought* are used to express a level of certainty in your subject. They are difficult verbs to use as the choice of which one to use is rather like the choice of tense and the article. The choice reflects the writer's or speaker's point of view.

For the EAL learners working at high level, continuing support for writing will be needed for the organization of extended contributions. To avoid misapplying formulaic phrases without understanding, it is important to maximize opportunities for planned practice in expressing the concepts in different ways: e.g. comparisons of size and quantity, similar to the reformulations we have referred to throughout Chapters 4, 5 and 6.

This overview of monitoring EAL learner emerging subject literacy at four PiE levels has shown what we can expect and how we can support progression. This trajectory is associated with the increasing complexity of thinking skills required as their learning progresses towards Exam-level study at Upper Secondary level.

Perhaps this profile of subject literacy helps you to revisit how you grade conceptual knowledge and the accompanying patterns of language development in home learners as well.

For all learners, the strategy for reaching the subject literacy targets is the same: to provide opportunities for learning to support the learner to reach their potential with a *language aware pedagogy*. Based on this monitoring, we can summarize the approach to planning progression in four steps.

Four steps in planning progression

Step 1: Be aware of the complexity level of the subject literacy that you are monitoring

It is the teacher's responsibility to be aware of how subject literacy develops and match this with the mindset of the EAL learner in the classroom. Your classroom is a place where everyone is equally valued. The normal practice is active learning that includes talk. You use board work all the way through the lesson for visual support and an approach to engagement that ensures all learners take part. You use extensive *oral practice* to develop academic language and hypothesizing skills, which will support development in independent *writing* (Edmunds 2000: 156).

You know how to plan your lesson demonstrating an awareness of the role of language in learning. Based on the *language aware adaptation of Kolb's teaching and learning cycle* presented in Chapter 2 (pages 58–9), your lesson will include a focus on the communication purpose and the main language features to model the subject literacies of the topic, taking account of challenges and offering planned opportunities for talking to build knowledge.

As mentioned in the Introduction, time spent on language features integrated into your lesson is time well spent (Ofsted 2011, Clark personal communication). All learners have the chance to learn at a deeper level, rather than memorize from a onetime exposure to the topic.

Inclusion policy documents published in 2002 for a range of subjects at Lower Secondary level all mention the importance of *securing progress for pupils learning EAL* at the outset (Department for Education and Skills 2002: 4). Aimed at head teachers and local authorities, the document asks

- Does the current marking policy support diagnostic marking and the identification of targets for pupils?
- Have language learning targets for EAL pupils been clearly identified?
- Are opportunities for planned talk maximized in group tasks and plenary sessions?
- Does planning allow all pupils to contribute or give feedback over the course of a half-term?
- What is the departmental policy on the effective use of pupils' first languages to support learning in lessons? To support development of English?

We can see here an emphasis on whole school commitment to these practices to support EAL learners in transition from Primary to Lower Secondary and, by implication, their progression to Upper Secondary study. We suggest that this approach can be adapted to support Upper Secondary learners.

The aspects of subject literacy mentioned most frequently through the chapters in this book are the ones to focus on: *communication purpose, expanding vocabulary (for appropriate word choice), saying more in fewer words (word class shift in noun phrases) and managing the grammar flexibly to support the meaning with confidence.*

But it is important to include the EAL learner in this process to encourage a positive view of assessment as part of learning.

Step 2: Work together with the EAL learner to set targets

All teachers agree that planning progression is best done with reference to departmental policy, the curriculum, syllabus and the performance of the learners. This means not just your view of the performance of the learners but their view as well. Learning is a shared experience, and knowledge is created jointly by you, the learner, and the experiences you offer in the classroom.

For the EAL learner, shared learning might typically mean working with friends outside the classroom rather than within, where she and her peers are under the gaze of the teacher. So she needs to be reassured by your practice that your role is supportive, rather than judgemental. Ideally, within this context, your EAL learner is becoming an independent learner, who reflects on her own learning. This habit tends to develop in the kind of positive classroom culture set out above so that learners

- plan before beginning a task by setting goals, working out how to accomplish it;
- check their comprehension and what language they are using as they carry out the task;
- assess their own performance when they finish the task, asking questions such as *How well did my planned approach work? How well did my comprehension check deal with the challenges? How effective was checking my work?*

Using this approach a learner can get a sense of how to learn effectively and adopt the practice of self-assessment (Chamot 2009). It also means that assessment in the broadest sense is part of the learning cycle. *How well did I do? What can I do to make it better?* becomes *everyday* and *talked about*.

If we link this approach to including the learner within the school wide approach to supporting progression set out above, it also implies, for the purposes of transparency, a commitment to working together with the EAL learner to set targets, to share interpretations of assessment descriptors, to work on agreed areas to be assessed, and for a record keeping system to be in place for future reference (Leung 2017). This is set out in more detail in Step 3 of planning progression.

Step 3: Train yourself to assess systematically and inclusively

As you gather evidence of emerging subject literacy skills regularly and systematically, you will become more familiar with the components of objective assessment. You can use the criteria set out in Chapter 6 (page 174) as a starting point to monitor 'conceptual understanding' and 'control of subject literacy'. You can then adapt or add detail as you become more comfortable with the language of benchmarking. You can use descriptors set out in a reference document, for example, the adapted EAL PiE proficiency levels (Chapter 2, pages 42–3).

Formative assessment is key to monitoring progress and planning next steps (Rea-Dickins and Gardner 2000), so record keeping is part of the process. Table 7.4 works well for PiE descriptors to be recorded three times in a term.

Table 7.4 PiE Descriptors Recorded for Three Subject Literacy Criteria through the Term

Criteria	Start of term	Mid-term	End of term
Conceptual understanding			
Control of subject literacy			
Next steps advised			

Working with an EAL, Subject English or Modern Languages specialist in your school will be a useful start if you are unsure how to apply the descriptors confidently. This might be an idea to take to a departmental meeting for discussion and possible development.

Planning the departmental or school assessment policy together helps (Hawkins 2006: 11). Some schools use a system that involves designing similar tasks with agreed criteria to be measured across subjects at a particular time to give a cross-sectional snapshot of achievement. The significant decision in this process is how the assessment task will be formatted and what kind of response is expected. It is important to bear all modes of communication in mind because assessments in varied formats offer different kinds of opportunities to demonstrate different kinds of knowledge, and you will choose one to suit your subject.

Using the assessment evidence, the teacher is able to set informed targets and discuss next steps with fellow teaching staff, the EAL specialist, the learner and parents. Your EAL specialists will have access to detailed language learning materials that can support the learning of aspects that your learners might be having problems with.

As you become more experienced in this area, you may want to refer to more detailed descriptors such as those offered by the Bell Foundation (https://www.bell-foundation.org.uk/eal-programme/teaching-resources/eal-assessment-framework/) and develop your own range of criteria for measuring progress.

As mentioned in Step 2, sharing descriptors will include the EAL learner in the process. You could do this with our Chapter 2 EAL descriptors, the Bell Foundation descriptors, or consider the user-friendly self-assessment grid that is part of the Common European Framework of Reference for Languages. These self-assessments would encourage the EAL learner to take a positive view of their progress because all the descriptors start with the words 'I can' (available for download at https://www.coe.int/en/web/common-european-framework-reference-languages/table-2-cefr-3.3-common-reference-levels-self-assessment-grid – *find Table 2 and choose English*).

This approach to monitoring and planning progression is an iterative process that sustains itself by collaboration and reflection and, as suggested above, includes opportunities for consultation with learners and parents to build shared expectations and goals.

Assessment literacy is an invaluable skill for teachers: the more detail you can manage the better. As with other aspects of your subject literacy knowledge, intuition is a valid guide for assessment. You can now develop your subject literacy assessment skills in a systematic way.

Step 4: Plan your own progression

Monitor your own practice. Develop a criticality. Ask yourself, *Is this aspect of subject literacy in my practice? How could I add it?* Keep your eyes open for new ideas – not just in this book. You'll find them in the classroom and in the process of observing and talking to others. Watch videos of subject teachers with a critical eye to identify how they present and model key words and support their uptake.

Share your ideas about supporting subject literacy in departmental meetings. The suggestion for a shared system of signs (gesture, mime) to communicate basic ideas could be a starter. If this takes off in your own department, could it be part of whole school practice?

A survey of literature on teacher development sponsored by Oxford University Press in 2012 concluded that any teacher development needs to be concrete and classroom based (Walter and Briggs 2012). *Collaborative professional development* is the ideal format, along with *peer observation-* and *action-based research* where you set your own professional development targets. *Reflective teaching, outside expertise, mentoring* and *coaching*, along with *pedagogical leadership*, tend to sustain development activities over time. This will also ensure teachers have the required level of familiarity with policies, professional accountability and professional standards.

This book has brought together a familiarity with how language works, an understanding of working with EAL learners' resources, how language is learned and how subject literacy develops. It is not a grammar book for teaching English, but you have made a start.

You will now know where to find answers to the questions not answered in this book. You will also know what kind of support to offer learners at what stage and when to call on a specialist. You might consider adapting this approach for learners working at the Exam stage. Regarding the English language, you will appreciate that there is much more to understand about how language patterns work and how they develop. Just as there is more than one way to express a concept in your subject area, so there is more than one way to describe the structure of English.

If you wish to pursue any of these strands further, the advice is to find a description that suits you. It may be online, or in a book. Just as you might choose a phrase book or dictionary of a thickness appropriate to the length of time you will visit a country, so you will select a description and dictionary of English that suits the level of detail you want to know. Suggestions are offered in the Teaching Resources for this chapter.

Enjoy the riches of emerging subject knowledge and literacies as you work with learners in culturally diverse classrooms.

Teaching resources for further study of language

Grammar resources

About Language. Thornbury, S. (2006) Cambridge: Cambridge University Press – for TESOL teachers.

A New Grammar Companion for Primary Teachers. Sydney: Primary English Teaching Association Derewianka, B. (2011). Suitable for Secondary level too.

A very Simple Grammar of English (1985) Blisset, C. & Hallgarten, K. Hove: Language Teaching Publications. Brilliant if you are looking for a simple explanation.

Cambridge Grammar of English: A Comprehensive Guide Spoken and Written English Grammar and Usage (2006) Carter, R and McCarthy, M. Cambridge University Press.

English Grammar in Use: A Self-Study Reference and Practice Book for Intermediate Students of English. Cambridge: Cambridge University Press. Murphy, R. (2004). This series is also available for learners at beginner and advanced levels.

English Language Knowledge for Secondary Teachers Ross, A. (2013). Abingdon: Routledge. 2nd Edition. For subject English teachers.

How English works. Swan, M. and Walter, C. (2007) Oxford: Oxford University Press. For learners.

The British Council *Learn English* site: a useful section for Grammar https://learnenglish.britishcouncil.org/en/english-grammar

For general reference

Sounds English. O'Connor, J., and Fletcher, C. (1989). Sounds to focus on for learners from different language backgrounds. Full details in references.

Learner English. Swann and Smith (2001). Features of learner English influenced by different language backgrounds. Full details in references.

Continuing professional development

'How does Language work?' CPD to support development of subject literacies. http://www.aston.ac.uk/lss/research/research-centres/language-research/news-and-events/clera-events/events-2013/how-does-language-work-conference/ University of Aston: Link to short video on the work of the project: http://youtu.be/PUPadXFqRG4; where teachers talk about their practice: http://youtu.be/Wg50bJ1K_DI

Department for Education (2009) *Ensuring the attainment of more advanced learners of English as an additional language: CPD modules*. https://webarchive.nationalarchives.gov.uk/20110202101215/https://nationalstrategies.standards.dcsf.gov.uk/node/187758

References

Alexander, R. (2004) *Towards Dialogic Teaching: Rethinking Classroom Talk*. North Yorkshire: Dialogos.

Baker, C. (2011) *Foundations of Bilingualism and Bilingual Education* (5th Edition). Bristol: Multilingual Matters.

Barnes, D. (1996) *From Communication to Curriculum*. London: Penguin.

Bauman, J. and Culligan, B. (1995) Updated General Service List. http://www.eapfoundation.com/vocab/general/gsl/frequency/

Black, P. and Wiliam, D. (1998) *Inside the Black Box: Raising Standards through Classroom Assessment*. www.kcl.zc.uk/depsta/education/publications/blackbox.html

Bowyer, C. (2018) 'Making historians out of sixth formers'. *EAL Journal*, Summer: 34–6.

Breen, M. (2001) 'Syllabus design'. In R. Carter and D. Nunan (Eds), *The Cambridge Guide to Teaching English to Speakers of Other Languages*. Cambridge: Cambridge University Press, pp. 151–9.

Brown, D., Howat, R., Marra, G., Mullan, E., Murray, R., Nisbet, K., Thomas, D. and Thomson, J. (2002) *New Maths in Action S1^3*. Cheltenham: Nelson Thornes.

Brown, G. and Armstrong, S. (1984) 'Explaining and explanations'. In E. Wragg (Ed.), *Classroom Teaching Skills*. London: Croom Helm, pp. 121–48.

Brown, G. and Yule, G. (1983) *Discourse Analysis*. Cambridge: Cambridge University Press.

Brown, R. (1973) *A First Language: The Early Stages*. Cambridge, MA: Harvard University Press.

Bruner, J. (1966) *Towards A Theory of Instruction*. Cambridge, MA: Harvard University Press.

Cameron, L. (2002) 'Measuring vocabulary size in English as an additional language'. *Language Teaching Research*, 6(2): 145–73.

Cameron, L. (2003) *Writing in English as an Additional Language at Key Stage 4 and Post 16*. London: Ofsted. https://dera.ioe.ac.uk/4723/

Cajkler, W. and Hislam, J. (2010) 'Trainee teachers' grammatical knowledge: the tension between public expectation and individual competence'. *Language Awareness*, 11(3): 161–77.

Carrell, P. (1987) 'Readability in ESL'. *Reading in a Foreign Language*, 4(1): 21–40.

Chamot, A. (2009) *The CALLA Handbook: Implementing the Cognitive Academic Language Learning Approach* (2nd Edition). London: Pearson Education.

Chandler, M. (1998) *History Key Stage 3 Longman Homework Handbooks*. Essex: Addison Wesley Longman.

References

Coates, A., Fitzpatrick, B., Hughes, S., Keay, A., Liddell, G., and Robertson, R. (2008) *Turnstones 2: An English course for Scotland.* London: Hodder and Stoughton.

Coffin, C. and Donohue, S. (2014) *A Language as Social Semiotic-based Approach to Teaching and Learning in Higher Education.* Oxford: Wiley-Blackwell.

Coxhead, A. (2000) 'A new academic word list'. *TESOL Quarterly,* 34(2): 213–38. https://www.victoria.ac.nz/lals/resources/academicwordlist/publications/awlsublists1.pdf

Cummins, J. (1979) 'Cognitive academic language proficiency, linguistic interdependence, the optimum age question'. *Working Papers on Bilingualism,* 19: 121–9.

Cummins, J. (1981) *Bilingualism and Minority-language Children.* Toronto: Oise Press.

Cummins, J. (1984) *Bilingualism and Special Education: Issues in Assessment and Pedagogy.* Clevedon: Multilingual Matters.

Deignan, A. and Semino, E. (2018) 'Metaphor and climate science in UK secondary school discourse'. Presentation at the 2018 BAAL-Routledge Workshop, University of Glasgow January 2018.

Department for Education (2014) *National Curriculum.* https://www.gov.uk/government/collections/national-curriculum

Department for Education (2016) *School Census 2016–2017: Guide for Schools and LAs.* https://www.gov.uk/government/publications/school-census-2016-to-2017-guide-for-schools-and-las

Department for Education and Skills (2002) *Access and Engagement in Physical Education (KS3).* https://webarchive.nationalarchives.gov.uk/20110506101435/https://www.education.gov.uk/publications/eOrderingDownload/DfES%200659%20200 MIG165.pdf 11 other subjects available at http://wsh.wokingham.gov.uk/learning-and-teaching/mea/eal/eal-guidance/national-strategy/access-ks3/

Derewianka, B. (1990) *Exploring How Texts Work.* PETAA: Sydney.

Derewianka, B. and Jones, P. (2016) *Teaching Language in Context* (2nd Edition). Australia: Oxford University Press.

Dyson, M. (2004) 'How physical text layout affects reading from screen'. *Behaviour and Information Technology,* 23(6): 377–93.

Edmunds, C. (2000) 'Developing language aware teaching in secondary schools'. In M. Gravelle (Ed.), *Planning for Bilingual Learners: An Inclusive Curriculum.* Stoke on Trent: Trentham Books, pp. 125–57.

Emmott, C. and Alexander, M. (2014) 'Schemata'. In P. Hühn, J. Meister, J. Pier and W. Schmid (Eds), *Handbook of Narratology* (2nd Edition). Berlin: De Gruyter, pp. 756–64.

Foley, Y. Sangster, P. and Anderson, C. (2013) 'Examining EAL policy and practice in mainstream schools'. *Language and Education,* 27(3): 191–206.

Gardner, S. and Nesi, H. (2012) 'A classification of genre families in university student writing'. *Applied Linguistics,* 34(1): 1–29.

Gibbons, P. (2006) *Bridging Discourses in the ESL Classroom.* London: Continuum.

Gibbons, P. (2009) *English Learners, Academic Literacy, and Thinking: Learning in the Challenge Zone.* Portsmouth, New Hampshire: Heinemann.

Gibbons, P. (2015) *Scaffolding Language, Scaffolding Learning: Teaching English Language Learners in the Mainstream Classroom*. Portsmouth, New Hampshire: Heinemann.

Halliday, M. A. K. (1975) *Learning How to Mean: Explorations in the Development of Language*. London: Edward Arnold.

Halliday, M. A. K. (1993/2004) 'Towards a language-based theory of learning'. In J. Webster (Ed.), *The Language of Early Childhood, The collected Works of MAK Halliday Volume 4*. London: Continuum, pp 327–52.

Hawkins, M. (2006) *Marking Progress: Training Materials for Assessing English as an Additional Language*. External Evaluation. http://dera.ioe.ac.uk/5743/1/markingprogress.pdf

Hedge, T. (1988/2005) *Writing. Resource Books for teachers* (2nd Edition). Oxford: Oxford University Press.

Iser, W. (1972) 'The reading process: a phenomenological approach'. *New Literary History*, 3(2): 279–99.

Jones, J. and Wiliam, D. (2008) *Modern Foreign Languages: Inside the Black Box*. London: GL Assessment.

Kolb, D. (1984) *Experiential Learning: Experience as the Source of Learning and Development*. Englewood Cliffs: Prentice Hall.

Kövecses, Z. (2002) *Metaphor: A Practical Introduction*. Oxford: Oxford University Press.

Kress, G. (1982) *Learning to Write*. Abingdon, Oxon: Routledge.

Kress, G. and van Leeuwen, T. (2006) *Reading Images: The Grammar of Visual Design* (2nd Edition). Abingdon, Oxon: Routledge.

Langer E. and Alexander, C. (1990) *Higher Stages of Human Development: Perspectives on Adult Growth*. New York: Oxford University Press.

Leung, C. (2017) 'Assessing EAL: a question of knowing what'. *EAL Journal*, Autumn 2017: 15–35.

Littleton, K. and Mercer, N. (2013) *Interthinking: Putting Talk to Work*. London: Routledge.

Lunzer, E. and Gardner, K. (1984) *Learning from the Written Word*. Oliver and Boyd: Schools Council Publication.

Lynch, T. (2009) *Teaching Second Language Listening*. Oxford: Oxford University Press.

MacGahern, D. and Boaten, K. (2000) 'Planning for inclusion at Key Stage 4'. In M. Gravelle (Ed.), *Planning for Bilingual Learners: An Inclusive Curriculum*. Stoke on Trent: Trentham Books, pp 99–124.

Maclean, K. and Thomson, N. (2009) *S1-S2 Geography*. Paisley: Hodder Gibson.

Mercer, N. (1995) *The Guided Construction of Knowledge*. Clevedon Bristol: Multilingual Matters.

Mercer, N. (2008) *Three Kinds of Talk*. https://thinkingtogether.educ.cam.ac.uk/resources/5_examples_of_talk_in_groups.pdf

References

Mercer, N. and Dawes, L. (2008) 'The value of exploratory talk'. In N. Mercer and S. Hodgkinson (Eds), *Exploring Talk in Schools: Inspired by the Work of Douglas Barnes*. London: Sage, pp. 55–72 .

Meyer, B., Marsiske, M. and Willis, S. (1993) 'Text processing variables predict the readability of everyday documents read by older adults'. *Reading Research Quarterly*, 28(3): 235.

Mines, G. (2000) 'Particles'. In B. McDuell (Ed.), *Teaching Secondary Chemistry*. Association for Science Education. London: John Murray, pp. 47–79.

Mohan, B. (1986) *Language and content*. Boston: Addison Wesley.

Moll, L., Amanti, C., Neff, D. and González, N. (1992) 'Funds of knowledge for teaching: Using a qualitative approach to connect homes and classrooms'. *Theory into Practice*, 31(2): 132–41.

Morgan, J. (2012) *Teaching Secondary Geography as if the Planet Matters*. London: Routledge.

Myhill, D. (2018) 'Grammar as a meaning-making resource for improving writing'. *L1 Educational Studies in Language and Literature*, 18: 1–21.

Nagy, W., Anderson, R. and Herman, P. (1987) 'Learning word meanings from context during normal reading'. *American Educational Research Journal*, 24(2): 237–70.

NALDIC (2009) *Assessment for Learning: Working with pupils learning English as an Additional Language*. (DVD) Reading: University of Reading.

Nancarrow, P. (2018) 'Hard working words: extending vocabulary breadth and depth across the curriculum'. *EAL Journal*, Spring 2018: 42–4.

Nation, I. (2006) 'How large a vocabulary is needed for reading'. *The Canadian Modern Language Review*, 63(1): 59–82.

Nation, P. (2001) *Learning Vocabulary in another Language*. Cambridge: Cambridge University Press.

Nuttall, C. (2005) *Teaching Reading Skills in a Foreign Language* (3rd Edition). London: Macmillan.

O'Connor, J. and Fletcher, C. (1989) *Sounds English: Pronunciation Practice Book*. London: Longman.

O'Connor, M., and Michaels, S. (1993) 'Aligning academic task and participation status through revoicing: analysis of a classroom discourse strategy'. *Anthropology & Education Quarterly*, 24(4): 318–35.

Ofsted (2002) *The National Literacy Strategy: the first four years 1998-2002*. https://dera.ioe.ac.uk/17512/7/Ofsted%20-%20national%20literacy%20strategy_Redacted.pdf

Ofsted (2011) *Barriers to Literacy*. www.ofsted.gov.uk/publications/090237

Ofsted (2012) *Ofsted Annual Report 2011/12*. https://www.gov.uk/government/publications/the-annual-report-of-her-majestys-chief-inspector-of-education-childrens-services-and-skills-201112

Paver, M. (2004) *Wolf Brother*. London: Orion Children's Books.

Perera, K. (1984) *Children's Writing and Reading*. Oxford: Basil Blackwell.

Piaget, J. (1952) *The Origins of Intelligence in Children*. New York: International Universities Press.

Pollard, A. (2008) *Reflective Teaching: Effective and Evidence-informed Professional Practice*. London: Continuum.

Qualifications and Curriculum Authority (2000) *A Language in Common: assessing English as an Additional Language*. Qualifications and Curriculum Authority. Available at http://dera.ioe.ac.uk/4440/

Rea-Dickins, P. and Gardner, S. (2000) 'Snares and silver Bullets: disentangling the construct of formative assessment'. *Language Testing*, 17(2): 215–43.

Roddick, C. and Sliva- Spitzer, J. (2010) *Succeeding at Teaching Secondary Mathematics*. London: Sage.

Rose, D. (2006) 'Reading Genre: a new wave of analysis'. *Linguistics and the Human Sciences*, 2(1): 1–30. Available at https://www.readingtolearn.com.au/wp-content/uploads/2016/01/Reading-genre.pdf

Schleppegrell, M. (2004) *The Language of Schooling: A Functional Linguistics Perspective*. Mahwah, NJ: Lawrence Erlbaum.

Schleppegrell, M. (2010) 'Supporting a 'reading to write pedagogy with functional grammar'. *NALDIC Quarterly*, 8(10): 26–31.

Schleppegrell, M. (2012) 'Academic language in teaching and learning: introduction to the special issue'. *The Elementary School Journal*, 112(3): 409–18.

Schleppegrell, M. (2014) 'Supporting Language-Based Content Teaching with Metalanguage from Systemic Function Linguistics'. Presentation at CLaRA conference University of Aston, Birmingham, March 2014.

Shulman, L. (1986) 'Those who understand: knowledge growth in teaching'. *Educational Researcher*, 15(2): 4–14.

Skehan, P. (1996) 'Second language acquisition research and task based instruction'. In J. Willis and D. Willis (Eds), *Challenge and Change in Language Teaching*. London: Heinemann, pp 17–30.

Sökmen, A. (1997) 'Current trends in teaching second language vocabulary'. In N. Schmitt and M. McCarthy (Eds), *Vocabulary: Description, Acquisition and Pedagogy*. Cambridge: Cambridge University Press, pp 237–58.

Swenson, M. (1993) *The Complete Poems to Solve*. Digitally available in *May Swenson: Collected Poems*. Library of America, 2013.

Swann, M. and Smith, B. (2001) (Eds), *Learner English: A Teacher's Guide to Interference and Other Problems* (2nd Edition). Cambridge: Cambridge University Press.

Tennyson, A. (1833) 'Ulysses'. *Poems Vol 1* (1842). London: Moxon.

University of Melbourne (2001) *Building Understandings in Learning and Teaching (BUILT)* CD ROM. https://extranet.education.unimelb.edu.au/LLAE/BUILT/index.shtml

Vygotsky, L. S. (1978) M. Cole, V. John-Steiner, S. Scribner and E. Soubaman (Eds), *Mind in Society: The Development of Higher Psychological Processes*. Cambridge, MA: Harvard University Press.

Walter, C. and Briggs, J. (2012) 'What professional development makes most difference to teachers?' Report sponsored by Oxford University Press.

Wells, G. (1985) *The Meaning Makers: Children Learning Language and Using Language to Learn*. London: Hodder and Stoughton.

Williams, H. (2006) 'Maths in the grammar classroom'. *English Language Teaching Journal*, 60(1):23–33.

Wilson, H. and Mant, J. (2011a) 'What makes an exemplary teacher of Science? the pupils' perspective'. *School Science Review*, 93(342):121–5.

Wilson, H. and Mant, J. (2011b) 'What makes an exemplary teacher of Science? The teachers' perspective'. *School Science Review*, 93(343): 115–25.

Zacharias, S. (2018) *The Linguistic Representation of Abstract Concepts in Learning Science: A Cognitive Discursive Approach.* PhD, University of Nottingham School of Education.

Index

assessment, context
    education policy guidance   59
    initial interview   33
    school policy   32, 44, 220
    setting targets (teachers)   40
    setting targets (with EAL learner)   221
    in teaching cycle   172–3
assessment, purpose
    formative   172, 220
    knowledge of other languages   37–8
    monitoring subject literacy   174, 196, 220–1
    Proficiency in English (PiE) assessment   40–3, 56–7
    self-assessment guidance   185, 219
    self-assessment language grid   221
adjustment to new context   5, 31–2, 205

classroom discourse, aim
    culture of talk   6–8
    exploratory talk (in groups)   132, 146–9, 167
    exploratory talk (plenary)   6–7, 103–12, 119–22
    modelling the language   13, 57
    professional role   12
    signalling change of purpose   205
    talking about subject language   3–4
classroom discourse, type
    dialogic teaching   6, 17, 36–7
    figurative /metaphorical language   157–63, 168
    idioms   47, 57–8
    literal and inferential language   108
    mixed everyday and specialist language   25, 53–4
    organising language   12, 48
    questioning   13–4
collaborative classroom   6–7, 56–7, 98, 190

constructing knowledge
    abstract concepts   26
    analogy   158–62
    creating mental images   1–2, 11, 46
    developing ownership   6–7, 109
    engagement   58, 95, 99–100, 129, 137–40, 140, 166
    figurative language   119–24, 157–63
    high challenge/high support   132–3
    Kolb's teaching cycle   23
    language aware teaching cycle   58–9
    participation   6, 42–3, 56–8, 138
    practice   6, 25, 159–62, 186, 196, 207
    reciprocal process   6, 22–5, 27, 172
    role of language   2–4, 10, 25, 218
creating a school profile   4, 31–2, 203
    cultural expectations   33–7, 54
    of English language   40–3
    of other languages   37–40, 55

EAL learner language in the classroom
    everyday language (BICS)   42–3, 48–9
    home language   4–6, 55, 56–7, 140, 152
    language for study (CALP)   2, 49–54, 90
    period of development (CALP)   52
    period of development (BICS)   48
    shadowing an EAL learner   48
existing knowledge
    drawing on mental images   62–5, 98, 100–1, 119, 146, 154
    funds of knowledge   4–6, 9, 31, 137–9, 164, 203
    hooks   2, 91, 101, 120, 126
    mental representations   2–6, 11
    schemas contribution   64, 100, 149, 166
    schemas for language learning   38, 55
    schemas for reading   19–20, 101, 105
    triggers to activate schemas   5, 9, 98, 113, 119, 132–3

explanations
  communication purposes   61–7
  planning   93
  lesson framework   168
  macro-level templates   93–4

feedback activities   197
  choosing a tense   193
  general academic verbs   192
  groups shape a text   191
  logical linkers   183, 212
  matching specialist meanings   111–12
  precise noun phrases   192–3
  specialist versus everyday words   184
  using an outline   183–4
  using articles   194
  writing for the reader   183, 185–6
feedback contexts   167
  collaborative   185, 190–1
  for individuals   185, 190, 191
  in the moment   175–7, 189
  in plenary   183, 190, 192
  self-monitoring   185
  in the teaching cycle   173
feedback tools
  feedback codes for writing   198
  'find and fix' error feedback   191
  rewording   7
  self-assessment criteria   185, 197
  two stars and a wish   190

grammar basics   1–4, 18, 21, 45, 46
  active / passive voice   3, 73, 143–4, 162, 199
  adjectives/adj phrases   51–2, 74, 94
  adverbs/adv phrases   73–4, 95, 213
  articles, the/a/an   194–5
  modal verbs   213, 216–17
  nouns/n phrases   3, 17, 30
  prepositions   73–4, 95, 213
  tense examples   19–20, 73, 188–9, 193–4, 199
  tenses timeline   199
  verb action types   30, 156
  verbs/vb phrases   30, 52, 73, 79, 115, 124, 143, 180–2
  word classes   17–18, 30, 111, 117–18, 198

grammar of complex language   133. *See also* language patterns at micro-level
  being more precise   18–21, 51–2
  clarifying   113–15
  deconstructing   115–18, 213
  extending noun phrases   51, 72, 94, 111–12, 130, 133, 180–1
  information density   20, 52, 124
  paraphrasing meaning   20
  word class shift   25, 52, 57, 79, 219
grammar of sentences   29–30
  co-ordination   17, 30
  deconstructing sentences   113, 117–18, 213
  multi-clause sentences   30, 72, 86, 210
  sentence length   116, 133
  subordination   30, 72, 86, 133, 207, 210
  tasks   168, 186, 194, 207, 216
group work
  cultural attitudes   33–7, 56
  oral confidence   7, 209
  organising   56
  productive discussions   150
  setting up task   144
  types of talk   146–8

inclusive classrooms
  build on existing knowledge   4–6, 15, 159
  engagement   57–58
  group work   57
  inclusive practice   54
  intercultural awareness   4–6, 9, 32, 39, 56–7, 205
  language support policies   44, 55, 59–60
  participation   6–7, 99, 137–9, 142, 168
  policies   32, 59–60
  using the home language   4–6, 55, 140, 168
  welcoming the learner   4–6, 41, 56, 59–60, 203–5
independent learners
  asking for clarification   109, 114, 196
  buddies   56
  responsibility for own learning   36
  self-assessment/editing   21, 174, 185
  strategies in lesson plan   58–9
  using Google Translate   5, 57, 140, 160, 168

Index

language knowledge
- developing your own   3–4, 21, 27, 222
- early development in first language English   10–11, 29
- fluency versus accuracy   45–6, 208
- integrating into practice   8, 27, 58, 64, 99
- Primary curriculum (macro-level)   18–22
- Primary curriculum (micro-level)   17–18, 29–30
- supporting after transition   9–10, 12–14
- your intuitive knowledge   3, 6–8

language patterns at micro-level   94–6
- adding detail with adjectives   94
- adding detail with adverb phrases/ clauses   73, 95–6
- cause/effect   159–60
- claims, multi-clause statements   79
- comparison   214–16
- definitions, noun phrases /multi-clause sentences   72
- degrees of certainty   217
- description, adjective phrases   74
- presenting results   216
- procedures   78–9, 81
- processes, verb phrases, adverb, preposition phrases   73
- the right verb   23–4, 73, 76, 94
- setting the scene, multi-clause sentences   86

language register support   26–8, 48–9, 57, 191, 209
- continuum 1 Playground/classroom   17
- continuum 2 Informal/formal   18
- continuum 3 Dialect/Non-standard/ standard   19
- continuum 4 Everyday/specialist   23–5
- continuum 5 Speaking/writing   26–8
- continuum 6 Concrete/ Abstract words   29

language support policies   44, 55, 59–60
learning in a culturally diverse classroom   4–6

linking words   130, 134–5
- adding   134
- exemplifying   135
- offering alternative   135
- showing aim   131
- showing contrast   135
- showing reason   135
- showing result/effect   134
- showing sequence   135

linking words activities
- text jigsaw task   87, 129, 183
- hunting for logical linkers   128–9

listening   97–8
- evidence in PiE descriptors   42–3
- hearing new words   102–4
- predicting the topic   98
- pronunciation   102–4
- spelling   29, 107
- using the context to make meaning   101
- word stress/ syllables   130

literacy skills development (Primary level)   21–6

matrix for challenge/support/engagement   98
matrix for cognitive challenge   92

planning a lesson, framework
- engagement   58, 142, 166
- an explanation   88–90, 93
- explanation lesson   168
- a group discussion   139–49
- a group task   151–7
- high challenge/high support   132
- identifying challenges   92, 97–9, 113, 218
- language aware teaching cycle   58, 164
- a test   157–64

planning a lesson, language
- communication purpose   93
- distinguishing types of new words   110, 113, 135
- key words to integrate   58–9
- language patterns   142, 148–9, 161–3, 165, 178–9
- practice   160–2
- support materials   56–8, 142
- thinking skills   49, 56, 65, 91–2
- topic familiarity   92, 97–8

reading activities, general meaning
   applying to other subjects   125
   directed activities related to texts
      (DARTS)   99
   hooks to existing knowledge   119–21, 125–6
   post reading activities   124, 155–7
   pre-reading activities   119–22, 151–4
   while reading activities   122–4
reading activities, language and structure
   communication purpose   65
   deconstructing challenging text   116–18
   identifying key points   85, 127
   markers of opinion   128–30
   signalling words   128–9
   taking notes   127–8
   text organisation   93–4, 128
reading challenging texts   97–8
   familiar mental images   2, 154
   new words   108–9
   text difficulty   97–8, 115–18
reading process   100–1, 104–5, 118

spelling   33, 57, 107, 133, 135–6, 168, 207
subject literacy   1–4, 18, 26–7
   criteria for monitoring   174, 180–2
   emerging subject literacy   175–7, 181–2, 187–90
   at primary/secondary transition   7–8, 64, 219
   progression plan   202–3
   style shifting   20, 23–4
   subject oriented lens   61
   teacher's existing subject literacy   2–3, 19

talking, culture   6
   oral culture   34–6
   personal / social identity   12–16
   professional role   18–19
talking, in curriculum
   evidence in PiE descriptors   42–3, 209, 213
   importance   6–8
   oral style in Maths   78–80

   oral mode   22–4, 47–48
   planned practice   6–8, 160–2, 192–3, 206–7
   Primary level input   17
   spoken versus written style   12, 23–5, 183
talking, skill development
   articulating cause and effect   159–63
   articulating definitions   72, 94, 185
   charts and graphs   214–8
   early years   10, 29
   expanding vocabulary   6–8, 21–4, 175–8, 192–3, 210
   exploratory talk   108–9, 112–13, 119–21, 132, 147–8
   flexible rewording   7, 58–9, 107, 113–15
   in group discussions   150
   guided tasks   3, 17, 78–81, 160–1, 167
task design aim
   active participation   138, 143, 196
   cultural adaptation   27, 58–9
   high challenge/high support   132, 142–4
   oral practice   160
task design elements
   assessment task   220
   break into stages   131
   check list   164
   communication purpose   138–40, 165
   teacher expectations   139–40, 179
   template   139
task design examples
   cause and effect   159–60
   clarifying test purpose   162–3
   from describing to defining   204
   an enquiry task   115–24, 151–7
   a group discussion   144–5
   a test   157–63
   wording   113–15, 155–6, 178
text patterns at macro-level, noticing
   change and description   71, 75
   discussion report   125–31
   events/cause and effect   83, 86, 88, 151, 189
   existing professional knowledge   64
   factual description   18–20

Geography (typical features)   75
History (typical features)   87
Maths (typical features)   79
narrative   20
procedure   78, 81
text literacy at Primary level   22–30
text patterns at macro-level, practice
   for concepts and contributing factors   88
   for organising text   128–31

using home language   4–6, 42, 55, 140, 152

visuals
   Google images   26, 141, 151, 158
   for support   23, 40, 45–7, 56–8, 113, 142–3, 150, 179, 218
   as triggers   5, 6–7, 101–3, 119–21, 126, 139, 152–3
   using mime/gesture   56, 145, 166, 168, 175, 204, 221
   visual literacies   63, 75, 84, 89, 99, 101–2, 206

word choice, extending
   general academic vocabulary   188–9
   general vocabulary   192
   how many new words   109–10
   vocabulary range   175–6
word choice, noticing   7, 136, 192
   abstract concepts   25, 50–5, 85, 90–2, 116, 141, 166, 211
   general academic words   110–11
   keyword hunts   74, 79, 86, 213
   mixing everyday and specialist   25, 53
   saying more in fewer words   20, 25, 51, 57
   specialist words   18–22, 57
word choice, practising   45, 108
   in classroom process   23–5
   develop continuums   209
   evidence in PiE descriptors   43–45
   in meaningful contexts   54, 108–9, 111–12
   refer to continuums   27–8, 57, 191
   specialist words   162–3, 185

word choice, register. *See also* language register support
   everyday for specialist purposes   50, 57, 72, 112–13
   general academic words   110–11
   specialist words   111–12
word forms
   in early years   29
   language origin   135
   prefixes/suffixes   135
   pronunciation   56, 105–7, 132, 135, 139, 207
   similar forms   26, 50, 136
   spelling patterns   17, 29, 45, 105, 204
   word stress rules   134
word frequency   109, 136,
word meanings, finding
   from buddies   55
   from complex language   113–15, 133, 175–6
   from context   106, 108–9
   dictionaries   45, 57, 113, 122, 132–3, 150, 204
   glossaries   58, 121
   Google Translate   5, 57, 140, 160, 168
   from language knowledge   213, 218
word meanings, practising
   making sentences   161–2
   matching meanings   106, 185
   new words   105–9
   paraphrasing concepts   116–18, 168
   synonymous phrases   111–12, 157
writing skill development
   advanced subordinators   30, 210
   assessment   40–3
   basic subordinators   207
   evidence in PiE descriptors   42–3, 210, 213
   modal verbs   210–12
   organisation   211–12, 216
   at Primary level   3, 16–18, 21–2
   teaching grammar   17–18
   writing for the reader   23–4, 181–3, 185–6

writing style, modelling
- argument structure   187, 215
- discussing charts/graphs   63, 214–17
- discussion report   127–8
- procedures   78–9
- sentence starters   209
- sequence/link events   87–8, 179–80, 183

writing style, noticing
- communication purposes   66–7
- cross-cultural approaches   34–6
- literary style   119–20, 123
- logical linkers   128–30
- long noun phrases   57, 130, 133
- markers of opinion   129–30

writing style, practising
- discussion report   128
- editing   21, 174, 185
- history essay   187
- logical linkers   211–12
- markers of opinion   211–12
- science test answer   178–80

writing style, templates
- causes and effects   159, 163
- enquiry report   157
- explanation   183–4
- notes/explanations   93–4
- procedures   93
- process description   93, 184
- sequence of events   94
- strategic use   89
- survey results   131